Seven Puzzles of Thought and How to Solve Them

Seven Puzzles of Thought and How to Solve Them

An Originalist Theory of Concepts

Mark Sainsbury and Michael Tye

UNIVERSITY PRESS

OXFORD
UNIVERSITY PRESS

Great Clarendon Street, Oxford, OX2 6DP,
United Kingdom

Oxford University Press is a department of the University of Oxford.
It furthers the University's objective of excellence in research, scholarship,
and education by publishing worldwide. Oxford is a registered trade mark of
Oxford University Press in the UK and in certain other countries

© R. M. Sainsbury and Michael Tye 2012

The moral rights of the authors have been asserted

First published 2012
First published in paperback 2013

All rights reserved. No part of this publication may be reproduced, stored in
a retrieval system, or transmitted, in any form or by any means, without the
prior permission in writing of Oxford University Press, or as expressly permitted
by law, by licence or under terms agreed with the appropriate reprographics
rights organization. Enquiries concerning reproduction outside the scope of the
above should be sent to the Rights Department, Oxford University Press, at the
address above

You must not circulate this work in any other form
and you must impose this same condition on any acquirer

Published in the United States of America by Oxford University Press
198 Madison Avenue, New York, NY 10016, United States of America

ISBN 978-0-19-969531-7 (Hbk)
ISBN 978-0-19-968894-4 (Pbk)

Contents

Preface ix

1. The Puzzles 1
   - 1.1 The Puzzle of Hesperus and Phosphorus 2
   - 1.2 The Puzzle of Twins 4
   - 1.3 The Puzzle of the Cat and le Chat 9
   - 1.4 The Puzzle of Paderewski 12
   - 1.5 The Puzzle of Pure Demonstratives 13
   - 1.6 The Puzzle of Empty Thoughts 16
   - 1.7 The Puzzle of Thinking About Oneself 18

2. Roads Not Taken 20
   - 2.1 Naïve Millian Views 21
   - 2.2 Fregean or Descriptivist Views 22
   - 2.3 Sophisticated Millianism: The Hidden Indexical Theory 26
   - 2.4 Sophisticated Fregeanism: Two-dimensional Semantics 30

3. Overview of an Originalist Theory of Concepts 40
   - 3.1 Origins 41
   - 3.2 Individuation by Origin 44
   - 3.3 Contents 45
   - 3.4 Thoughts 47
   - 3.5 Isomorphism 50
   - 3.6 Indexicality 51
   - 3.7 Cognition 53
   - 3.8 "Mastering" or "Grasping" Concepts 55
   - 3.9 Conclusion 57

4. The Originalist Theory Defended and Elaborated — 58
   - 4.1 Words — 58
   - 4.2 Concepts are Non-eternal Abstract Continuants — 63
   - 4.3 Fission and Fusion — 66
   - 4.4 Reference: Fixing and Preserving — 69
   - 4.5 Information, Composition — 72
   - 4.6 Mates Cases and the Demise of Two-level Fregean Semantics — 76
   - 4.7 Multi-level Fregeanism — 79
   - 4.8 Knowledge and Conceptual Mastery — 81
   - 4.9 Comparison with Fodor — 85
   - 4.10 Comparison with Millikan — 87

5. Concept Externalism, Originalism and Privileged Access — 90
   - 5.1 Formulating IKCC — 91
   - 5.2 IKCC and Switching — 92
   - 5.3 The Empirical Implausibility of IKCC — 95
   - 5.4 IKCC and Rationality — 98
   - 5.5 The Privileged Access Thesis — 101
   - 5.6 Privileged Access and Switching Cases — 102
   - 5.7 Introspective Evidence — 103
   - 5.8 Privileged Access and McKinsey's Recipe — 105
   - 5.9 McGinn's Externalism — 106
   - 5.10 Burge's Externalism — 108
   - 5.11 Originalist Concept Externalism — 109

6. The Metaphysics of Thought — 110
   - 6.1 The Metaphysics of Belief and Thought: The Positive Account — 110
   - 6.2 Arguments for the Orthodox View — 112
   - 6.3 Evaluating the Orthodox Arguments — 114
   - 6.4 Attitude Ascriptions — 116
   - 6.5 De Re, De Se, De Dicto — 121

7. The Puzzles Solved — 124
   7.1 The Puzzle of Hesperus and Phosphorus — 124
   7.2 The Puzzle of the Twins — 127
   7.3 The Puzzle of the Cat and le Chat — 127
   7.4 The Puzzle of Paderewski — 131
   7.5 The Puzzle of the Two Tubes — 138
   7.6 The Puzzle of Empty Thoughts — 139
   7.7 The Puzzle of Thinking About Oneself — 144

8. Further Applications: Originalism and Experience — 150
   8.1 The Content of Hallucinatory Experience — 150
   8.2 The Trouble with Gappy Content — 152
   8.3 An Alternative View of the Content of Visual Experience — 157
   8.4 The Epistemic Role of Experiences — 160
   8.5 The Knowledge Argument — 163
   8.6 Knowing What It Is Like — 164
   8.7 Mary's Discovery — 166
   8.8 Conceivability: Preliminary Remarks — 167
   8.9 The Zombie Argument — 169

9. Objections and Replies — 173

References — 187
Index — 193

Preface

Originalism's central thesis is that concepts, the constituents of thoughts, are to be individuated by their origin, rather than epistemically or semantically. This is the view we elaborate and defend in this book.

Our methodology resembles Russell's:

A logical theory may be tested by its capacity for dealing with puzzles, and it is a wholesome plan, in thinking about logic, to stock the mind with as many puzzles as possible, since these serve much the same purpose as is served by experiments in physical science. (Russell 1905: 484–5)

In Chapter 1, we stock the mind with seven familiar puzzles. Familiar solutions, even if in some cases prima facie very plausible, often conflict with one another or else lead to implausible treatments of other puzzles. It's like a balloon with seven protuberances. Push in on the balloon at one of the seven and, lo and behold, it swells further at another. The trick is to eliminate all the protuberances without simply bursting the balloon. That is what we propose to do in this book. Originalism provides simple and natural solutions to all the puzzles, and has further valuable consequences for the nature of thought, our knowledge of our own thoughts, the nature of experience, the epistemology of perception-based beliefs, and for arguments based on conceivability.

We do not attempt to consider or refute all the things philosophers have said in response to the seven puzzles. Chapter 2 indicates some approaches we do not adopt, due originally to Mill and to Frege. Our positive theory is set out in Chapters 3 and 4. Some consequences of originalism are spelled out in Chapters 5 and 6, and the theory is applied to the puzzles in Chapter 7. Chapter 8 indicates further applications of the theory, going beyond the seven puzzles, and Chapter 9 briefly lists some objections and our replies.

In our opinion, thought is special but there is no special mystery attaching to the nature of thought.

We would like to thank many people for their comments: participants in Arche's workshop on conceivability and imaginability (St Andrews, Spring 2010), participants in New York University's workshop on judgeable content (Florence, June 2010), in particular our respondent Paul Horwich, our exceptionally able graduate class of Spring 2011 at the University of Texas, Ruth Millikan, who responded to an Aristotelian Society paper in which originalism was first published, and the following: Paul Boghossian, Jessica Brown, Ray Buchanan, Alex Byrne, Herman Cappelen, Jonathan Cohen, Jonathan Dancy, Cian Dorr, Ephraim Glick, Terry Horgan, Hans Kamp, Aidan McGlynn, Jesse Prinz, Gideon Rosen, Stephen Schiffer, Nicholas Shea, Barry Smith, David Sosa, Aaron Zimmerman, and two referees for Oxford University Press.

The work is fully collaborative. The (alphabetical) order of the authors' names has no significance.

Parts of Chapter 3 appeared in R. M. Sainsbury and Michael Tye, "An Originalist Theory of Concepts" *Proceedings of the Aristotelian Society, Supplementary Volume* 85: 101–24 (2011). They are reprinted here by courtesy of the Editor of the Aristotelian Society, ©2011.

1
The Puzzles

What is it to think? You cannot just think, as you can just swim or just sneeze. When you think, you must think something or other—that life is good, that Manchester United is the greatest football team in the world, that mojitos are refreshing to drink.[1]

Suppose you think that pigs cannot fly. Your thought has accuracy or truth conditions. It is accurate or true if pigs cannot fly and false otherwise. Given the actual facts, your thought is true. It represents that pigs cannot fly, and that is how things are.

In representing that pigs cannot fly, the thought has what is called a "representational content". It is generally held that there is a close connection between the conditions under which a thought is true (its "truth conditions") and its representational content. At a minimum, thoughts that differ in their truth conditions differ in their representational content. We adopt this framework.

Concepts, as we use the term, are mental representations of a sort deployed in thought; they are representational constituents of thoughts. Thoughts are made up of concepts, and what thoughts as a whole represent is a function of their component concepts: what they represent and how they are combined. In this way, thoughts are like pictures and sentences.

To illustrate: take a picture of a ball on a box. It has a part representing a ball, a part representing a box, and the way those two parts are combined in the picture (the former on top of the latter) enables the picture to represent that a ball is on a box. Now take the sentence, "A ball is on a box". It has a part representing a ball (the words "a ball"), a part representing a box (the words "a box"), and a further part (the words "is on") representing the spatial relation of being on. These parts are combined so as to generate a sentence that represents that a ball is on a box. Similarly, the thought that a ball is on a box is formed out of various concepts (the concept BALL, the concept BOX, for example), combined in a particular way.

Since concepts represent things and they make up thoughts, they too have representational contents. Their contents combine to generate the representational content of the thoughts of which they are components. For example, Antonio's thought that

---

[1] You can also think *about* things: about London or about Napoleon. Although this sometimes involves thinking *that* something or other is the case (concerning London or Napoleon), it seems possible merely to think about something, without thinking a "*that*-thought". However, *that*-thoughts are the main topic of this book.

Armani is an Italian designer is composed of concepts. There is a concept representing Armani, a concept representing the property of being Italian and a concept representing the property of being a designer.² The first concept can be expressed using the name "Armani", the second using "Italian" and the third using "designer". Each of these concepts has its own content. It is standard to refer to a concept by using an expression of the form "the concept F": the concept ARMANI, the concept ITALIAN, and so on. The representational content of the thought that Armani is an Italian designer is a function of the contents of its component concepts and the way they are combined in the thought. There is no such thing as *the* concept *of* Armani: he may be conceptualized in any number of ways, using the concept THE MOST FAMOUS ITALIAN DESIGNER, the concept MY SON (if one is one of Armani's parents), the concept THE GUY IN THE FANCY SHIRT, or whatever. By contrast, there is a unique concept, the concept ARMANI.

1.1 The Puzzle of Hesperus and Phosphorus

According to the usual story, the name "Hesperus" was introduced by the ancient Babylonians as a name for the heavenly body seen at a certain position in the sky in the evening.³ The name "Phosphorus" was introduced for the heavenly body seen at another position in the sky in the morning. It was not until much later that it was discovered that the two names pick out the same heavenly body, namely the planet Venus.

The ancient Babylonians certainly realized that Hesperus is the same as Hesperus. How could they not? The claim that Hesperus is Hesperus is trivial, a mere instance of the law of identity. But they did not realize that Hesperus is Phosphorus. Intuitively, what the Babylonians thought in thinking that Hesperus is Hesperus is not what astronomers later thought in thinking that Hesperus is Phosphorus. On this very natural view, the thought that Hesperus is Hesperus is a different thought from the thought that Hesperus is Phosphorus. The puzzle is to say in what this difference consists. The former thought is true if and only if Hesperus is identical with Hesperus (that is, Phosphorus). The latter thought is true if and only if Hesperus is identical with Phosphorus (that is, Hesperus). So, by one natural reckoning, the two thoughts have exactly the same accuracy- or truth-conditions. What, then, accounts for their difference?

There is a linguistic version of the puzzle that goes as follows. Consider the two sentences:

1. Hesperus is Hesperus.
2. Hesperus is Phosphorus.

---

² Here, and throughout the book, we take properties to be different from concepts. Properties are things in the world that concepts represent. They do not themselves represent anything. On some views, properties are universals—types or kinds that may have many instances or tokens.

³ The puzzle in this form goes back to Frege (1892).

(1) is trivial, a mere instance of the law of identity. But (2) is informative—it represents a significant empirical discovery. How is this possible? One answer derives from Frege. Assume

   3. "Hesperus" has the same meaning as "Phosphorus".

Given

   4. The meaning of a sentence is a function of the meanings of its component words and the way they are combined,

it follows that the replacement of "Hesperus" by "Phosphorus" in a sentence cannot change the meaning of that sentence. Hence, it follows that (1) has the same meaning as (2). This result is at odds with the difference in informativeness between (1) and (2). (2) cannot represent a significant empirical discovery if it has the same meaning as (1), since (1) is trivial. So, either (3) or (4) is false.

Frege held that (3) is false, and developed a conception of "sense" (*Sinn*, in German) according to which "Hesperus" and "Phosphorus", though referring to the same thing, differ in sense. On a standard interpretation of his view, the sense of each proper name is given by a definite description, and even in the case of names that refer to the same thing the descriptions may be different, giving rise to different senses. The sense of "Hesperus" is, say, "the planet seen at position x in the evening sky" and the sense of "Phosphorus" is, say, "the planet seen at position y in the morning sky". Then (2) is informative, because it expresses the truth that one and the same planet is seen at position x in the evening sky and at position y in the morning sky, whilst (1) is trivial because the truth that it states is simply that the planet seen at position x in the evening sky is the same as the planet seen at position x in the evening sky.

The trouble with this Fregean view is that it is not plausible to hold that proper names are really definite descriptions. The main reason, developed further in Chapter 2, is that people who share a common understanding of a name may differ in what definite descriptions they associate with it. But if there really is a common understanding, there should be a single sense.

When one thinks about what a proper name means, there seem to be only two resources: there's what it refers to, and there are associated descriptions, of the kind used in Fregean sense. If the Fregean view is rejected, it would seem that there is no way of finding any difference of meaning between the names "Hesperus" and "Phosphorus", for they both refer to the same thing.[4] Without a difference of meaning, it's hard to see how one could explain the difference of informativeness between (1) and (2).

---

[4] More strongly, we assume that the terms "Hesperus" and "Phosphorus" are rigid designators, that is, each term picks out in any counterfactual situation the very thing it picks out in actual fact (Kripke 1972/1980).

Returning now to the puzzle at the level of thought, it appears that one can reason in a corresponding way. Suppose

5. The concept HESPERUS has the same content as the concept PHOSPHORUS.

Given

6. The representational content of a thought is a function of the contents of its component concepts and the way they are combined,

it follows that the thought that Hesperus is Hesperus has the same content as the thought that Hesperus is Phosphorus. But this seems problematic. The thoughts are strikingly different, one trivial and the other informative. How is this possible? The Fregean response, applied now to concepts rather than words, is to say that the concepts HESPERUS and PHOSPHORUS are mental representations akin to definite descriptions, so (5) is false, and the two thoughts have different descriptive contents. One who thinks that Hesperus is Phosphorus thinks that one and the same planet seen at position x in the evening sky is seen at position y in the morning sky, whereas one who thinks that Hesperus is Hesperus thinks that the planet seen at position x in the evening sky is the planet seen at position x in the evening sky.

For reasons similar to those regarding Frege's suggestion about proper names (of which more in Chapter 2), it cannot be the case that the concept HESPERUS and the concept PHOSPHORUS function in our thoughts in the same general way as definite descriptions do in public language. So, how can (5) be false? This question becomes even more pressing given that the two concepts refer to the very same thing (the planet Venus), not just in the actual world but also in all possible worlds in which they refer to anything.

Puzzle 1: Hesperus and Phosphorus

The concept HESPERUS would seem to represent just what the concept PHOSPHORUS represents. So how can there be a difference between the thought that Hesperus is Hesperus (trivial) and the thought that Hesperus is Phosphorus (an important empirical discovery)?

1.2 The Puzzle of Twins

Strictly speaking, there is no such thing as *the* puzzle of twins. Rather, there are several different, though closely related, twin puzzles. We begin with a thought experiment that finds its origin in the work of Hilary Putnam (1975) and Tyler Burge (1982).[5]

---

[5] Putnam's concern in his discussion of twin-earth was with the meanings of natural kind terms, and so related wholly to language. Burge extended Putnam's thought experiment to thought and belief.

Water/twater: Suppose that there is another planet (far, far away)—call it "twin-earth"—which is exactly like our planet earth except in one respect: where on earth there is water, made of H_2O molecules, on twin-earth there is a similar-looking and tasting liquid made up of XYZ, a compound unknown in earthly chemistry. We'll refer to this stuff as "twater", though this word belongs neither to the language used on earth, nor that used on twin-earth. Like water, twater is colorless, tasteless, odorless, and wet. On twin-earth, twater comes out of taps, fills lakes, falls from the sky, and so on. On twin-earth, there is no water. The twin-earth word "water" refers to the local water-like stuff, twater.

Earth and twin-earth are so similar that everyone on earth has a duplicate on twin-earth: duplicates have all their intrinsic properties in common.[6] When anyone on earth does anything, their duplicate on twin-earth does something intrinsically the same. Moreover the English spoken on earth is duplicated on twin-earth by a language that sounds and is spelled just the same: twin English. On earth, there's a word "water," which refers to water. On twin-earth there's a similar sounding word. But it cannot refer to water, for there is no water on twin-earth. Rather, "water" in twin English refers to twater.

Tim, on our planet earth, is holding a glass of water. Speaking sincerely in English, he says, "Water is wet". He expresses the belief that water is wet, so his belief is true if and only if water is wet. Whether twater is wet is irrelevant to the question whether Tim's belief is true.

Tim's intrinsic duplicate, Tom, on twin-earth, is holding a glass of twater. Speaking sincerely in twin English, he says, "Water is wet". He expresses the belief that twater is wet, so his belief is true if and only if twater is wet. Whether water is wet is irrelevant to the question whether Tom's belief is true.

Tim's belief, which is about water, is not the same as Tom's belief, which is about twater. How is this possible? Tim and Tom are intrinsic duplicates. Intrinsically, there is no difference whatsoever between them. So how can there be a mental difference, a difference between their beliefs? If beliefs are states of the brain, one cannot have a belief the other lacks, for their heads and brains are exactly alike. If beliefs are states of the soul then, since Tim and Tom are intrinsic duplicates, their souls are exactly alike. Again, it follows that one cannot have a belief the other lacks.

One possible reaction is that the scenario has been misdescribed: the stuff called "water" on twin-earth really *is* water. It is just a different kind of water from the stuff called "water" on earth.[7] Then Tim and Tom's beliefs don't differ, for they both believe that water is wet, and there is no puzzle. On this view, water is like jade. Just as

---

[6] Distinct photocopies of the same original are examples of intrinsic duplicates (assuming the photocopier has behaved properly). They may differ in relational properties: e.g. one photocopy may be ours, the other yours.

[7] For example, heavy water is counted as water, even though distinct from H_2O: "Heavy water is water containing a higher-than-normal proportion of the hydrogen isotope deuterium" (Wikipedia).

there are two different kinds of jade (nephrite and jadeite) with little chemically in common,[8] so there are two different kinds of water, H_2O and XYZ.

A problem for this reaction is that it cannot easily accommodate the following revised scenario. Suppose that Tim gets in a spaceship and goes to twin-earth. How would he react upon seeing twater? He might immediately say such things as "There is plenty of water around here", but if he were to find out that the liquid he had taken to be water was nothing like water chemically, it seems entirely appropriate for him to retract his initial view and say, for example, "There is a liquid on this planet that looks just like water and tastes just like water, but it isn't really water". If Tim, in using the word "water", is expressing a concept of his that applies equally well to water and twater, then it is hard to make sense of Tim's correction of what he had said earlier. Likewise, were Tom to make a corresponding journey to earth he would no doubt initially claim that the stuff on earth he is inclined to call "water" is the very stuff that is so plentiful on twin-earth. But when he learns that it is chemically quite different from twater, it will be entirely appropriate for him to retract this claim. In twin English, the sentence "This looks just like water, but isn't really" would be true. It would mean that this looks just like twater, but isn't really.

If this does not deter the theorist who claims that twater is really a kind of water, there are other twin-earth scenarios for which a view of this sort is unavailable.

Aluminum/molybdenum: Let's start with two things which are incontrovertibly different in kind, since they both exist on earth: the very different metals aluminum and molybdenum.[9] Suppose that in twin English aluminum is called "molybdenum" and molybdenum is called "aluminum". Further, suppose that things made of aluminum on earth are made of molybdenum on twin-earth and vice-versa. Molybdenum superficially is very like aluminum (both are shiny metals), so much so that to non-experts on earth and also on twin-earth, there is no way of telling the two apart just by inspection. Hence the switch in the roles played by the metals on the two earths is compatible with the supposition that Tim and Tom are intrinsic duplicates: where the one is affected in a certain way by the one metal, the other is affected in just that way by the other.

When Tim (on earth) holds up an aluminum pot and, speaking English, sincerely says, "Pots and pans are often made of aluminum", what he believes is that pots and pans are often made of aluminum. By contrast, when Tom (on twin-earth) holds up a superficially identical pot made of molybdenum and makes the same sounding remark in twin English, what he believes is that pots and pans are often made of molybdenum.

---

[8] "Jade is the gem name for mineral aggregates composed of either or both of two different minerals, Jadeite and Nephrite. Jadeite is a sodium-rich aluminous pyroxene; nephrite is a fine-grained, calcium-rich, magnesium, iron, aluminous amphibole" (http://www.geo.utexas.edu/courses/347k/redesign/gem_notes/jade/jade_main.htm).

[9] "Aluminium (or aluminum...) is a silvery white and ductile member of the boron group of chemical elements [group 13]. It has the symbol Al and its atomic number is 13." "Molybdenum is a Group 6 chemical element with the symbol Mo and atomic number 42" (Wikipedia entries).

Tim's belief and Tom's belief have different truth conditions and different representational contents. So, their beliefs are different. How can this be, if Tim and Tom are intrinsically exactly the same? One cannot avoid the puzzle by claiming that molybdenum is a kind of aluminum (paralleling the suggestion that twater is a kind of water), for this is patently not the case. The metals are known to be distinct.

Some thoughts are "twin-earth-able": they can be different while all the intrinsic facts remain the same. In each such case, there is a concept contained in the thought that is itself "twin-earth-able". Whether the concept WATER is one such concept may be disputed, though we share the widely held view that it is. Still, it seems undeniable that some concepts are twin-earth-able under scenarios of the sort described above, for example the concept ALUMINUM. A distinguishing feature of these concepts is that they are natural kind concepts, where a concept is a natural kind concept only if it picks out a natural kind.[10] Those who deny that the concept WATER is twin-earth-able typically hold that the concept WATER is not a natural kind concept. On this view, the concept WATER is like the concept JADE or the concept AIR.[11] These are concepts that refer to what are sometimes called motleys: things that can be chemically constituted in many ways (jade), or are mixtures of various things (air).

Arthritis/tharthritis: Twin-earth thought experiments have been extended to thoughts involving non-natural kind concepts. On some twin-earth scenarios, what varies is not the external, physical environment but the linguistic practices of two communities. Such scenarios trace back to Burge (1979).

In Burge's famous example, there is a man (let's call him "Albert") who goes to his doctor with the complaint that he has arthritis in his thigh. After the doctor explains to him that arthritis is an inflammation of the joints, Albert could refuse to accept the doctor's correction and insist that, whatever the doctor may think, he really does have arthritis in his thigh. However, such a person would be highly atypical. The usual response would be to accept the doctor's correction, thereby indicating that there is a shared concept in play, the concept ARTHRITIS, about whose application the doctor knows more. One who rejects the doctor's claim that arthritis is found only in the joints is operating with some other concept. But that's not what Albert does.

Consider another (counterfactual) community in which it is correct to apply the term "arthritis" not only to inflammation of the joints, but also to other inflammations that feel similar. In this community "arthritis" refers to tharthritis (though neither community uses the word "tharthritis"). Suppose that in this community, there is an intrinsic duplicate of Albert who goes to his doctor just as Albert does and who reports

---

[10] A natural kind is a kind in nature. Each such kind has an essence describable within one of the physical sciences.

[11] "Air is mainly composed of nitrogen, oxygen, and argon, which together constitute the major gases of the atmosphere. The remaining gases are often referred to as trace gases, among which are the greenhouse gases such as water vapor, carbon dioxide, methane, nitrous oxide, and ozone." (Wikipedia entry for "Atmosphere of earth.")

to the doctor, "I have arthritis in my thigh". What does twin Albert believe when he makes this report? Intuitively, his report is true, given how the word "arthritis" is used in the counterfactual scenario, as is the belief it expresses. Twin Albert cannot be expressing the belief that he has arthritis in his thigh, for that belief would be false.[12] So twin Albert, though Albert's intrinsic duplicate, has different beliefs. But how can they have different beliefs, given that they are intrinsic duplicates?

Some philosophers deny that there is any difference in their beliefs. They say that when Albert says, "I have arthritis in my thigh", he has a true object-level belief and a false metalinguistic belief. What he really believes is that he has tharthritis in his thigh (which is true, since tharthritis is any condition that feels like arthritis) and he further believes that "arthritis" stands for tharthritis (which is false). Twin Albert has these beliefs too, but his beliefs are true since in the twin scenario, it is correct to apply "arthritis" to tharthritis.

One reason to reject this suggestion is that it doesn't satisfactorily explain Albert's behavior at his doctor's office. Albert accepts his doctor's superior judgment, and concludes he was mistaken. But on the proposal just made, he would not be mistaken about his medical condition, for he does have tharthritis in his thigh. His mistake is about how the term "arthritis" is correctly used, in which case it would be more natural for him to reply: well, it's what *I* call "arthritis".

Another reason to reject the suggestion is that it does not do justice to the way in which speakers of different languages can share beliefs. It entails that a monolingual French speaker cannot believe what an English speaker believes when the latter says, "I have arthritis in my thigh". That's because, generalizing the analysis, the French speaker's beliefs would include a metalinguistic belief about the French language, whereas the English speaker's beliefs would not. This seems unacceptable.

This thought experiment has very wide application. Wherever there is a deferential concept, that is, a concept about whose application its user is disposed to accept correction, the thought experiment involving a small change in the meaning of the relevant word will go through.

Colors: Here is one further illustration, showing that a very wide range of concepts are twin-earth-able. Color concepts can be over- or under-extended. For example, someone might have the usual beliefs about which common objects are red and might normally agree with others about which presented color patches are red; yet they might think that in one particular case, the shade of that object over there is clearly red even though everyone else agrees that it is on the border between orange and red. Such a person would likely accept correction from others who confidently agree about the right way to classify the given shade. In this way, color concepts are deferential.

---

[12] Twin Albert must lack the concept ARTHRITIS, or at least its presence could not show up in his overt behavior. For he uses the word "arthritis" just as his community does, referring to tharthritis.

Consider a counterfactual linguistic community in which this person has an intrinsic duplicate and in which it is correct to apply the term "red" to objects with the given shade. The twin person, viewing the same object in the same setting, in saying, "That object over there is red", has a true belief. So, as in the arthritis case, the content of the belief in the counterfactual situation is different from the content of the actual belief.

These thought experiments suggest that thoughts are individuated in part by, and thus depend upon, external, environmental matters (for example, the presence of water) or socio-linguistic facts (for example, the fact that the word "arthritis" has a certain meaning in the linguistic community as a whole), knowledge of which requires empirical investigation by the thinker. Yet no such investigation is required for the thinker to know his or her own thought. Thinkers have privileged access to their thoughts—they can know them simply by introspection—but prima facie they don't have privileged access to external facts. Prima facie, then, thoughts are intrinsic. But they can't be, if the thought experiments show what they seem to show. Twins, it seems, are very puzzling creatures indeed.

Puzzle 2: Twins

Someone can be the same in all intrinsic respects as their "twin"—their duplicate on twin-earth or in a twin community—even though they think different thoughts. Mental properties are intrinsic, and thoughts are mental, so twins shouldn't be able to think different thoughts!

1.3 The Puzzle of the Cat and le Chat

Suppose that Paul is an English speaker who has been brought up by a French nanny in a sheltered environment.[13] She talks to Paul about many things and she does so in English, with one exception: she refers to the cats in the nursery and elsewhere in the house and grounds as chats. She never calls them "cats". Paul picks up the word and he uses it as his nanny does. He says such things as, "All chats have tails". What does Paul believe in making this remark? It seems very natural to suppose that he has acquired the concept CAT. A French person who competently uses the term "chat" in the course of speaking French surely expresses the same concept as an English person who competently uses the term "cat", namely the concept CAT. Paul's nanny is well aware of what "chat" means in French, so in her mouth it expresses the concept CAT. Paul uses "chat" as his nanny does. So Paul uses it to express the concept CAT. So Paul, in saying "All chats have tails", expresses the thought that all cats have tails.

This conclusion is reinforced by reflection upon the general phenomenon of deference. One theme in much recent work on concepts is that of "partial understanding". People can properly be credited with grasp of a concept, even if they are ignorant

---

[13] This puzzle is due to Brian Loar (1987).

of some things, and even some pretty important things, about what the concept refers to. For example, Alfred grasped the concept ARTHRITIS, even though he did not know that arthritis was confined to the joints. One explanation of how this is possible is that a thinker's linguistic community in part determines which concepts she possesses, for thinkers come to grasp many concepts through linguistic interaction with others. This dependence on the community is manifest in the phenomenon of deference. For example, Alfred rightly thinks the doctor is more likely to be right about whether or not he has arthritis than he himself is. In using his concept ARTHRITIS, Alfred defers to the doctor's presumed superior knowledge of arthritis.[14]

Deference to experts and correction by them helps ground the view that experts and those who are not experts share the same concepts. The experts simply know more about what the concepts apply to. The right thing to say about Paul, on this view, given his competence with the word "chat" and his preparedness to defer to his nanny, is that in using "chat" he is to be credited with beliefs involving the concept CAT.

When considering concepts like ARTHRITIS and MOLYBDENUM, it is natural to suppose that there is a privileged class of experts who should be deferred to: in these cases doctors or chemists. But dependence on the linguistic community does not require any privileged class of experts. You know more than we do about the colors of the pens on your desk, but each of us knows more than you about the colors of the pens on his own desk. So, we'll defer to you about your pens and you'll defer to us about ours. On this view, the truth is simply that we all defer to anyone else we think might know more than we do. When we do so defer, we agree with those to whom we defer. And this agreement typically involves shared concepts. Paul, in deferring to his nanny, is accepting what his nanny believes, namely that cats have tails (among other things). Thus, Paul, like his nanny, is using the concept CAT.

Suppose Paul's parents meet with Paul from time to time in a London hotel and they speak to him of animals they call "cats". During these visits, there are no pictures of cats in the hotel room and there are no cats permitted in the hotel. Paul does not realize that cats are really just chats. However, Paul's parents tell him a number of stories involving cats and in the course of listening to these stories, Paul learns (among other things) that all cats have tails. But isn't that something he believed already?

There's some temptation to say no. The belief Paul expresses in uttering "All chats have tails" explains why, for example, he says "That's not a chat", upon seeing a Manx cat outside his house. The belief Paul expresses in uttering "All cats have tails" explains why, for example, when his nanny mischievously asks him to tell her about cats on his return from a visit with his parents, he reports, "All cats have tails". Furthermore, if subsequently Paul's nanny decides to tell him that cats are really just their familiar chats, and he believes her, he certainly seems to make a discovery. How can this be?

---

[14] The linguistic counterpart to this claim is Putnam's (1975) thesis of the division of linguistic labor.

There are powerful reasons to say that the belief that Paul expresses with "All cats have tails" is the same as the belief he expresses with "All chats have tails" and also powerful reasons to deny this. Clearly something has to give. But what exactly? It is not easy to say.

The puzzle of the cat and le chat is similar to Kripke's (1979) puzzle of London and Londres. In that puzzle, Kripke asks us to imagine a monolingual French boy, Pierre, who reads French books about London and who, on the basis of what he reads and the pictures he observes in the book, forms a belief he expresses in the sentence "Londres est jolie". It can properly be inferred that Pierre believes that London is pretty. Subsequently, Pierre moves to London but he does not realize that London is the city he calls "Londres". He learns English in the same way as native English speakers, and not by translating words from French into English. He lives in a depressing, ugly part of London and he picks up the name "London" in connection with the city he lives in. He comes to believe that London is not pretty. It seems, then, that Pierre has inconsistent beliefs: he believes both that London is pretty and that London is not pretty. But Pierre is not irrational. How can he have such obviously contradictory beliefs?

In the puzzle of the cat and le chat, "chat" translates "cat". Likewise, in the related puzzle of London and Londres, "Londres" translates "London". These puzzles bear some affinity to the puzzle of Hesperus and Phosphorus. They differ in that it seems more promising to make a Fregean response to Hesperus/Phosphorus cases: it seems reasonable to say that "Hesperus" and "Phosphorus" differ in meaning, or that the concept HESPERUS contributes differently to thought than does the concept PHOSPHORUS. By contrast, "cat" translates "chat", and "Londres" translates "London", so it seems hard to find a difference of linguistic meaning, or a difference of conceptual contribution.

Cat/chat puzzles are connected to a worry raised by Benson Mates. Mates (1952) asked whether synonyms can be substituted *salva veritate* (i.e. without changing truth value) in propositional attitude contexts, contexts in which thoughts (for example, beliefs, fears, hopes) are ascribed. If they can, then (assuming, as Mates did, that "Greek" and "Hellene" are synonyms) from

   7. James wonders whether all Greeks are Hellenes

it follows that

   8. James wonders whether all Greeks are Greeks.

But surely one cannot infer (8) from (7): (7) could well be true, but unless James is very unusual (8) will be false. So, synonyms are not always substitutable *salva veritate* in propositional attitude contexts.

If this is correct, analogous considerations make room for the possibility that the thought Paul expressed by "All chats have tails" differs from the thought he expressed by "All cats have tails". As one might say: Paul could wonder whether all cats have tails without wondering whether all chats have tails. Yet we have also seen that there are grounds for saying that both sentences express the same thought, namely the thought that all cats have tails.

> Puzzle 3: Chats and cats
>
> Paul seems to make a discovery when he learns that cats are chats. But the thought that cats are chats seems to represent just what the thought that cats are cats represents. In that case, there is nothing to be discovered.

1.4 The Puzzle of Paderewski

Ignace Paderewski (1860–1941) was a very popular pianist. He gave many concerts over several decades in Europe and the United States, playing Beethoven, Chopin, and Liszt as well as some of his own works. We are told that he was a striking presence on stage, having a mop of golden red hair and looks that made many a woman's heart flutter. Paderewski also had a political side. Shortly before the First World War, Paderewski began to speak out on behalf of the cause of Polish independence and sometimes his concerts combined both music and political matters. Paderewski quickly became known as the most famous advocate of the Polish cause, and after the war, having raised a lot of money for Polish independence as well as for famine relief, he became prime minister of Poland. Once Poland had established itself as a separate state, Paderewski resigned as prime minister and returned to the concert hall. When Poland was invaded at the beginning of the Second World War, Paderewski returned to political activities in support of his country, giving up his musical career.

Paderewski started to interest philosophers with the publication of Saul Kripke's 1979 paper "A Puzzle About Belief". That paper is largely concerned with the example of London and Londres, but there is a short passage about Paderewski in which a puzzle is presented that goes as follows. Suppose that Peter reads about a pianist named "Paderewski" and also independently comes to know a Polish statesman named "Paderewski". It never strikes Peter that they are one and the same person. On the contrary, given their very different activities, he believes that they are two people sharing a common name. Peter also believes that no politicians have musical talent and that no pianists are political figures. Knowing all the relevant facts, it certainly seems plausible to attribute to Peter both the belief that Paderewski had musical talent and the belief that Paderewski did not have musical talent. But which belief does he have? He cannot have both, it seems, for they are straightforwardly inconsistent and Peter is fully rational.

This case differs from Hesperus/Phosphorus cases, of which we now present a further example. James is a schoolboy who learns in Latin class that Cicero was a Roman orator. He also reads of Tully, but he pays little attention and confusedly forms the belief that Tully was a gladiator. In fact, Cicero is Tully. Believing that no gladiators are orators, James believes that Cicero was a Roman orator and also that Tully was not a Roman orator. In this case, it seems plausible to claim that two different concepts are operative in James's beliefs: the concept CICERO and the concept TULLY. Since James cannot link the referent of the one concept with the referent of the other except by empirical investigation, James has no *contradictory* beliefs (though he does have a conjunctive belief that cannot possibly be true, namely the belief that Cicero was a Roman orator and Tully was not).[15] In the Paderewski case, however, it seems that Peter really does believe contradictory things. If so, Peter is irrational. But *ex hypothesi* he is not. How can this be? How can Peter have straightforwardly contradictory beliefs and yet it be the case that no amount of logical acumen on his part will enable him to uncover their inconsistency?

That's what we call the standard puzzle of Paderewski, and the one to which Kripke and his commentators have devoted most of their attention. Kripke also mentions another puzzle, and we call this the strengthened puzzle. If you get Peter to think about politics and you ask him "Does Paderewski have musical talent?" the likely answer is "No". In many circumstances, this gives good reason to say that the subject does not believe that Paderewski has musical talent. But we've already seen that there are strong reasons to suppose that Peter *does* believe that Paderewski has musical talent. In the standard puzzle, the contradiction is confined to Peter's beliefs, and the puzzle is how a rational person could have such beliefs. In the strengthened puzzle, the very description of the case seems to involve a contradiction: Peter both does and does not believe that Paderewski has musical talent.

> *Puzzle 4: Paderewski (standard version)*
>
> *Peter believes that Paderewski has musical talent. Peter is perfectly rational. Peter believes that Paderewski lacks musical talent. These beliefs are contradictory. But a rational person does not have contradictory beliefs!*

1.5 The Puzzle of Pure Demonstratives

Consider the thought I express by uttering, "That is a coin", as I view a coin before me, and further the thought I express by uttering, "That is a coin", as I reach out and feel a coin with my hand. Suppose that I am participating in a psychological experiment on visual illusions and, although I can see a hand touching the coin, I wonder to myself whether it is really my hand. So wondering, I also wonder whether that (the coin I am seeing) is one and the same as that (the coin I am feeling).

---

[15] The same points can be made in the Hesperus/Phosphorus case, if James believes that Hesperus is seen at a certain position in the evening sky and he also believes that Phosphorus is not seen at that position in the evening.

In both cases, I am thinking about the same object via the demonstrative concept THAT and I am also exercising in my thought the same general concept COIN. Am I thinking the same thing twice? It would seem not; for in the given situation it can be a discovery to me that that is the same as that. But if I am thinking two different things, what accounts for this difference?

One natural idea is that I associate the coin with different properties in the two exercises of the demonstrative concept THAT. For example, I think of the coin as being felt by me as I reach out and touch it, and I think of it as being seen by me as I view it. The representational content of my first thought would be more perspicuously expressed by "That which I am feeling is a coin" and the representational content of my second thought by "That which I am seeing is a coin". My discovery is then that that which I am feeling is that which I am seeing.

This proposal may be put by saying that the demonstrative concept THAT, on these different occasions of its exercise, utilizes different modes of presentation, and these ensure its content is different on the different occasions. In the one case, there is a tactual mode of presentation and in the other a visual one, where the relevant modes of presentation are properties the thinker apriori associates with the demonstrative concept on the two occasions of its exercise. David Austin (1990) has constructed an example designed to rule out this kind of response: the puzzle of the two tubes.

Suppose that there is a person, Jonathan, who is capable of focusing his eyes independently and who looks with each eye through a small hole in a vertical, black board. Attached to the other side of the board are two separate black tubes. Each tube extends away from one of the holes to a vertical screen, on which there is a red circular patch with a diameter the same as that of the tubes. Jonathan cannot tell just how the two tubes are oriented. In fact, the two tubes merge into one as they get close to the screen, so Jonathan is seeing just a single red patch.

Jonathan believes that he may be subject to a complex medical condition, the effect of which is that he cannot tell reliably on the basis of his visual and bodily experiences where objects are located, or even which eye he is using to see which object. He asks himself whether that (referring to the red, circular region that he is actually seeing with his left eye) is identical with that (referring to the red, circular region that he is actually seeing with his right eye). This question is not a trivial one. Jonathan does not know the answer. In considering whether that is the same as that, Jonathan thinks to himself that that is the same as that, but he does not know whether to endorse the thought or reject it. There is nothing in the thought that tells Jonathan whether it is true or false. Jonathan's thought, then, cannot simply be of the form $a = a$. So, what is its form?

It is tempting to suppose that this case should be handled in the same general way as the coin case. Yet there seems to be no difference in the properties Jonathan apriori associates with the referent of the demonstrative concept THAT on the two occasions of its exercise in his thought. Evidently, Jonathan's perplexity is not explained by supposing that he is really thinking that that which he is seeing is that which he is seeing. Nor does it help to suppose that, in referring to the object as "that" he apriori associates with it the property of being focused on with the left eye in the one case and being focused on with the right eye in the other. Since Jonathan cannot tell which eye he is using on which occasion, he might be unwilling to associate either of these properties with what he is seeing.

Perhaps it will be suggested that Jonathan apriori associates different appearance properties with the two applications of the demonstrative concept in his thought. In wondering whether that is that, he is wondering whether that patch which is presented to him as appearing to be to the left of a red patch is the same as that patch which is presented to him as appearing to be to the right of a red patch. But this cannot be right. Jonathan, via the use of his left eye, has a visual experience as of a red patch and, via the use of his right eye, he also has a visual experience as of a red patch. But he does not have a visual experience as of two spatially connected patches. How, then, can it be a discovery for Jonathan that that is that? How can it be a matter of some confusion to him as to whether that is that? Herein lies the puzzle of pure demonstratives.

Another case involving pure demonstratives arises in connection with the color scientist Mary (Jackson 1982). The example has been used to provide an argument against physicalism (the view that all objects and all facts are physical[16]). Mary is locked in a black and white room. She has been there all her life and she has only ever experienced things in black, white, and shades of grey. Using the computers in her room, which come equipped only with black and white monitor screens, and an extensive library, Mary comes to know a great deal about color vision. Indeed, she comes to have exhaustive knowledge of the physical facts of color vision. She comes to know all there is to know about, for example, the surfaces of red objects, the way they reflect light, the subsequent changes in the retina, the optic nerve, and the visual cortex. But there is something she doesn't know; indeed there is something she cannot know while she remains in her room. This is shown by the fact that when she finally leaves her room and sees something red for the first time, she makes a significant discovery, one she might express as, "So *this* is what it's like to see red". She comes to know something she was unable to know before. Since, by hypothesis, she knew all the physical facts before she emerged from the black and white room, it seems that the fact she discovers must be non-physical. Hence there are non-physical facts. Hence physicalism is false.

This argument is often called the "Knowledge Argument".[17] In the present context, our interest is in showing how Mary's situation gives rise to a puzzle involving pure demonstratives. Suppose that when Mary leaves her room and experiences red for the first time, she introspects her experience and thinks of its subjective character using the concept THIS. Suppose also that she is interested in keeping track of her brain states as

---

[16] This statement of the thesis of physicalism is oversimplified (harmlessly so for present purposes). For a detailed treatment, see Tye (2009, ch. 2).

[17] Mary's situation is fantastic, of course, but it is not so very far removed from real-world situations. Knut Nordby, a well-known Scandinavian color scientist, is also an achromatope: he sees the world in black and white.

she undergoes new color experiences and that she has strapped to her head an autocerebroscope—a device that enables her to scan her own brain. As she sees something red, she turns her attention for a moment to the brain state registered in her visual cortex by the autocerebroscope and thinks of it using the concept THIS. Some physicalists hold that the subjective character of Mary's experience of red is one and the same as the registered brain state. Suppose that physicalism of this variety is true. Then if Mary thinks to herself that this—the subjective character she introspects—is the same as this—the registered brain state—her thought, it seems, is trivial; for it is of the form $a = a$. But that seems wrong. Intuitively, Mary has a thought expressing a significant empirical discovery, at least if physicalism of the above sort is true.

One possible reaction to this scenario is to say that Mary doesn't really make a discovery and that the case undermines the physicalist view that the subjective character of experience is a state of the brain. But whatever one's views on physicalism it is not obvious that this is the right response, as we shall show later.

Another possible reaction is to insist that Mary apriori associates different properties with the relevant brain state when she introspects it and when she views it through the cerebroscope. The trouble now is that Mary, in her room, is supposed to know all the physical facts (past, present, and future) and thus, if physicalism is true, all the facts there are. So, even if it is the case that Mary associates apriori different properties with the relevant brain state, this cannot fully explain the *discovery* she supposedly makes when she thinks to herself that this is this. For physicalists, this should be a physical fact, and so a fact Mary knew before she left the room.

Puzzle 5: Pure demonstratives

One can use two demonstratives to think something of the form that is that. But if the demonstratives refer to the same thing, how could one fail to know whether or not the statement of identity is true?

1.6 The Puzzle of Empty Thoughts

If a child thinks that Santa Claus lives at the North Pole, the child certainly thinks something. But what exactly is the child thinking? Her thought cannot concern a certain real individual, Santa Claus, ascribing to him the property of living at the North Pole; for there is no such individual. So, the child's thought cannot have truth conditions that involve this individual.

Consider another case. Leverrier believed that there was such a planet as Vulcan, and that Vulcan's proximity to Mercury explained at least some of the observed perturbations in Mercury's perihelion.[18] Leverrier was wrong: Vulcan does not exist. Leverrier's

---

[18] We here follow philosophical tradition in oversimplifying the history of astronomy; see Roseveare (1982).

beliefs did not concern any real thing. Did they concern some unreal thing? That seems more than a little far fetched, and would create trouble for understanding what is generally believed today. For when we say now that Vulcan does not exist, we surely take ourselves to be denying that there is such a thing rather than affirming that there is such a thing but that it is unreal.

Reflections of the above sort have led some philosophers to suppose that in those cases in which a thought involves an empty concept, the representational content of the thought is descriptive (like the Fregean view of the representational content of the thought that Hesperus is a planet). On this view, the concept VULCAN is really the concept THE INTRA-MERCURIAL PLANET. Similarly, the concept SANTA CLAUS is the concept THE JOLLY FELLOW WHO DRIVES A SLEDGE AND BRINGS CHILDREN PRESENTS AT CHRISTMAS (or something of this sort). Thus, one who thinks that Vulcan does not exist thinks that it is not the case that there is exactly one intra-Mercurial planet; this negative existential thought is straightforwardly true. Similarly, one who thinks that Santa Claus lives at the North Pole thinks that there is exactly one jolly fellow who drives a sledge and who brings children presents at Christmas and that individual lives at the North Pole; this thought is straightforwardly false.

The trouble with the above view is that people can agree in their beliefs even when they associate dramatically different descriptions with their concepts. Consider the belief that Vulcan is a small planet. Suppose that, before Galle looked through his superior German optics at the part of the sky where Vulcan should have been and did not see it, thereby disconfirming Leverrier's hypothesis, some anti-intellectual disturbance hit Europe, so that scientific research was brought to a standstill, and there was a rapid decline into superstition and darkness. Leverrier's supposed "discovery" of Vulcan was never tested, but news of it reached the popular press, and Vulcan-stories abounded. Astrologists claimed that those born when Vulcan was in the ascendant would have the ability to resist mercury poisoning, and naturopaths claimed that a pinch of dust from Vulcan, taken with a glass of Irish bog water, would protect against syphilis. In time, the way the name "Vulcan" was introduced was forgotten, and some rational people came to doubt that Vulcan lay between Mercury and the sun.

In the story just told of descent into a dark age, it is still believed that Vulcan is a small planet, just as Leverrier thought. To this extent, there is agreement. But it is no longer believed that Vulcan is the intra-Mercurial planet. So, the thought that Vulcan is a small planet cannot be the thought that there is exactly one intra-Mercurial planet and that planet is a small planet. So, what is the nature of the thought? In particular, what is the nature of the concept VULCAN (and other empty concepts)?

Puzzle 6: Empty thoughts

One can quite well think that Vulcan does not exist, or that Santa Claus brings presents at Christmas. But the concepts VULCAN and SANTA CLAUS do not refer to, and do not represent anything. How can genuine thoughts involve these concepts?

1.7 The Puzzle of Thinking About Oneself

In 1885, Ernst Mach reported:

> Not long ago, after a trying railway journey by night, when I was very tired, I got into an omnibus, just as another man appeared at the other end. "What a shabby pedagogue that man is, that has just entered," thought I.

Mach continued:

> It was myself: opposite me hung a large mirror. The physiognomy of my class, accordingly, was better known to me than my own.

In this example, the following three claims are all true:

9. Ernst Mach believed that that man was a shabby pedagogue.
10. That man was Ernst Mach.
11. Ernst Mach did not believe that he himself was a shabby pedagogue.

How can all three of (9)–(11) be true? What is required of one to form a first person thought or belief about oneself *as* oneself, a belief one can express in a sentence of the form "I am *F*"? This is the puzzle of thinking of oneself.

Normally, when one fails to know something, one lacks knowledge of some state of affairs in the world. But cases of the sort Mach describes can be developed in such a way as to show that this cannot be the right account: one can know everything there is to know about the composition of the world and yet still lack self-knowledge. Consider an example due to John Perry (1977). An amnesiac, Rudolf Lingens, is lost in the Stanford library. He reads many books in the library. Among them is a biography of Lingens and a detailed floor plan of the library itself. Lingens keeps reading. No matter how much he reads, no matter how large his store of knowledge becomes, he won't know who he is until he is ready to say (in Perry's words), "*This* place is aisle five, floor six, of Main Library, Stanford. I am Rudolf Lingens."

A related case is given by David Lewis (1979). Lewis asks us to imagine a world in which there are two gods. Each god knows every state of affairs that obtains in the world they inhabit. In this way, each god is omniscient. Still, Lewis claims, it makes sense to suppose that they suffer ignorance in that neither one knows which god he is. Imagine, for example, that one of them lives on top of the coldest mountain and flings down thunderbolts. The other lives on top of the tallest mountain and throws manna. As Lewis puts it:

> Neither one knows whether he lives on the tallest mountain or the coldest mountain. Neither one knows whether he throws manna or thunderbolts. (Lewis 1979: 520)

These cases strongly suggest that there is a way of thinking of oneself that is different from third person, objective ways of thinking of oneself.

It may be tempting to suppose that the concept I is a special sort of recognitional concept.[19] But though the concept I sometimes seems to function in a recognitional manner, it does not always do so, as the following passage from Wittgenstein makes clear.

> There are two different cases in the use of the word "I" (or "my") which I might call "the use as object" and "the use as subject". Examples of the first kind of use are these: "My arm is broken", "I have grown six inches", "I have a bump on my forehead".... Examples of the second kind are: "I see so and so", "I hear so and so", "I try to lift my arm", "I think it will rain", "I have a toothache". One can point to the difference between these two categories by saying: The cases of the first category involve the recognition of a particular person, and there is in these cases the possibility of error, or as I should rather put it: The possibility of an error has been provided for... It is possible that, say in an accident, I should feel a pain in my arm, see a broken arm at my side, and think it is mine, when really it is my neighbour's. And I could, looking into a mirror, mistake a bump on his forehead for one on mine. On the other hand there is no question of recognizing a person when I say I have a toothache. To ask "are you sure that it's you who have pains?" would be nonsensical... And now this way of stating our idea suggests itself: that it is impossible that in making the statement "I have a toothache" I should have mistaken another person for myself.... (*The Blue and Brown Books*)

Wittgenstein's point may be put by saying that in some (though not all) cases of thought about oneself, there is immunity to error through misidentification. Again, how can this be? A full solution to the puzzle of thinking of oneself must explain how first person thought differs from third person thought, and how (and why) in some cases it involves immunity to error through misidentification.

> *Puzzle 7: Thinking about oneself*
>
> *What is it for someone to think about herself as herself? An appropriate concept, it seems, must do more than just represent the subject, for she is represented in many ways. Does this special way of thinking about the subject engender some special immunity to error?*

---

[19] Our usual convention of presenting words that refer to concepts in small capitals (as in "the concept WATER") does not work well for the first-person concept, since in English the word expressing it is already in capitals. We therefore use a distinct with-serif font: I (as opposed to I).

2
Roads Not Taken

This chapter reviews two familiar approaches to the puzzles of thought. One stems from Frege and the other from Mill, so they may be called Fregean and Millian theories. In each case, we describe a straightforward version of the view first, and then look at more sophisticated (and recent) versions: the hidden indexical theory of section 2.3 is a sophistication of Millian views, and the two-dimensionalism of section 2.4 is a sophistication of Fregean views.

The aim is not to refute these alternative theories, but rather to bring out difficulties they encounter. Our positive view, originalism, which we believe does not confront these difficulties, is initially set out in Chapter 3.

The views discussed here are typically applied to language, whereas our interest is in applying them to thought. We offer fairly simple-minded refashioning of the views to apply them to thought. Proponents of the views might adopt different and perhaps more sophisticated ways of transitioning from language to thought. That's why we can't claim to refute any position in this chapter. But we can show that at least simple-minded applications to thought of familiar views about language have a hard time explaining the puzzles.

Concepts are components of thoughts. As noted in the last chapter, we use phrases like "the concept WATER" to refer to a unique concept, one expressed by the word "water" in English. The idiom should be distinguished from "the concept of water". Since water can be conceptualized in many different ways, there is no such thing as *the* concept of water. "Concept of water" is true of all the concepts that refer to water: the concept H_2O, the concept STUFF IN MY GLASS RIGHT NOW, and so on. Concepts must be distinguished from conceptions. We and you may share the concept WATER yet have very different conceptions of it. Perhaps you are a chemist, and have as part of your conception of water that its enthalpy of fusion is 333.55 kJ·kg^{-1} at 0°C, whereas we are scientifically uninformed, so that our conception of water contains nothing of the kind. This difference of conception does not prevent us sharing the concept WATER, and hence sharing thoughts involving the concept, for example the thought that water tastes best cold.

Concepts come in various different kinds. Atomic and nonatomic concepts have already been distinguished (e.g. the concept WATER as compared to the concept H_2O).[1]

---

[1] The distinction is not entirely straightforward. Is the concept CAPE COD atomic or nonatomic? There is some pressure to say it is nonatomic, for it would seem to contain the concept CAPE. But the same pressure

There are other distinctions corresponding to different parts of speech in language. Corresponding to names and other referring expressions, we speak of *nominative concepts*. Corresponding to predicates, there are *predicative concepts*. There are logical concepts like the concept AND, intensifying concepts like the concept VERY, and so on. In discussing the puzzles, the main focus is on nominative concepts.

Concepts are public and shared. No doubt we and you think of Austin in somewhat different ways. But we all have the same concept AUSTIN, shown by the sameness of some of our thoughts, and logical relations among others. If you and we think that Austin is a cool city, we think the same thought, and hence share the concepts that constitute it, and hence share the concept AUSTIN. If you think that Austin is the music capital of the world and we disagree, we think a thought that conflicts with yours, and this is again explicable in terms of our sharing the concept AUSTIN. This is consistent with our associating the concept with different information, which is what makes us say that we think of Austin in different ways. This helps locate concepts at a certain level of description of mental states. If one tries to provide too much detail, one will miss out on what is in common between the mental states of many people when they think of Austin as Austin.

Thoughts are structures of concepts. Their content is *compositional*, a function of the properties of the composing concepts. The nature of conceptual content is a central area of debate, and our own view is not presented until Chapter 3. However, every theorist must agree that many concepts are *true of* things: the nominative concept AUSTIN is true of, or applies to, Austin, and so does the predicative concept CITY.

These general points are presupposed when we apply familiar views in philosophy of language to the nature of thought.

2.1 Naïve Millian Views

Mill held that the meaning of a proper name is simply its bearer.[2] Transposing this view from language to thought, a Millian view is that the content of an atomic nominative concept is simply its reference. Hence atomic concepts which agree in their reference agree in their content: the content of the concept HESPERUS is the same as the content of the concept PHOSPHORUS, the content of the concept CAT is the same as the content of the concept CHAT, and so on.

Views of this kind have been very popular in the last fifty or so years. Their popularity may stem from an undeniably valuable feature: Millians present the mind as in direct contact with objects in the world, by means of atomic concepts or names. As philosophers have increasingly repudiated various kinds of idealism, according to

---

might incline us to say that the concept DARTMOUTH is nonatomic, despite the fact that, if Mill is right, it would continue to apply to the town it now applies to even if the River Dart changed course.

[2] This is probably not exactly what Mill said (see Mill 1843), but it's a standard oversimplification.

which the primary objects of thought are ideas or other mental entities, Millianism's robust realism has seemed attractive.

Yet two puzzles from Chapter 1 pose serious problems for Millian views, ones we regard as insuperable. One puzzle is to explain how the thought that Hesperus is Hesperus differs from the thought that Hesperus is Phosphorus; or how the thought that Hesperus is visible differs from the thought that Phosphorus is visible. The pairs of thoughts have the same content, and Millians seem to have no further resources to which they can appeal to explain these differences, differences we'll refer to as "the Fregean data".

The other puzzle is that of empty content. The concept VULCAN has no reference, so a Millian must say it has no content. Millians seem to have no further resources to which they can appeal to explain how, even so, such concepts apparently have a use in the construction of thoughts. To test his hypothesis, Leverrier had to think things like: if the perturbations in the orbit of Mercury are really caused by Vulcan, then Vulcan must be pretty large. Millians are apparently unable to explain how such thoughts can be contentful.

These are familiar problems for Millian views. Fregean or descriptivist theories are often motivated by an attempt to avoid these problems.

2.2 Fregean or Descriptivist Views

Naïve Millianism seems to mischaracterize atomic nominative concepts in two ways. It's too demanding, since it requires that every such concept has a referent, whereas intuitively there are usable nominative concepts that do not. This makes it impossible for Millians to give any natural account of empty content. It's not demanding enough, since Millian atomic nominative concepts contain no resources with which to accommodate the Fregean data. Descriptivist views, which go back to (one reading of) Frege, address both problems.

Frege's view was applied to language. Every expression[3] has a sense, "wherein the mode of presentation [of the reference] is contained"; and the sense of an expression determines its reference. By a thought (*Gedanke*), Frege understood a structure of senses. Senses, and the thoughts they compose, are abstract mind-independent entities, and our minds engage with them in thinking.

Frege's claim that a sense is a mode of presentation[4] needs to be elaborated. Following a common exegetical practice, we attribute to him the view that a sense

---

[3] Frege (1892) explicitly attributes sense only to proper names, though this category is construed very broadly, so as to include definite descriptions and whole sentences. It seems to us that his overall view requires the attribution of sense to all expressions, so as to provide materials for Fregean thoughts, which are structures of senses.

[4] Strictly speaking, he says that a sense *contains* a mode of presentation. We follow most commentators in ignoring any distinction between a mode of presentation and a container for a mode.

can be made fully explicit by a definite description.[5] For language, the sense of an expression like "Hesperus" can be made explicit by a description like "the evening star". It follows that a thought expressed by, for example, "Hesperus is visible", is a structure of senses whose initial element can be expressed by a definite description. Whereas the sentence starts with an apparently semantically simple expression, the thought starts with a complex sense. Distinct but coreferring expressions can introduce distinct senses, and this leads to a straightforward explanation of how "Hesperus is Hesperus" and "Hesperus is Phosphorus" express different thoughts, and how it is possible to think the thought expressed by "Hesperus is visible" without thinking the thought expressed by "Phosphorus is visible". The pairs coincide in reference, but differ in sense. The picture also provides a straightforward explanation of the possibility of empty thought, like the thought that Pegasus was a horse. The associated descriptive sense, for example the sense made explicit by the definite description "the winged horse tamed by Bellerophon", is one that nothing satisfies, so there is sense without reference.

This picture implements an idea that we believe is profoundly mistaken, and which we take to be the deep motivation for descriptivist approaches like Frege's. The idea is that a particular object cannot come before the mind directly and as such, but only through the intermediary of certain properties or attributes, the ones introduced into the sense. On this view, one may try to think of Hesperus just as such, but the best one can do is to think of certain attributes, like *being the first star to become visible in the evening*. One reaches out mentally to Hesperus as the unique possessor of these attributes. The attributes function as a medium between our minds and the objects. By contrast, we believe, as Mill did, that one can think of objects simply as such, without reaching out to them through the intermediary of properties. This is the intuitively natural view of how objects can come before the mind, and the Fregean picture is open to decisive objections.

Chapter 1 gave a standard reason for dissatisfaction with descriptivist views of empty content, as applied to the concept Vulcan. It seems that people could continue to exercise the concept Vulcan without exercising the concept THE INTRA-MERCURIAL PLANET. For example, people might forget that Leverrier initially introduced the concept Vulcan to apply to a supposed planet lying between Mercury and the sun; a new generation of exercisers of the concept Vulcan might have no idea that Vulcan was, supposedly, the intra-Mercurial planet. That can't be the same as having no idea that the intra-Mercurial planet was the intra-Mercurial planet. Hence the concept Vulcan cannot be the same as the concept THE INTRA-MERCURIAL PLANET, and cannot have *being the intra-Mercurial planet* as its sense. It would seem that an argument of this kind can be produced for more or less

---

[5] This interpretation of Frege is resisted by, for example, Evans (1982). No one doubts that Frege at least sometimes uses definite descriptions as a way of describing the sense of proper names, as in footnote 4 of "On sense and reference" (1892).

any descriptive (nonatomic) concept that is offered as being a candidate for the sense of the concept VULCAN.

A related familiar reason for dissatisfaction with descriptivism is the following. Intuitively, the concept HESPERUS is widely shared. We and you all possess it, despite the many differences between us in astronomical knowledge and other matters. One manifestation of this is that we all can use the word "Hesperus" in successful communication. If you say "Hesperus is visible" and we agree, we agree with the very thought that you express with those words, because we use the same concept HESPERUS as you use. Descriptivists must therefore find a shared descriptive sense or concept. But precisely which descriptive concept do we all share? We gave as a candidate the descriptive concept THE INTRA-MERCURIAL PLANET. But perhaps some people think of Vulcan through the descriptive concept THE PLANET, LYING BETWEEN MERCURY AND THE SUN, THAT CAUSES THE OTHERWISE UNEXPECTED PATH OF MERCURY. This is plainly a different concept from the other one: it contains the concept PATH, which the other does not. There are a whole range of possibilities (THE PLANET NAMED BY JACQUES BABINET, THOUGH FREQUENTLY SUPPOSED TO HAVE BEEN NAMED BY LEVERRIER; THE PLANET HYPOTHESIZED BY LEVERRIER, BUT FOUND NOT TO EXIST; and so on). The only basis for choice would seem to be what goes on in thinkers' minds. But at this level of detail, there will be variation from thinker to thinker, as just illustrated, whereas what we wish to say is that all these thinkers share a common concept, the concept VULCAN.

The phenomenon appears to be quite general. It might be that you associate the word "Hesperus" with the concept THE EVENING STAR, whereas we associate it with the concept THE PLANET OCCUPYING SUCH-AND-SUCH A POSITION IN THE EVENING SKY, and some confused person associates the word with the concept THE MORNING STAR. Yet we all use the single concept HESPERUS. The descriptivist faces the challenge of explaining how all of us can, at some level of description, count as thinking of Hesperus in the same way, using the common public concept HESPERUS.

The intuitive commitment to such shared public concepts emerges in ways in which we think about belief and communication. If I assert that Hesperus is visible, it won't do for you to say, "Well, I think that Hesperus is not visible, though of course I'm not committed to disagreeing with you, since I may be using a different concept HESPERUS". On the contrary, in such cases there is a genuine disagreement, a disagreement concerning a shared thought, even if the subjects associate different information with the shared concept HESPERUS.

Descriptivists face a structural difficulty. They see conceptual complexity where others do not. Yet they must allow that there are atomic concepts, for the nonatomic concepts need atomic ones as their basic building blocks.[6] There are two strategies for addressing this need. One, followed by Russell, is to allow that there is a privileged class of atomic

---

[6] Another way of putting this is: anything like Frege's view needs to allow for "primitive" concepts, ones whose sense is identical to the concept itself, so that grasping it does not require one to grasp distinct concepts.

nominative concepts. Another is to deny that there are any atomic nominative concepts at all. We'll briefly review each strategy.

The Russellian strategy, transposed into our framework, selects as the only atomic nominative concepts those whose referents are sense-data (the immediate objects of perception).[7] Russell chose these as privileged objects because he thought they had special features which would prevent Frege puzzles from arising:

1. One could never think that a sense-datum was before one's mind when there was nothing (a victim of Descartes' evil genius scenario would have just the same sense-data as an inhabitant of our world);
2. If on two occasions one were presented with a sense-datum, one could never make a mistake about whether the same sense-datum had been presented twice, or whether two sense-data had been presented.

The second point can be regarded as aimed to prevent problems of the Hesperus/Phosphorus kind when the referents are sense-data, and the first can be regarded as supposed to prevent puzzles about empty content. But sense-data won't help deliver an account of public concepts. As Russell said, sense-data are not shared, we don't have any concepts for them, and if we did they would be highly idiosyncratic and would not form a good basis on which to construct public concepts.[8]

The alternative strategy is to deny that there are any atomic nominative concepts. On this view, it is properties that are the fundamental objects of conceptualization. We cannot bring an individual object under a concept directly; only indirectly, by constructing some set of properties, conceptualized in a nonatomic concept.[9]

A view of this kind must allow some atomic nominative concepts, since otherwise there's no chance of constructing suitable nonatomic nominal concepts. The nominative concept BARACK OBAMA cannot be just the concept THE PRESIDENT OF THE US, for there have been many presidents. Some indicator of time is needed, say THE PRESIDENT OF THE US IN 2009. The concept 2009 has a year as its referent; it's a nominative concept. One can disagree about whether or not it is atomic, but a standard view is that, atomic or not, its referent is ultimately fixed in terms of some atomic indexical concept, for example the concept NOW. So atomic nominative concepts will feature somewhere in this account. Likewise, names of places will ultimately need to be tied down by some atomic concept like the concept HERE. Descriptivists commonly allow that there are atomic indexical nominative concepts, like the concepts NOW, HERE, and I. In that case, why not go further, and allow nonindexical atomic nominative concepts, like the

---

[7] In his framework (which has no room for concepts) the question is: what are the objects of immediate acquaintance? See Russell (1912, ch. 5).
[8] Russell was well aware of this, and explicitly committed himself to the view that language was essentially idiosyncratic.
[9] This is the view McDowell (1977: 173) refers to as a "suspect conception of mind".

concept HESPERUS? The descriptivist's exclusive preference for indexical nominative concepts seems unmotivated.

Kit Fine has mounted an impressive attack on conventional Fregean theories, which he characterizes in a highly revealing way: Fregeans are motivated by the thought that *every cognitive difference must be reflected by a semantic difference* (2007: 35).[10] Fine himself preserves this principle, though setting it in an unconventional framework. By contrast, we take the principle to encapsulate very neatly the underlying assumption we challenge. On our view, some cognitive differences spring not from anything semantic, but from mere difference among concepts, where conceptual difference does not entail semantic difference. As will be elaborated in Chapters 3 and 4, the vehicles of content can affect cognition in ways that do not depend on their semantic properties.

Fregean descriptivist views became unpopular after Kripke's attacks in *Naming and Necessity* (1972/1980). Nowadays, the only forms of descriptivism with a significant following are those set in the framework of two-dimensional semantics, the topic of section 2.4 of this chapter; and our own theory is firmly non-descriptivist. Before turning to two-dimensionalism, we'll consider how Millians can refine their view so as to accommodate some of the data that seemed important to descriptivists, in particular the datum, or apparent datum, that someone could believe that Hesperus is visible without believing that Phosphorus is visible.

2.3 Sophisticated Millianism: The Hidden Indexical Theory

The key feature of Millian views of nominative concepts is that two atomic such concepts having the same referent also have the same content. This means that, as far as content goes, there is no difference between thinking of Hesperus as Hesperus, and thinking of it as Phosphorus, or as Venus. Intuitively, there is a difference: it's one thing to think of Hesperus as Hesperus, another to think of it as Phosphorus. This is what makes it possible to believe that Hesperus is visible without believing that Phosphorus is visible. Sophisticated Millians attempt to do justice to this intuition by allowing that there is more to thinking of an object than bringing it under a nominative concept.[11] In addition to the concept, there is also a *guise* (Salmon 1986), or *mode of presentation* (Schiffer 1992), or *notion* (Crimmins and Perry 1989). All these theories attempt to mitigate the conflict between Millian theories and Fregean data. We think the most promising approach is Schiffer's hidden indexical theory, which we discuss in more detail. (Schiffer himself does

---

[10] Fine himself thinks Fregeans are wrong to hold that every cognitive difference must be reflected by an *intrinsic* semantic difference. The point of his book is to develop a theory of *relational* semantic differences, a theory that vindicates the principle emphasized above.

[11] The theories are theories of language, so, in a standard formulation, "name" would replace "atomic concept". For our purposes, we adapt the theories to apply to thought.

not accept the theory, though he does think that it is the best theory available given some broad theoretical assumptions.[12])

The hidden indexical theory aims to do justice to some Fregean data while remaining within a fundamentally Millian framework. Schiffer (1992: 509) requires a successful theory to acknowledge that Lois Lane can believe that Superman flies without believing that Clark Kent flies.[13] This acknowledgement is unavailable to unsophisticated Millians, for whom belief is simply a relation to a proposition, since they count the proposition that Superman flies as the same as the proposition that Clark Kent flies. For these Millians, believing that Superman flies is the same as believing that Clark Kent flies.

The hidden indexical theory retains the fundamental Millian conception of meaning or content: for names or nominative concepts, their content is their reference, so sameness of reference is enough for sameness of content. The theory shares the Millian conception of the content of a thought, a "proposition": the proposition expressed by an atomic thought is the sequence of objects which are the referents of the concepts in the thought. The result is that, like unsophisticated Millians, for hidden indexical theorists the proposition that Superman flies is indeed the proposition that Clark Kent flies. The departure from unsophisticated Millianism consists in construing belief as a three-place relation between a subject, a proposition, and a mode of presentation of a proposition. The departure from Frege is that modes of presentation can vary from person to person and time to time, unlike Fregean senses, which are supposed to be invariant across a language community.[14]

These departures are both at work in the hidden indexical account of belief reports. The central contention is that a sentence or thought like

1. Lois Lane believes that Superman flies

should be understood on the following lines:

2. $\exists m(\phi^* m \ \& \ B(\text{Lois Lane}, <\text{Superman, flies}>, m))$.

The quantification is over modes of presentation. The condition ϕ^* is a context-dependent restriction on modes of presentation. It fixes a mode of presentation of each element in the proposition, and thereby fixes a mode of presentation of the proposition as a whole. For example, in order that (2) should be true and equivalent to (1), Lois's modes of thinking of Superman must be restricted to Superman modes, rather than Clark Kent modes; that is, ϕ^* must ensure that she thinks of Clark Kent as Superman, and not as Clark Kent. With this restriction on ϕ^* in place, the following is just as true as (2):

3. $\exists m(\phi^* m \ \& \ B(\text{Lois Lane}, <\text{Clark Kent, flies}>, m))$.

---

[12] Schiffer ends up using his criticisms of the hidden indexical theory to undermine the theoretical assumption that there are compositional theories of truth or meaning for natural languages.
[13] Superman examples require one to pretend that the fiction is fact.
[14] "The sense of a proper name is grasped by everybody who is sufficiently familiar with the language" (1892: 158).

On the other hand, and despite the truth of (3), the theory can also do justice to the truth of

    4. Lois Lane does not believe that Clark Kent flies.

Intuitively, this is true when Lois thinks of Clark Kent under the Clark Kent mode of presentation, whereas what made (3) true was her thinking of him under the Superman mode of presentation. Assuming that ϕ' restricts modes of presentation to Clark Kent ones, the following can be true, as an account of (4), and consistently with (3):

    5. $\exists m(\phi' m$ & not B(Lois Lane, <Clark Kent, flies>, m)).

Schiffer offers three criticisms of the hidden indexical theory, of which we will present just one. This is that is it incorrect to suggest that those who use sentences like "Lois Lane believes that Superman flies", or who think the thoughts these sentences express, are in general able to think of a suitable $\phi*$, a property of modes of presentation that restricts them to the very ones the subject of the belief attribution used. This is not so obvious in very simple and familiar examples like the beliefs attributed to Lois Lane, but becomes entirely clear in straightforward cases like this:

    6. Harold believes that TWA is offering a New York–Paris return fare for $318.

The attribution is perfectly ordinary, and can readily be made by someone who has no idea even how to begin to devise a $\phi*$ that suitably restricts Harold's ways of thinking about TWA, offering, New York, Paris, a fare, and $318. Hence it cannot be correct to represent the thought in (6) as one involving a thought of the $\phi*$-involving kind that the hidden indexical theory requires.

It is unclear how the hidden indexical theory would address more complex attributions of belief. For example, one might expect the following to be true:

    7. Jerry Siegel believes that Clark Kent flies, but Lois Lane doesn't.[15]

There is only one overt occurrence of "believes" and, intuitively, the implicit second occurrence of it copies the first occurrence: there is a relation of believing, there is something to be believed or not (that Clark Kent flies), and Siegel but not Lois is said to stand in that relation to that thing. By contrast, the hidden indexical theory must say that the relation involving Siegel is different from that involving Lois, for they are related to different modes of presentation. Siegel thinks of Clark Kent under some sort of composite mode, merging the Clark Kent and Superman modes, whereas Lois thinks of him under a Clark Kent specific mode. It seems as if we are beginning to explain difference of mode of presentation in terms of difference of belief, whereas the explanatory direction was supposed to be the opposite. In any case, the hidden indexical proposal seems absurdly ad hoc for such cases.

---

[15] Jerry Siegel is the author of the original Superman stories.

Perhaps one should retain the idea that belief is a three-place relation involving a subject, a proposition and a mode of presentation, but drop the restriction on the modes of presentation, thus removing at least the difficulty associated with (6). Then the original Lois Lane thought (1) will be represented simply as

8. $\exists m(B(\text{Lois Lane}, <\text{Superman, flies}>, m))$.

This modification, the removal of the hidden indexical, results in more or less Salmon's theory (1986), though Salmon speaks of "guises" rather than modes of presentation. As Salmon is well aware, the upshot is that Lois Lane *does* believe that Clark Kent flies, for there is a guise under which she thinks of Clark Kent, namely the Superman guise, and believes him to fly. Salmon tries to mitigate the implausibility of this upshot by appealing to pragmatic mechanisms: although it may sound false to utter "Lois Lane believes that Clark Kent flies", the reality is that our utterance is true but highly misleading. It is misleading because it suggests, though it does not entail, that Lois Lane thinks the relevant proposition under the Clark Kent guise, whereas she only thinks it under the Superman guise.

Salmon is right to say that there are cases in which we wrongly classify a misleading utterance as false. Suppose you know Jones and his sister well, but you wish to keep the fact that you know Jones (a notorious bad hat) to yourself. When asked "Do you know Jones?", you reply "I think I may know his sister". You have not said anything false. Even so, when the questioner finds out that you do know Jones, you could well be accused of deception or even of lying. So the phenomenon on which Salmon wishes to rely is genuine: it may be misleading to assert a truth. However, the phenomenon does not apply to the cases under discussion. Although Salmon was mostly interested in language, our interest is in thought, which need not involve the kind of interpersonal interaction which is the home of pragmatic phenomena. Most people believe that Lois Lane does not believe that *Clark Kent* flies; she believes that *Superman* flies. We can have these beliefs without saying anything, and so without triggering the pragmatic mechanisms on which Salmon relies. It must be admitted that we might be mistaken about what we believe. But if defending a theory requires holding that people are generally mistaken, some explanation of how the mistake arises is required. We are not aware of any plausible account of how we come to be mistaken in taking it that Lois Lane believes that Superman flies but not that Clark Kent does.[16]

There are more straightforward reasons for dissatisfaction with the hidden indexical theory, regarded as an attempt to reconcile Millian preferences with Fregean data. As presented by Schiffer, the theory applies to only one kind of Fregean datum: for verbs of propositional attitude V, pairs of sentences "S Vs that p" and "S Vs that q" may differ in truth value even when "p" and "q" do not differ at the level of reference (e.g. "p" is "Clark Kent flies" and "q" is "Superman flies"). But this does not exhaust the Fregean data. An adequate theory will have also to deal with contrasts like:

---

[16] A detailed criticism of Salmon's appeal to pragmatics is given by Schiffer (1987).

9. It's obvious that Hesperus is Hesperus but not that Hesperus is Phosphorus.
10. It was an empirical discovery that Hesperus is Phosphorus, but not that it is Hesperus.
11. One cannot know apriori that Hesperus is Phosphorus.

Extending the hidden indexical theory to these cases will lead at best to a complicated and unintuitive account.

Finally, the hidden indexical theory does not address the problem of empty content and has no resources with which to do so. If there is no such thing as Vulcan, it seems there could not be a mode of presentation of Vulcan.

Originalism, as will become clear in Chapter 3, has similarities with Millian theories. According to originalism, the content of atomic concepts is just their reference, so atomic concepts that agree in reference agree in content. Originalism differs from Millianism in finding no use for propositions, conceived as sequences of objects and properties. It accounts for many Fregean data in terms of sameness and difference among concepts, rather than in terms of guises, notions or modes of presentation. In Chapter 6, using no additional apparatus, originalism is extended to an account of ascriptions of beliefs and other attitudes that accommodates Fregean data.

2.4 Sophisticated Fregeanism: Two-dimensional Semantics

Taken in the broadest sense, a semantics is two-dimensional if it ascribes two systematic aspects of meaning. Fregean descriptivist semantics is, in this broad sense, two-dimensional: there is the referent of a word or concept, and then there is the sense, or associated description.

Two-dimensional semantics is normally understood more narrowly, as a theory that will reveal the epistemic aspects of our use of language in such a way as to permit a definition of what it is for a sentence or thought to be knowable apriori. On this understanding, it's a fairly recent phenomenon, originating in work by Jackson (1998b) and Chalmers (1996, 2004b, 2006). It's certainly not essential to this book that the reader should understand just how this approach differs from the one offered in Chapters 3 and 4. But for those who have encountered recent two-dimensionalism, the remainder of this section provides a survey and a discussion which, in the nature of the case, is rather complex. Skipping directly to Chapter 3 will induce no sense of discontinuity.

In a philosophical tradition that goes back at least to Kant, there was no need to distinguish necessity and apriority: it was held that any necessary truth is knowable apriori, and anything knowable apriori is necessary. Kripke's work in the 1970s convinced most philosophers that this was wrong (examples in the next paragraph). This meant that even if one had some satisfying account of necessity, say in terms of truth at all possible worlds, the notion of apriority required separate attention. The basic idea behind the two-dimensionalism to be discussed here is that an account of apriority should be added to standard possible worlds semantics by adding something structurally similar: just as necessity is treated in terms of universal quantification over possible worlds, capturing one aspect of meaning, so apriority will also be treated as universal quantification over entities similar to worlds, thereby capturing a distinct aspect of meaning. The aspect captured by relations to possible worlds is called an expression's "secondary intension"; the other aspect, distinctive of two dimensional semantics, is called the expression's "primary intension".

The non-equivalence of apriority and necessity is exemplified by sentences like "Hesperus is Phosphorus" and "Water is H_2O". These are not merely true, they are necessarily true, true however things might have been, true at every possible world.[17] Yet they are not knowable apriori, since one needs observation and empirical information to come to know that Hesperus is Phosphorus or that water is H_2O. There are arguably also sentences which are knowable apriori but are contingent, for example "I am here". You don't have to be where you are, so the sentence states something contingent; yet it can be known in advance and apriori that if you utter this sentence what you state is true.

Two-dimensional semantics[18] are motivated by the idea that apriority is in some sense a semantic phenomenon. Both primary and secondary intensions involve base elements, possible worlds or similar entities, but they are structured differently in order to do justice to different aspects of meaning. Call the world-like things that are the base elements in the primary intension "scenarios". The idea is to implement the following analogy:

Just as
Sentence s is necessarily true iff, for all possible worlds, w, s is true at w
so:
Sentence s is knowable apriori iff, for all scenarios, c, s is true at c.

Necessity is truth at all possible worlds, apriority is truth at all scenarios.[19] Being apriori is structurally like being necessary, and not being apriori is structurally like being contingent. The primary and secondary intensions together aspire to do justice not just to those aspects of meaning that give rise to the distinctions between necessarily true sentences and others, but also to those aspects of meaning that give rise to the distinctions between apriori sentences and others.

Similar issues arise for thought as for language.[20] The thoughts that Hesperus is Phosphorus or that water is H_2O are necessary but not knowable apriori. It would be useful if

---

[17] Might not water have been made of something other than H_2O? No! The truth is that it might have been that what makes up the oceans and falls as liquid from the sky was not H_2O, but this liquid would not have been water.

[18] There are various versions, some of which are overtly descriptivist (e.g. Jackson 1998b). See Davies and Stoljar (2004) for a review. We focus on a version developed by David Chalmers (1996, 2004b, 2006).

[19] See Chalmers (2006: 587): "it is crucial to the two dimensionalist position that typical a posteriori identities involving proper names or natural kind terms, such as 'Mark Twain is Samuel Clemens' or 'water is H_2O,' have a primary intension that is false in some scenario."

[20] Chalmers is explicit that his two-dimensionalist approach applies as much to thought as to language (e.g. 1996: 65; 2006: 596–7). Most of his discussions relate to language, so our transposition to thought may not coincide with what he would have said.

two-dimensional semantics could be applied to thoughts, capturing their epistemic aspects. Sometimes we'll transpose some of the crucial ideas of linguistic two-dimensional semantics to thought. At other times, and especially when paying close attention to details, we'll keep with the more familiar formulations in terms of language.

The conventional semantic dimension for thoughts, the secondary intension, starts with the notion of an *extension*. The extension of a nominative concept is its referent (just as for naïve Millianism), of a predicative concept the things of which it is true, and of a thought, its truth value. This notion can be relativized to worlds. The extension of the concept FEATHERLESS BIPED at our world is just humans, but at other worlds there are distinct featherless biped species, and at yet other worlds no such species. With some artificiality, the notion of extension can be applied to thoughts: true thoughts have the True as their extension, false thoughts the False.[21] More generally, the extension of a thought is its "truth value", which is the True if the thought is true, and the False if it is false. The extension of the thought that there is just one natural satellite of the earth is the True with respect to our world, but the False with respect to worlds at which the earth has fewer than one or more than one moon. Many nominative concepts, like the concepts HESPERUS and WATER, are "rigid": their extension is the same at every other world as it is at the actual world. This fits with the necessity of identity-thoughts that involve such concepts.

World-relativized extensions are standardly replaced by *intensions*: functions from worlds to extensions. The secondary intension of the concept FEATHERLESS BIPED is the set of ordered pairs whose first member is a possible world and whose second member consists of the featherless bipeds at that world. The secondary intension of a nominative concept like the concept WATER is a constant function, pairing each world with the stuff water. The intension of a sentence like "Water is liquid" is a function from worlds to truth values: to the True if water is liquid at the world, and otherwise to the value the False. Two-dimensionalists wish to incorporate these classical or conventional intensions into their theory, but to add further "primary" intensions, ones that will do justice to the cognitive aspects of concepts. The truths that are knowable apriori will have primary intensions true at every world, whereas the truths that are not knowable apriori will be assigned the False at some world by their primary intension.

"A primary intension is a function from scenarios to extensions" (Chalmers 2006: 585). The notion of a scenario is unclear, and Chalmers himself says that there is more than one way of cashing out what scenarios amount to. We review three options, and suggest that the third provides the clearest picture of the two-dimensionalist view.

1. Scenarios are possible worlds: "A scenario is a centered world: an ordered triple of a possible world along with an individual and a time in that world" (Chalmers 2006: 586).

---

[21] This idea, and the terminology, goes back to Frege (1892), and has now become common parlance, carrying no commitment to other Fregean views.

This cannot be what Chalmers really intends, for "Water is H_2O" is not apriori, and so is false at some scenario, but, as Chalmers agrees, it is true at every possible world.

2. Scenarios are possible worlds considered as actual: It might turn out that our world is an XYZ world: the stuff we take to be water (it falls as rain, fills the lakes and seas, and so on) is in fact XYZ and always has been (see the puzzle of the twins from Chapter 1). The chemists have somehow been fooled into thinking that water is H_2O when it is not.

If we were to discover that the oceans and lakes in the actual world contained XYZ, we would judge that water is XYZ... if the XYZ-world is actual, then water is XYZ. (Chalmers 2004b: 178)

In telling the XYZ story, we have "considered the XYZ world as actual", rather than as counterfactual. Maybe that's how we need to think of scenarios: they are possible worlds considered as actual, as opposed to possible worlds considered as counterfactual, and many of Chalmers' formulations take precisely that form.[22]

To consider a world as actual is not to consider whether or not, were we to use language in an XYZ world as similarly as possible to the way we actually use it, our word "water" would refer to XYZ. It's hard to dispute that this would be so. The question, rather, is whether the word "water" we actually use refers to XYZ in such a world, considered as actual.

Chalmers claims that, at the XYZ world considered as actual, our word "water," with the very meaning it actually has, would apply to XYZ. As stressed in the previous paragraph, this is different from the indisputable claim that, at the XYZ world, we would use the word "water" to apply to XYZ, and would not be wrong. The indisputable claim is consistent with the further claim that XYZ-uses of "water" do not have the same meaning as actual world uses. Chalmers' claim is debatable: as he recognizes, it will be resisted by those who think that the meaning of our word "water" essentially involves what it actually refers to.

A world is what it is, however we consider it. If there is no possible world at which water is XYZ, there is no possible world that we can consider as actual at which water is XYZ. "Considered as" marks a metaphor that requires explanation.

One explanation invites us to think of sentences as true not at single worlds, but at pairs of worlds: necessity, metaphysical or epistemic, is "double-indexed."[23] The first element in the index is the world that is actual in the model, and the second element is the world of

---

[22] "One might worry about how a metaphysically possible world (the XYZ-world) can verify a metaphysically impossible statement ('Water is XYZ')? But two-dimensional evaluation makes this straightforward: 'Water is XYZ' is true at the XYZ-world considered as actual, but false at the XYZ- world considered as counterfactual. The metaphysical impossibility of 'Water is XYZ' reflects the fact that it is false at all worlds considered as counterfactual. But this is quite compatible with its being true at some worlds considered as actual" (2004b: 186).

[23] The idea goes back at least to Segerberg (1973), who cites Kamp (1971), Prior (1968), and Vlach (1973) as precursors. We draw on Davies and Humberstone (1980), discussed in various places by Chalmers (e.g. 2004b: 163–4). They informally gloss the first of their two indices as specifying which world is to be "considered as actual". However, the double indexing in their theory only makes any difference when the target sentence contains an "actually" operator.

evaluation. The claim that "Water is water" is true at every (metaphysically) possible world, or world *considered as counterfactual*, is an abbreviated way of writing:

For all possible worlds, w, "Water is water" is true at $<@, w>$

where @ is the actual world, the one we and you in fact occupy. On this view, our familiar claims of necessity and possibility hold constant the first element of the index (which is why this first element is often not made explicit). But there are other claims that allow the index to vary. Let w^* name the XYZ world.[24] One way to understand the claim that "Water is XYZ" is true at w^* *considered as actual* is:

"Water is XYZ" is true at $<w^*, w^*>$.

Given that $w^* \neq @$, that's consistent with holding that

for all w, "Water is XYZ" is false at $<@, w>$.

The first index tells you which world matters for determining the referent of the expressions in the sentence; the second index is the world at which, with referents thus fixed, the sentence is to be evaluated for truth.

On this version of two-dimensionalism, both primary and secondary intensions will be double-indexed. Primary intensions will focus on "twin" pairs of worlds (e.g. $<w, w>$), those whose first member is the same as the second, since twinning interprets what it is to evaluate a sentence at "a world considered as actual." The definition of apriority would become:

Sentence s is knowable apriori iff, for all worlds, w, s is true at $<w, w>$.

Given what was just said about w^*, "Water is H_2O" comes out as not apriori, the desired result.

This is a coherent account, but it essentially depends upon the view that the referent of an expression depends upon which world is actual. Of course, understood in one way, that's trivial: if a world in which "pigs" was used to refer to birds was actual, then at that world (considered as actual) "pigs" would refer to birds. This can hardly tell us anything of interest about the actual semantics of "pigs," or about whether pigs can fly, or about any relevant apriority. When two dimensionalists say that, at the XYZ world, "water" refers to XYZ they mean that this is consistent with, and indeed reveals an aspect of, the actual meaning of "water" (its meaning at @).

As Chalmers is well aware, the upshot is that the meaning of a word like "water" does not essentially involve the referent water.[25] In the originalist theory developed in

---

[24] More exactly, an arbitrary XYZ world than which none more closely resembles our world (@). This resemblance ensures that XYZ at w^* plays just the role water actually plays.

[25] See Chalmers (2004b: 170): "*if* the referent of 'water' is essential to the word, as many theorists hold, then Twin Oscar's 'water' is a different word." Twin Oscar inhabits Twin-Earth, where the substance playing the role that water actually plays is XYZ. We accept the antecedent of the conditional (as intended in the context), whereas Chalmers rejects it. That's the main difference between his view and ours.

Chapter 3, concepts like the concept WATER have their actual reference essentially: there is no possible situation in which the very concept WATER that we use refers to something other than what we use it to refer to, that is, water. That's one difference between originalism and two-dimensionalism, and it extends to many concepts other than the concept WATER.

For two-dimensionalists, water itself plays no part in fixing the meaning of "water", so they need to say how its referent is fixed. We've already seen a rough suggestion: "water" refers to the liquid that fills the oceans and lakes.[26] We think that's wrong in principle, because it treats the word's meaning as not essentially involving the object, water. It may also be wrong in detail. For all we know apriori, water is not a liquid (at normal temperatures). Consider a "pink scenario"—one in which wherever we take there to be a body or sample of water, there is really a pale pink, granular stuff. This granular stuff is made up of conglomerations of tiny, pink particles, each about the size of a grain of sand. These particles form clouds in the atmosphere. The pink, granular stuff does not appear to us to be pink or granular but rather colorless and liquid. When we dip our fingers in it, we have the sensation of touching a liquid; and so on. When we use the term "water", we are really referring to this pink, granular stuff. We just don't realize this; we take the referent of "water" to be colorless and liquid, but we are wrong. The example shows that, even conceding the two-dimensionalist approach in general, there remain difficulties in saying exactly how reference is fixed. Is it fixed by the condition that it refers to something that is *really* a liquid? Or that *appears* to be a liquid?

At the heart of a two-dimensionalist's conception of primary intensions is the view that, holding meaning constant, an expression may have different referents with respect to different scenarios (different worlds considered as actual, on the present formulation). We certainly agree that there are such expressions: indexicals. However, they do not support the kind of disquotation that Chalmers seems to want, moving from "Water is XYZ" is true at the XYZ world to the claim that, at the XYZ world considered as actual, water is XYZ. Such moves are not always valid for expressions with contextually sensitive referents. Compare:

If (at some world) "water" refers to XYZ, then water is XYZ (at that world).
If (at some context) "I" refers to you, then I am you (at that context).

---

[26] Chalmers (2006: 593): "one might roughly characterize the primary intension of a typical use of 'water' by saying that in a centered world w, it picks out the dominant clear, drinkable liquid with which the individual at the center of w is acquainted."

for all w, "water" refers at <w, w> to whatever liquid fills the oceans and lakes at w.

(By contrast, our view is that "water" refers at w to the liquid that fills the oceans at @.) We also need to allow for the centering of the worlds, which can be accommodated by adding the final phrase from the quotation from Chalmers just given.)

We believe that the second example, plainly false, should guide our assessment of the first. This is not intended as a refutation of two-dimensionalism; Chalmers explicitly contrasts the way indexicals affect reference with the way he aims to specify for primary intensions (e.g. 2004: 175–6). Rather, it's a request for an explanation of how reference-fixing for words like "water" works differently from reference-fixing for words like "I", and in such a way as to permit the kind of disquotation at issue.

We think that it's no doubt true that if the watery stuff around us were in fact XYZ we would use the word "water" to refer to it, and we would be free from error.[27] We can also imaginatively project ourselves into such a situation, imagining that we are part of a linguistic community in which "water" is thus used. But we also think that this means that the word would have had a different meaning. We accept that the way in which a word is introduced, or a concept formed, helps determine what its referent is, but we don't see these ways as exhausting the meaning of a word: the referent also contributes to meaning, in a way the two-dimensional picture ignores. So we think that "Water might turn out to be XYZ" is clearly true if it means that it's not apriori that water is not XYZ. But if it means that there are circumstances such that, consistently with what "water" actually means, the word would have referred to XYZ, we demur.

The two-dimensional apparatus fails to connect in a natural way with the notion of apriori knowledge. It is not knowable apriori that there are dogs. The explanation, however, is not that the things we take to be dogs might in reality be fake dogs, things that stand to real dogs as XYZ stands to water. It is indeed so that we might be fooled in this way. But that's not the explanation of why our knowledge that there are dogs is not apriori. The real explanation is that we need observation and experience to come to know about dogs. Even if there could not be fake dogs, it's still not apriori that there are dogs. Likewise, the explanation of why it's not apriori that water is H_2O is simply that it took considerable empirical work to figure this out. Even if "water" designates rigidly, and so refers to water no matter which world is actual, we still can't know apriori which chemical kind its referent is.

The two-dimensionalist assumes that apriori knowledge is grounded in knowledge of meaning. Otherwise, the primary intension could not simultaneously register an aspect of meaning, and also be used to define apriority.[28] It has long been recognized that it is hard to explain apriori mathematical knowledge in terms of knowledge of meaning. Moreover, real debates about whether or not something is known apriori make no

---

[27] This holds on a standard understanding of counterfactual conditionals: the worlds most similar to ours, except that for containing XYZ wherever our world contains water, are ones in which we use "water" to refer to XYZ. Here the word "water" is, as Chalmers puts it, individuated orthographically, not semantically (Chalmers 2004b: 169). On our view, it does not mean what our word "water" means and, as we explain in Chapter 3, we see no merit in the idea that a word can be individuated orthographically.

[28] Chalmers envisages at least one way in which primary intensions can be defined independently of the notion of apriority (2004b: 183–4).

connection at all with two-dimensionalist ways of thinking. When Kenneth Appel and Wolfgang Haken first offered a proof of the four-color theorem it was held to be inadequate, for the mathematicians had used a computer to investigate each of the possible kinds of maps (they had established that there were just 1,936 possibilities). Tymoczko (1979) claimed that this could not count as an *apriori* proof, since it was not apriori that the computer had done its job correctly. While we offer no view about who was right, the character of the debate seems to us entirely fitting to the question at hand: does using a computer in this way count as "observation or experiment," or is its use consistent with the result being genuinely apriori? This debate about apriority is far removed from the issues a two-dimensionalist would have us consider; no alternative worlds considered as actual figure in the debate, and there are no questions about reference-fixing.[29]

3. *Scenarios are "maximal epistemic possibilities"* (*Chalmers* 2004b: 177)[30] Thus understood, "A scenario corresponds, intuitively, to a maximally specific way the world might be, for all one can know a priori" (2004b: 177). One way to add detail to this thought is to start with what it is for a sentence D of a language L to be "epistemically complete":

> D is epistemically complete for L iff D is epistemically possible (i.e. cannot be ruled out a priori) and there is no sentence S in L such that D & S and D & ¬S are both epistemically possible. (Chalmers 2004b: 188)

Since there are no doubt hypotheses that we cannot rule out apriori and which we also cannot express in English, we should think of L as an idealized language, with a fully expressive vocabulary and no restriction on the length of its sentences. We can then identify scenarios with epistemically complete sentences in some idealized language,[31] and define the verification of a sentence by a scenario as the scenario implying the sentence (where implication is understood as a relation that makes available rational apriori inference). Apriority is, as always, truth at every scenario, that is, being verified by every epistemically complete sentence.

Chalmers says that one might worry that if primary intensions are defined in terms of epistemically complete sentences, the result will be trivial: verification will become simply

---

[29] We don't think this observation as such constitutes an argument against two-dimensionalism (we are sympathetic to Chalmers's remarks about apriority in general (2004b: 208–9)). It's just that one possible way of justifying two-dimensionalism, by showing that it connects naturally with real debates about apriority, is in fact unavailable.

[30] We share the view that Chalmers expresses thus: "One might reasonably hold that since we want epistemic intensions to be constitutively connected to the epistemic realm, we need not invoke the metaphysical modality at all. Instead, we can do things wholly in terms of the epistemic modality" (2004b: 187).

[31] More exactly, a scenario is a class of equivalent epistemically complete sentences (2004: 189). It seems to us that epistemically complete sentences should also be the smallest ones that will resolve every issue (see 2004b: 199). E.g. if D' is like D except that D only implies whereas D' contains "Water is H_2O", then D is smaller than D'.

being part of (2004: 195). For all we know apriori, water is H_2O, and for all we know apriori, water is not H_2O. The worrisome trivialization is that this means that every epistemically complete sentence has to contain as a conjunct (a translation of) either "Water is H_2O" or "Water is not H_2O".

We find it hard to say exactly what the trivialization consists in, but the discussion at this point makes clear an essential part of the two-dimensionalist's project. The idea is that there's a rational inference from "information about the appearance, behavior composition, and distribution of objects and substances in one's environment", recorded in an epistemically complete sentence, D, to such conclusions as that water is H_2O, or that water is XYZ (as the case may be).[32] What makes the availability of this inference of interest is precisely that D does not contain the expression "water". It's knowledge of the meaning of this expression that combines with the information in D to deliver the apriori inference to a truth expressed using "water". The crucial idea of two-dimensional semantics is that correctness of such inferences reveals a fact about the meanings of terms that feature in their conclusions, but not their premises. These meanings warrant the inferences, and describing the patterns of inference indirectly describes the relevant meanings.

To reject that crucial idea is to reject the core claim of two-dimensionalism. It's straightforward to demarcate a kind of semantic view that, as Chalmers recognizes, constitutes such a rejection: the view that the meaning of expressions like "water," or concepts like the concept WATER, essentially involve their referent. On this view, once you've been told that there's a liquid that falls from the skies and fills the lakes you still don't know whether it's water (maybe it's XYZ, and so not water). Likewise, once you've been told that there's a star that is first to appear in the evening, you still don't know whether it's Hesperus; it's possible that some other heavenly body should appear earlier than Hesperus. When such remarks are made in connection with scenarios defined as worlds considered as actual, a two-dimensionalist can say that we are not doing justice to the "considered as actual" requirement. But here scenarios are simply epistemically complete sentences, so no such move is available. We think that a sentence, D, that does not contain the word "water" cannot give one enough information to infer, using only apriori inference, that there is water. D may contain "the lake-filling liquid is H_2O", in which case it *necessitates* that there is water. But this is not apriori inference: it depends on the background non-apriori necessary fact that water is H_2O. Likewise, a sentence that does not contain the word "Napoleon" (or a synonym) cannot provide an adequate basis on which to tell whether a world that verifies the sentence does or does not contain Napoleon: perhaps it is a world in which some distinct individual shares all Napoleon's properties, or perhaps it is a world in which Napoleon lived a very different life.

---

[32] "There is a relatively limited vocabulary V such that for any truth S, there is a V-truth D such that D implies S" (Chalmers 2004b: 198).

3

Overview of an Originalist Theory of Concepts

Atomic concepts are to be individuated by their historical origins, as opposed to their semantic or epistemic properties. Distinct concepts have different origins, and may not differ intrinsically. Originalists reject the view that cognitive differences need to be explained by semantic differences: the puzzle cases introduced in Chapter 1 are best explained in terms of distinctness of concepts. Individuating concepts in a non-epistemic way makes them available as independent sources of explanation for epistemic features. Individuating concepts in a non-semantic way shows that the explanation does not rely on semantic properties of the concepts themselves.

This chapter offers a brief overview of originalism, giving a preliminary indication of how it provides simple and straightforward resolutions of the puzzles. A fuller defense and development is given in Chapter 4, along with comparisons with some alternative views. An originalist account of ascriptions of propositional attitudes is offered in Chapter 6. Detailed application of the theory to the puzzles comes in Chapter 7.

Concepts are constituents of thoughts, vehicles of representation, tools used in thinking. Atomic concepts are individuated historically. They can be combined into larger structures, including thoughts; these are distinguished by the fact that they can be evaluated as true or false, can stand in logical relations to other thoughts, and can be elements in propositional attitudes. The thought that snow is white is true, and it can be believed, affirmed, questioned, and so on.

Typically, atomic concepts have reference: nominative concepts, for example the concept WATER, typically refer to things, for example water; predicative concepts, for example the concept WET, typically refer to properties, for example the property of being wet, and so indirectly refer to objects possessing those properties. Some concepts fail to refer, but this does not prevent them having a role in thought. Distinct thoughts, even if they are referentially isomorphic, can play different cognitive roles. This enables originalism to make room for Fregean data, for example that the thought that Hesperus is visible is distinct from the thought that Phosphorus is visible. The concept HESPERUS and the concept PHOSPHORUS were introduced on distinct occasions, one at dusk, the other at dawn, so they are distinct. Hence the thought in part composed of the one concept is distinct from the thought in part composed of the other, and so someone could believe one thought and not the other. Likewise, since the concept

Here, we think, we have identified the crucial disagreement between two-dimensionalism and our own approach. We do not think that we have refuted two-dimensionalism (that would be a very different project from the one we undertake here); but we hope we have given a clear indication of how that theory differs from our own.

PEGASUS is distinct from the concept VULCAN, the thought that Pegasus is a horse is distinct from the thought that Vulcan is a horse, even though there is no difference at the level of reference.

3.1 Origins

Atomic concepts come into existence (and perhaps go out of existence); they are non-eternal abstract continuants. For example, the concept QUARK did not exist in 1950 but it exists now. It's natural to infer that there was a first moment at which it came into existence. We have a rough idea what that first moment was: the concept was introduced by Gell-Mann in 1963.[1] We expect everyone to agree that concepts have histories. Our more controversial claim is that no single concept can have two historical origins: distinct events in which the concept was introduced.

The metaphysics of concepts is similar to that of words. Words, like concepts, are non-eternal abstract continuants. They are invented or created, so there are times at which they did not exist. For example, the word "quark"[2] probably did not exist until the 1920s when James Joyce was writing *Finnegan's Wake*. Words are not individuated by their spelling, since the same word can be spelled in different ways (e.g. UK "colour", US "color"). Words are not individuated by their pronunciation, for the same word can be pronounced in different ways (e.g. "lieutenant"). Words are not individuated by some combination of spelling, pronunciation and reference, for there might have been two orthographically and phonetically indistinguishable names for the same thing (Kaplan 1990: 115; Wetzel 2009, ch. 3).[3] Rather, words are individuated by their origin. There are two words spelled "bank", one deriving from the Norse and the other from the French. The different histories are what ensure difference of word. Sameness of history ensures sameness of word.

Like a word, a concept, though itself abstract, has many concrete correlates, which we call *uses* or *tokens*. A subject's use of a concept is a dated particular event. Uses of concepts stand to concepts rather as the utterings or inscribings of words stand to the words themselves. A use is essentially the use of a concept by a given subject, but the same subject may use a concept more than once, and distinct subjects may use the same concept, at the same or different times. You and we all possess the concept AUSTIN. The uses we make of the concept are distinct, since we are distinct subjects. But the concept is shared. The motivation for saying this is that thoughts are structures

---

[1] According to Gell-Mann (1994: 180) himself. A standard view is that the *same* concept was introduced independently by George Zweig. On our view, a single concept cannot have distinct origins, so the Gell-Mann/Zweig case needs redescription. This is argued for in Chapter 4.

[2] That is, the word used by Gell-Mann for quarks, as opposed to the similarly spelled and pronounced word for a kind of cheese, which was invented earlier.

[3] Suppose a wag introduces a word "Phosphorus" for the evening star (knowing full well that a same-sounding word already exists for that star, thought of as the morning star). There would be two words "Phosphorus" with the same spelling, sound, and reference.

of concepts, and many thoughts are capable of being shared. If you and we think that Austin is an attractive city, we share the concept AUSTIN. According to originalism, concepts are language-like, but they are not the property of individual subjects, as Fodor (1975) holds. Hence it might be misleading to say that originalist concepts are elements in "the language of thought", for that phrase will suggest Fodor's different view. (See Chapter 4 for more detailed comparisons with Fodor.)

A given individual may use a concept for the first time in one of two ways. It may be the first time the concept has ever been used. In this case, the use constitutes the introduction of the concept, and we call such use an *originating* use. Alternatively, the concept may already be in existence, and the individual's first use of it constitutes his becoming a member of an existing concept-using community. In this case, the use is not an originating use. Non-originating uses are marked by both of the following features:

1. The use involves deference to other uses, by the same subject or other subjects.
2. The use makes possible the accumulation of information from other uses, by the same subject or other subjects.

When Gell-Mann originated the concept QUARK, he was in no way deferring to other uses of the concept, whether by himself or by other scientists. (That's consistent with his having borrowed the word "quark" from James Joyce.) By contrast, our current uses of the concept QUARK involve deference: we aim to conform in our usage to our previous usage, and to the usage of those in our conceptual community, especially the usage of the scientifically informed. This is typical of non-originating uses. The deference takes the form of intending to use the concept as it has been used by oneself or others on previous occasions. Using it in the same way does not require one to use it to think the same thoughts, nor does it require one to believe that those to whom one defers are in a privileged epistemic position regarding the subject matter: one can change one's mind or disagree with others.[4] But this kind of change of mind or disagreement requires agreement in concepts. Shifting concepts would be a kind of equivocation, rather than a genuine change of mind or disagreement. In a non-originating use, a suitable kind of conformity with an existing practice is required, and this must exercise some normative force. For example, conformity is intended, so failure to conform is failure to act as one intended, and in this sense is to make a mistake. One characteristic of originating uses is the absence of any such conformist requirement.[5]

---

[4] As we use the notion of deference, it has nothing special to do with expertise (and so little or nothing to do with Putnam's use of the notion (Putnam 1975)), nor even with superior epistemic position. In taking someone to have wrongly applied a concept (perhaps because she is in an epistemically inferior position relative to oneself), one still aims to use the very concept she used, and in that manner one defers to her usage.

[5] Developmental psychologists speak of infants forming expectations that are falsified (e.g. a child is surprised at seeing two objects when a screen is lifted). They attribute to the child use of the same concept in the falsified expectation as was used in the habituation condition: the concept used when surprised is supposed to conform with that used during habituation. This is not conformity by intention (it would be baseless to attribute such intentions to infants); rather, the conformity is marked by our counting the case as the use of an old concept in a

In typical non-originating uses, information is brought forward and integrated from other uses; it is "accumulated". This is manifest in adult uses: to learn about quarks is to make further use of the concept QUARK in the course of adding to the information the concept is used to register. It is also a feature of infant cognition. Studies suggest that infants respond to, for a example, a red block, not merely with separate thoughts, ones that might be verbalized as "That's red" and "That's a block", but also with conjoined thoughts, in which the information is accumulated: the information *is red* and the information *is a block* are subsumed under a single concept.

Originating uses are characterized as ones not governed by any conformist norm (for example, not involving deferential intentions) and not involving any informational accumulation. They are of various kinds. Explicit intentional introductions of concepts, like Gell-Mann's introduction of the concept QUARK, are easy enough to describe and understand. However, they involve intentional actions, and having intentions of the kind in question requires using concepts. Hence not all concepts can come into existence through explicit intentional introductions.

Originating uses that are not explicit intentional introductions arise in normal behavioral and neurological development. The cognitive architecture of many species, including our own, ensures that concepts arise in young organisms as part of normal development, prior to language use. Developmental psychologists study when babies first come to possess concepts, and what the concepts are concepts for. Originating uses of these concepts occur through the operation of subpersonal processes. They involve nonconceptual contact between the mind and objects of thought. That there are nonconceptual ways in which the mind can make contact with other things has been argued for theoretically (Tye 2005, 2010) and hypothesized in the course of empirical work (Pylyshyn 2007). This is fortunate, for otherwise it would be hard to explain how concepts could arise in a being lacking concepts (this was Fodor's (1975) "doorknob" puzzle).[6]

According to originalism, the concepts infants form on their own are typically supplanted by public concepts when they become full members of their surrounding linguistic community. An infant might originate a concept for cats. But as the child becomes a member of his conceptual community, that concept will be supplanted by one or more public concepts, most likely the concept CAT. One mark is the child's willingness to accept correction: if she was using an idiosyncratic concept, rather than the public concept CAT, there's no reason to think that an adult correction ("That's not a cat; it's a small dog") would be treated as relevant. Linguistic immersion is also conceptual immersion. In learning and coming to use the public language in our community, we thereby acquire

---

falsified expectation, rather than as the correct use of a new concept; the latter description leaves the surprise unexplained. Conformity can acquire normative force without being intended.

[6] We find no need for the assumption that we are born with concepts, though we are of course born with mechanisms which, as they mature and interact with the environment, generate concepts. Fodor's views are discussed in Chapter 4. Prinz (2002) offers a detailed critique of various versions of nativism.

and come to use the concepts these words express. This is the source of the majority of the enduring concepts we use.

3.2 Individuation by Origin

Originalism answers the question: what are the necessary and sufficient conditions for the concept C1 to be the same concept as the concept C2? According to originalism, every concept has exactly one originating use,[7] and every originating use of a concept is an originating use of just one concept. The following is a necessary and sufficient condition for concepts to be the same:

> (O) Necessarily: concept C1 = concept C2 iff the originating use of C1 = the originating use of C2.

Following an originating use, there are (zero or more) "descendant" uses: uses that count as uses of that very same concept thanks to standing in the ancestral[8] of a deference-involving relation R to the originating use. We first came into contact with the concept QUARK at a lecture by Gell-Mann. When we first used it, we were trying to use it as he had used it in the lecture. We have maintained those efforts. Maybe we have now forgotten that early learning experience, but in trying today to use the concept as we used it yesterday we are maintaining a link of R-dependence with our first use; and so, indirectly, with Gell-Mann's originating use.

In this picture, each use U of a concept is a use of the unique concept that lies at the origin of the R-linked chain of uses to which U belongs. From the point of view of metaphysics, all facts of identity and difference among concepts are settled. This is not how we typically distinguish concepts: originalism fixes the metaphysics of concepts, not their epistemology.

Filling out and defending the picture involves the following:

1. Justifying the claim that every concept has a unique originating use.
2. Justifying the claim that every originating use introduces just one concept.
3. Explaining in more detail the relation R of "descent:" the relation that binds subsequent uses of a concept to its originating use.

Some of these tasks are taken up in Chapter 4.

---

[7] For all we know apriori, there is an infinite human past, and so, for many concepts, no moment at which they were introduced (thanks to Brian Cutter for the observation). It is an indisputable aposteriori fact that our concepts are not like this. A claim both fully general and apriori would be that concepts are individuated by their unique histories.

[8] An object a stands to an object b in the *ancestral* of a relation R iff there are objects $x_1, \ldots x_n$ such that a stands in R to x_1, x_1 to x_2 etc., ... and x_n stands in R to b.

3.3 Contents

There are many different kinds of atomic concepts: nominative concepts like the concept Hesperus, predicative concepts like the concept barks, concepts for logical operations like the concept and, concepts associated with intensifiers like the concept very, and so on. The relevant taxonomy mirrors the appropriate taxonomy for public language expressions, expressions for concepts. Concepts expressed in a public language have the semantic properties of the words that express them. Natural language semantics is an ongoing project, so we cannot help ourselves to a finished semantic theory. However, for illustrative purposes we will adopt a very simple-minded style of semantics. Our aim is to show that one does not need sophisticated semantics to explain Fregean data and related puzzles. Indeed, the main thrust of originalism is to show that most such puzzles are to be explained not in terms of semantic differences, but in terms of conceptual differences. We highlight this point by adopting very coarse-grained contents for concepts, and by allowing that there are concepts that can be used successfully in thought, while lacking content altogether.

In this illustrative vein, we will presume that the contents of contentful atomic nominative concepts, like the concept Hesperus, are the individual objects to which the concepts refer, in this case the planet Venus; and the contents of contentful atomic predicative concepts, like the concept happy, are the properties which the concepts introduce, in this case the property of being happy. Nominative concepts may lack any content, like the concept Pegasus. Likewise for predicative concepts: one may hold a theory of properties according to which there is no such property as *being phlogiston*, but this would be no barrier to the existence of the concept phlogiston.

The concept Hesperus has the same content as the concept Phosphorus, since they refer to the same thing. However, the concepts are distinct, having different origins. This explains how it can be one thing to think that Hesperus is visible and another to think that Phosphorus is visible. Similarly, the distinctness of the concepts Pegasus and Vulcan explains how thinking that Pegasus is a horse is different from thinking that Vulcan is a horse.

The simplest picture is that concepts acquire their content at their origin, and then maintain it. On this simple picture, the same causal structure that ensures that various uses are uses of the same concept also ensures that these are uses of a concept with the same content. We'll see shortly that the simple picture is too simple. In any case, the first question is how an originating use of a concept comes to have the content it has. There is an analogous question for language: how did the word "Hesperus" come to refer to Hesperus (that is, to Venus)? The intentions of whoever first introduced the word clearly have a role to play. On a simple view, Venus was present to someone's mind, and he coined the word "Hesperus", intending the word to refer to the object in question. The "baptism" was successful, and a practice of using the word for that object was initiated. We can adopt a similar story for concepts: the concept Hesperus acquired the content Hesperus thanks to the intention that it should refer to that object. On this story, it needs to be possible for an object to come before a thinker's mind, and be the object of an intentional state, without having been brought under the very concept being originated. In perception, a subject can attend to an object without bringing it under any concept. This makes attention available as a precursor of concept-creation.

A nominative concept may lack content for two reasons: one is error, as in the case of the concept VULCAN. The other is fiction- or myth-making, as was presumably the case for the concept PEGASUS (and certainly the case for the concept SHERLOCK HOLMES). In the case of error, nothing satisfied the originating intentions. In the case of fiction, nothing (in our reality) was even supposed to answer to the concept.

There is a great deal more to be said about the fixing of the original content of a concept expressed by a word in a public language. We say a little more in Chapter 4, but for the most part we are happy to borrow from the work of semantic theorists on analogous problems. In the case of concepts without linguistic expression, as in the concepts psychologists attribute to infants and creatures without language, we can draw on their expertise. An infant's concept OBJECT is determined as having the content it has by a complex interaction among how its uses are caused, with what they co-vary, and how they relate to behavior.

Once original content is fixed, there is a further question how it is maintained. Does a concept have its original content forever, as envisaged in the simple picture above, or can it be modified in the course of time? And if it can be modified, how are the modifications effected?

The concept MEAT used in the fifteenth century had as its referent anything edible; in our terms, its content was the property of *being edible*. The concept MEAT we use now has as its referent only flesh; in our terms, its content is the property of *being flesh*. One option is to say the earlier concept is the same as the current concept, but that its content has changed. Another option is to say that a new concept, expressed by a word spelled and pronounced the same way, was introduced at some point, and each of the two concepts have retained their original and distinct contents. We prefer the first story. It is a case of gradual drift, with no event that seems a good candidate for the introduction of a new concept.[9]

Likewise, there are versions of the Madagascar case, modeled on that given by Evans (1973), which seem best described in terms of a single concept that shifts reference. For us, this amounts to a change in the content of the concept MADAGASCAR. We have something to say in Chapter 4 about the principles underlying such cases. For present purposes, it is enough that these problems are not special to originalism: they need to be solved by any account.

---

[9] A possibly more striking case: seventy years ago a two-story five-bedroom house might have qualified as an instance of the concept MANSION. Thanks to gradual upsizing, this is no longer so. But there seems no case for saying the current concept MANSION is distinct from the earlier one. (Thanks to Richard Davies for the example.)

Originalism entails externalism with respect to the individuation of concepts: thinkers who are intrinsic duplicates may use distinct concepts, for their concepts may originate in numerically distinct events. That's what we are asked to imagine in twin-earth cases. A user of the earthly concept WATER may be an intrinsic duplicate of a user of the twin-earthly concept TWATER, but they use distinct concepts, originating in different events, on different planets.

Individuative externalism for concepts does not entail semantic externalism for concepts. It might be that though the concept WATER is distinct from the concept TWATER, having very different origins, they nonetheless coincide semantically in virtue of their internalistically duplicated use. However, the right semantics for concepts is externalist, as shown by twin-earth cases. Tim's concept WATER is an intrinsic duplicate of Tom's concept TWATER, but they have different semantics; in our terms, they differ in content, one having twater as its content, the other water. Similarly, the users of the word "arthritis" in Burge's example are intrinsic duplicates, yet they use concepts that differ in their content, one having as its content the property of *being an inflammation in joints*, the other the property of *being any inflammation resembling inflammation in joints*. In Chapter 5, we explore the consequences of this externalism for knowledge of concepts and their content.

3.4 Thoughts

A thought is a well-formed structure of concepts. The thought that Pegasus is a horse is such a structure and so is the thought that Vulcan is a horse. Since one thought contains the concept VULCAN where the other contains the concept PEGASUS, they are distinct thoughts. Their distinctness can make all the difference. No one, so far as we know, has (until encountering this chapter) entertained the thought that Vulcan is a horse, but the thought that Pegasus is a horse has been widely entertained, thanks to a famous myth.

Atomic concepts combine together in systematic ways. The nonatomic concept THE MORNING STAR contains the concepts MORNING and STAR as proper parts. This nominative concept has a referent, namely Phosphorus, the same referent as the atomic concept PHOSPHORUS and as the atomic concept HESPERUS. Whereas the content of the atomic concepts is defined on our account—for both concepts, it is Phosphorus itself—we have not defined the notion of content for nonatomic concepts. (The relevant options are well known: readers may adopt their preferred approach.) Hence, though the concepts THE MORNING STAR and HESPERUS have the same referent, we are not committed to their having the same content.

However, we do define content for a crucial kind of complexes of concepts: thoughts. The structure of a thought can be represented as a tree, in a way familiar from linguistic analysis, but with atomic concepts, rather than words, as the terminal nodes. Originalism requires that there be rules relating the content of whole thoughts to their composing concepts and the contents of these concepts. Originalism is not committed to any specific version of such rules, but we illustrate with ones that associate thoughts with a (possibly empty) set of possible worlds, as a function of the contents (if any) of the constituent atomic concepts, and their mode of combination. On this basis, the notion of content is extended from atomic concepts to thoughts: the content of a thought is the associated set of possible worlds.

The association of thoughts with sets of possible worlds presupposes a classification of thoughts by their structures, which will include:

> *unary atomic thoughts:* thoughts consisting just of an atomic nominative concept and a predicatively associated predicative concept, for example the thought that Fido barks.
> *negative thoughts:* thoughts dominated by a concept of negation, for example, the thought that it is not the case that Fido barks.
> *conjunctive thoughts:* thoughts dominated by the concept of conjunction, for example the thought that Fido barks and pigs fly.

The familiar kind of recursion requires the definition of a world-relativized notion of content for atomic concepts. There are various options to choose from, even for just nominative and predicative atoms, but for illustrative purposes we propose:

> *Content for atomic nominative and predicative concepts:*
> For any world w, the content of an atomic nominative concept with respect to w is its actual referent, if any; if it has no referent, it has no content at any world.
> For any world w, the content of an atomic predicative concept with respect to w is its actual referent, if any (we will assume this to be the property to which it actually refers, if any); if it has no referent, it has no content at any world.

Here are some examples of the recursive clauses:

1. A unary atomic thought is associated with the set W of worlds meeting this condition: $w \in W$ iff both concepts have a content with respect to w, and the content of the nominative concept at w possesses the property that is the content of the predicative concept at w;[10]
2. A negative thought is associated with the set W of worlds meeting this condition: $w \in W$ iff w does not belong to the set of worlds associated with the thought that is negated;
3. A conjunctive thought is associated with the set W of worlds that is the intersection of the sets associated with each of the conjoined thoughts.

---

[10] Although the rules we offer are in general only illustrative, we do need the rule for atomic thoughts to have the free logical character of the rule offered here. We rely on this in addressing the puzzle of "empty content". If one thinks of properties in a "sparse" way (see Lewis 1986), many predicative concepts will lack content. If one thinks of properties as functions from worlds to sets of objects (the extension of the property at that world), no predicative concepts will lack content.

Thoughts have kinds of complexity going well beyond these simple cases, but dealing with the many other types of combination is not a problem specific to originalism: it arises in just the same way for language. In particular, there are some constructions, for example higher-order thoughts concerning propositional attitudes,[11] in which the content of the whole thought is not determined just by the contents of the atomic constituents. That's what makes it possible for the thought (T1) that the Babylonians wondered whether Hesperus is Hesperus to be false, even though the thought (T2) that the Babylonians wondered whether Hesperus is Phosphorus is true. The thoughts T1 and T2 differ in content, even while having atomic components that agree point-by-point in content.[12]

The *content* of a thought is the associated set of worlds. Every thought has a content. A thought is true iff the actual world is a member of the associated set, and is otherwise false.

As in the case of contents for atomic concepts, the recursive clauses just mentioned are merely illustrative. We choose very crude semantics in order to emphasize that our solutions to the puzzles do not depend upon semantics. However, one semantic feature is important. According to originalism, concepts are not individuated semantically, so concepts with no semantic content are no embarrassment. This means that thoughts may have a content, even if some of their constituent concepts lack contents. This is ensured by the free-logical spirit of the condition for atomic thoughts: if a nominative or predicative concept lacks a referent with respect to the actual world, any atomic thought containing it is false. For example, the unary atomic thought that Vulcan is a planet has a nominative concept with no referent with respect to the actual world, and so no content, and so the set of worlds associated with the thought is empty, so the actual world is not a member of the associated set, so the thought is false. This yields a very straightforward account of true negative existential thoughts, like the thought that Vulcan does not exist. The thought that Vulcan exists is false, for the same reason as the thought that Vulcan is a planet is false; the negation of a false thought is true. So the negation of the thought that Vulcan exists, that is, the thought that Vulcan does not exist, is true. For originalism, the main requirement is that an atomic concept's failing to have a content should not prevent a thought built from it having a significant role in cognition.

---

[11] The attribution of propositional attitudes is discussed in Chapter 6.

[12] This consequence of originalism makes it preferable to Millian theories. We reject naïve compositionality (contents are determined by nothing but constituents' contents), but retain a form of compositionality sufficient to explain the productivity and systematicity of thought: the content of a thought is wholly determined by its constituent concepts, their arrangement and content. For further discussion, see Chapter 4.

3.5 Isomorphism

Treating thoughts as structured entities makes it possible to define interesting similarity relations among thoughts, for example:

> *Isomorphism:* Thoughts are *isomorphic* iff they share a complete tree structure, and their corresponding terminal nodes are concepts with the same content.

Isomorphism is not necessary for sameness of content (though it is sufficient in extensional contexts). The thought that Odysseus is a Greek is isomorphic to the thought that Odysseus is a Hellene; these thoughts have the same content.[13] The thought that identity is transitive has the same content as the thought that 2 + 2 = 4, for both are true at every world. They are not isomorphic. The thought that Odysseus is a Hellene is not isomorphic to the thought that the inventor of the Trojan horse is a Hellene, for the latter has a more complex tree structure, preventing any content-preserving one-one correlation of concepts in terminal nodes. (For example, the latter thought will have the concept HORSE at a terminal node, whereas no terminal node in the former thought will have a concept with the same content.) However, we can define a weaker notion, based on the manifest similarity between the pair of thoughts just mentioned. Intuitively, they share an overall subject–predicate structure, and the only difference is that one has an atomic nominative concept where the other has a nonatomic nominative concept with the same referent.

> *Sub-isomorphism:* thoughts are *sub-isomorphic* iff they share a partial tree structure, and each terminal node either corresponds to a coreferential concept at the corresponding node in the other, or else falls under a higher node that is coreferential with a corresponding terminal node in the other.

The definition ensures that the thought that Odysseus is a Hellene is sub-isomorphic with the thought that the inventor of the Trojan horse is a Hellene.

We can also define a more demanding notion, in which thoughts related by it also match with respect to their internal patterns:

> *Super-isomorphism:* thoughts are *super-isomorphic* iff (i) they are isomorphic and (ii) if any two terminal nodes in one contain the same concept so do the corresponding terminal nodes in the other.

The thought that Hesperus is Hesperus is isomorphic to, but not super-isomorphic to, the thought that Hesperus is Phosphorus. It is super-isomorphic to the thought that Phosphorus is Phosphorus.

In what follows, and especially in connection with the adequacy of reports of beliefs and other thoughts, such structural relations will play a significant role.

---

[13] This requires that the property of being a Greek is the same property as the property of being a Hellene.

3.6 Indexicality

We introduced our first-person concepts I in the twentieth century; Hume introduced his in the eighteenth. So the concepts are distinct. There is no single concept I we all share. We'll speak of the *concept-template* I, contrasting this with a given subject's specific concept I. Only specific concepts are concepts. A concept-template is not a concept, but rather a recipe for forming concepts, or a pigeon-hole to hold many different but similar concepts.

The thought you would express by the words "I am hungry" is distinct from the thought that someone else would express with those words; the thoughts are not even isomorphs, since their first elements differ in content. The thought that you are hungry gets closer, for it is an isomorph of the thought you think. But your concept I was introduced on a different (and much earlier) occasion from that on which we introduced a specific concept YOU for you, so the concepts are distinct. Hence the thought that we think, when we think that you are hungry is not the same thought as the one you thought. We have reached a somewhat Fregean position from a quite different starting point.[14]

Likewise for other indexicals: there is a demonstrative concept-template THAT, and many specific concepts THAT, used on specific occasions with specific intentions. Questions of content arise only for specific concepts; the notion does not apply to concept-templates.

It is one thing to reuse a specific demonstrative concept THAT, another to introduce a new specific demonstrative concept THAT. A subject may use specific THAT concepts quite independently, for manifestly different objects. In this case, there is more than one specific concept forged from a single concept-template. But a subject may also exercise the very same specific THAT concept more than once.

Gareth Evans uses a case involving indexicals (owed to John Perry) to support Fregean views:

> Suppose a person can see two views of what is in fact one very long ship, through two windows in the room in which he is sitting. He may be prepared to accept "That ship was built in Japan" (pointing through one window), but not prepared to accept "That ship was built in Japan" (pointing through the other window). Now suppose we try to describe this situation in terms of the ordered-couple conception of Russellian thought. We have a single proposition or thought content—<the ship in question, the property of having been built in Japan>—to which the subject both has and fails to have the relation corresponding to the notion of belief. Not only does this fail to give any intelligible characterization of the subject's state of mind; it appears to be actually contradictory. (Evans 1982: 84)

The example helps bring out the difference between traditional views and originalism. The two uses of the complex demonstrative concept-template THAT SHIP involve distinct specific demonstrative concepts, one introduced in connection with the first sighting of the ship,

---

[14] Frege says that "everyone is presented to himself in a special and primitive way, in which he is presented to no-one else" (1918/1984: 359). In comparing originalism with Frege's theory, one should not rush to equate our thoughts with Fregean *Gedanke*. The elements of a Fregean *Gedanke* are individuated semantically.

the other introduced in connection with the second. This can be inferred from the speaker's intentions and reactions. For example, he has no inclination to bring forward the information *was built in Japan* when having the thought associated with the view from the second window. Our description of the case can accordingly appeal to two concepts, concepts originating in distinct acts of concept introduction.[15]

Once we have distinct concepts, no further difference is needed to "give an intelligible characterization of the subject's state of mind", for distinctness of concepts yields distinctness of thoughts. We ascribe the same content to the thought the subject accepts as to the thought he rejects, just as does the "ordered-couple" conception that Evans attacks. Both specific demonstrative concepts have the same content. Hence the set of worlds at which the first thought is true (the thought expressed by the first utterance of the words "That ship was built in Japan", and which the thinker accepts) is the same as the set of worlds at which the second thought is true (the thought the thinker rejects). Subjects do not relate directly to sets of worlds. We can't infer that the set of worlds in question has the contradictory properties of being both accepted and rejected by the subject; sets of worlds are not the kinds of thing that can be accepted or rejected. Rather, we relate to sets of worlds via thoughts, and there are distinct thoughts. The situation is exactly like one in which a subject is prepared to accept the thought expressed by "Hesperus is visible", but is not prepared to accept the thought expressed by "Phosphorus is visible". The explanation is based on conceptual difference, not semantic difference.

Cases like the ship seen through different windows are problematic for Fregeans, since applying the standard Fregean strategy requires uncovering distinct senses, one but not the other of which the subject is prepared to accept. But it's hard to explain what the different senses of "that ship" might be. By contrast, originalists have no such difficulty. We do indeed need two of something, but we have two specific demonstrative concepts, and their distinctness is characterized in the originalist way: they are concepts with different origins.

There is considerable variety among different indexical and demonstrative concepts. Thinkers have a great deal of freedom in introducing and using specific concepts THAT. Perhaps one should use a specific concept THAT for things further away (literally or metaphorically) from things for which one uses a specific concept THIS, but even on this point there is no very firm rule. By contrast, the concept NOW is highly constrained. A specific concept NOW must be used for a stretch of time containing a contextually salient moment, typically the moment of the thought.[16] The thinker has freedom with respect to

---

[15] It's a feature of indexical concepts that a speaker can introduce them for himself, independently of other thinkers. This contrasts with public concepts acquired by immersion, like the concept PADEREWSKI. It's not up to individual users to settle anything about the nature or semantics of that concept.

[16] In narrative thinking, a specific concept NOW may refer to a past time: Finally he caught sight of the monster. Now his determination would be put to its greatest test.

the breadth of the region of time containing the determining moment: it can range from a fraction of a second to many years. But a thinker is not free to exclude the salient moment.

Consider the thought: now you see it, now you don't. There are two uses of NOW. Are they uses of the same specific concept NOW? They are clearly supposed to introduce different temporal stretches, ones with incompatible properties, so if the uses are of the same specific concept, that concept must have changed its referent. Although we do not rule out this possibility in general (think of the concept MEAT) it's not the right treatment of this case. The normal thinker will not accumulate information across the two uses and will not, in her second use, be trying to use the very concept she had used in her first use. This case is best described as the use of distinct specific concepts NOW, each with a different content.

3.7 Cognition

A Fregean datum is that it's one thing to think that Hesperus is Hesperus, and another to think that Hesperus is Phosphorus; one thing to think that Hesperus is visible, another to think that Phosphorus is visible. We agree. Different thoughts are involved, that is, different structures of concepts, since the concept HESPERUS is distinct from the concept PHOSPHORUS. We disagree with Fregeans that the difference requires postulating any additional semantic layer. As illustrated in the example from Evans of the ship built in Japan, the differences can be fully and satisfyingly explained using just concepts (and their combination into thoughts) and their contents (conceived just as referents).[17]

Distinct concepts can, and typically will, play different roles in our cognitive activities, even if they have the same content. This can be so for more than one reason. One is that a thinker may not know that concepts she uses have the same content, even if they do, and even if she knows the content of each. This is how one can explain an ancient (pre-Babylonian) astronomer believing both that Hesperus is visible and that Phosphorus is not visible, and the ship-viewer believing that that ship, but not that ship, was built in Japan. Another role is this: a thinker who knows quite well that two concepts have the same content may nonetheless use them discriminatingly, for example, using one rather than another in reporting beliefs, as we just did in reminding you about the ancient astronomer. A third role for concepts in cognition is that their sameness and difference generate relational effects: the pattern exemplified by the thought that Hesperus is Hesperus is distinct from the pattern exemplified by the thought that Hesperus is Phosphorus. In the first, a single concept is used twice. In the second, two concepts are each used once. This may have an impact on informativeness. When a concept is used twice in an identity thought, the thought is typically

---

[17] Fodor asked: "Can distinctions in cognitive value be made in terms of the message without taking account of the medium? Or does the medium play a central role?" (Fodor 1990: 93). We agree with his answer: in Frege puzzles, the medium can do the explanatory work.

uninformative, whereas a thought similar in point of structure and content, but using two concepts, may be informative.

To vary the example: the thought that Greeks are Greeks is typically uninformative, whereas the thought that Greeks are Hellenes is potentially informative. In processing the first, only one concept is exercised, though on two occasions. Whatever processing effort is required has already been made by the time the second occurrence of the concept is encountered; the previous interpretive outcome can simply be brought forward. In processing the second thought, more effort is required, since a second concept needs to be processed from scratch. Corresponding to the extra effort, there is more informational value. To use a computer analogy: a comparison is made between distinct addresses, and the need for such a comparison is independent of the values held at the addresses.[18]

This difference in degree of informativeness can be made to affect truth value, if a suitable embedding is chosen. For example, the first of the following pair is true, the second false:

1. The thought that Greeks are Greeks is exactly as informative as the thought that Greeks are Greeks.
2. The thought that Greeks are Greeks is exactly as informative as the thought that Greeks are Hellenes.

This analysis shows that what have been lumped together as Fregean data come in at least two kinds. There's difference of informativeness that depends on difference in the patterning of concepts within a single thought, and not on the intrinsic features of the concepts themselves. Then there are differences between thoughts that differ only in their concepts, and not in their patterning or their content, like the difference between believing that Hesperus is visible and believing that Phosphorus is visible. Super-isomorphism preserves the internal patterning, so super-isomorphism is conducive to (though it does not guarantee) equality of informativeness. Isomorphic thoughts may easily not be equally informative. The originalist explanation has a degree of detail and accuracy that cannot be matched by other theories.

The work supposedly done by difference of sense can be done better by difference of concept. Chapter 7 shows in detail how conceptual difference can account for various cases (like two tube cases) that were designed to resist explanation in terms of difference of sense. Unlike sense, which raises tricky questions about its identity and its metaphysical status, concepts have clear identity conditions based on their origin and are required by any reasonable account of the mind. Hence one should not appeal to a mysterious difference of sense when one can instead appeal to the clearer notion of difference of concept.

---

[18] Further distinctions can be made. See Chapter 7, section 7.1 for the related distinction between possibility-eliminating and cognitive discoveries.

3.8 "Mastering" or "Grasping" Concepts

Traditional theories often make no distinction between understanding a concept, grasping it, being able to use it correctly, mastering it, and knowing its content. For us, by contrast, there are important distinctions.[19] There's what it takes to acquire an atomic concept. There's what it takes to combine atomic concepts into complex structures, for example thoughts. There's what it is to know the content of a concept, if it has one, or to know that it has no content, and this takes different forms in atomic and nonatomic cases. And there's what it is to know the truth conditions of thoughts. Since some concepts lack contents, yet can be used correctly, we must firmly distinguish between being able to use a concept correctly and knowing its content (if this last phrase is so understood that the knowledge requires the concept to have a content).

There are three main ways in which concepts can be acquired: (i) by subpersonal processes, as part of normal development; (ii) by explicit acts of concept introduction; and (iii) by immersion in a concept-using practice. We acknowledge that there is work to be done in saying more about these modes of acquisition. But we think their reality cannot be doubted. These are indeed ways in which we come to acquire atomic concepts, that is, come to be in a position to use them. We think it highly unlikely that any analysis of what these ways involve would in general require mention of knowledge of their content (in our sense of "content").

This view is defended in Chapter 4. Here, we content ourselves with illustrations of ways in which a concept may be possessed by one who is ignorant of its content, in the sense of having false beliefs in which the concept features saliently. The young Burge, we know on his own authority, did not know that a fortnight was a period of fourteen days, and so did not know that the content of the concept FORTNIGHT was a period of fourteen days. Fodor tells us that he cannot tell an elm from an oak. One way to describe his situation is this: he can use the concept ELM to express the thought that he does not know what elms are, as opposed to oaks. More generally, concept possession is consistent with all sorts of mistakes and misunderstandings about the concept's subject matter (whales are fish, there are examples of witches, and so on). It may be that not just any false belief is consistent with possession of an atomic concept (and it is difficult to say anything general about when error prevents concept possession and when it does not), but the possibility of error is widespread enough to undermine attempts to forge a general link between concept possession and knowledge of content.

Indexical concepts call for an intimate connection between use and knowledge. These concepts are created from a template, which contains information analogous to Kaplan's

---

[19] In this respect, our view of concepts is sympathetic to Putnam's view of words (1975: 248). He says we should speak of "acquiring" a word, rather than "learning its meaning". However, Putnam places more emphasis on knowledge as a component of acquisition than we do. We agree with Putnam that if someone asks, concerning a snowball, whether it is a tiger, she will in many cases give us good evidence that she does not understand "tiger". But we disagree with Putnam's insistence that not asking such a question partially constitutes what it is to understand "tiger".

character for indexical expressions. For example, the concept I is to be used just for oneself, the concept you is to be used for an animate subject to whom one is addressing a thought or speech. Use of these concepts does require knowledge of this character; though, of course, this falls well short of knowledge of content.

Understanding and knowledge relate differently to concepts and to thoughts. In a long tradition, understanding sentences has been associated with knowing their truth conditions. Since, according to originalism, every thought T is associated with a set of worlds, specified recursively in terms of some condition, C(T), each thought is associated with a truth condition as follows: T is true iff the actual world belongs to the set of worlds meeting the condition C(T). Hence originalists have the resources to identify knowing the content of a thought with knowing such a truth condition, in conformity with the traditional view. This makes for a contrast between concepts and thoughts: thinking involves knowing truth conditions, but possessing a concept does not require comparable knowledge.

The justification for the traditional requirement derives from what is involved in thinking. A thinker must possess all the concepts in the thought's terminal nodes. The requirement that is harder to articulate is that the thinker must assemble these elements into an appropriate tree structure. This is where we see the need for something like knowledge of the semantic axioms that govern concepts, leading to knowledge of truth conditions. The concepts composing a thought should not simply be present together: they need to be structured in accordance with suitable rules, rules that will determine how the truth conditions of the whole thought emerge from the constituent concepts and their contents. The simplest way to model how this is done is in terms of the subject's applying the right semantic rules to the atomic concepts.

The simple model is unsatisfactory in at least two ways. First, it attributes to thinkers much more sophistication than they need have in order to think. It's obvious that young children do not have semantic concepts, and could not grasp semantic rules. Indeed, very few realistic semantic rules have been explicitly formulated, so far as we are aware. Second, there is something unsatisfactorily regressive about the model: applying a rule is thinking, but if every act of thinking needs a prior act of thinking, the process can never get started. We therefore have to appeal to a model of some less demanding kind.

The topic has been widely discussed in the context of language and, once again, we propose to take over whatever theory is best.[20] As a familiar label, we think that what is required is "tacit knowledge" of the semantic axioms: a thinker must incorporate a processing system that operates, in a subpersonal way, rather as a personal system would operate in applying explicitly known semantic rules. The subpersonal operations are not acts at all, and so are not acts of thinking; the regress is removed.

---

[20] See Stich (1978); Wright (1986); Davies (1987).

3.9 Conclusion

Originalism combines the best features of Fregean and Millian views. Fregeans should respond favorably to our making room for the data they say should be taken at face value, as well as making room for intuitively similar data that they are unable to accommodate (e.g. Mates cases, discussed in Chapters 4 and 7). Millians should respond favorably to originalism's one-level view of content. Fregeans are right to think that something more than reference is needed in a complete account, but wrong to think that this something more needs to be epistemically or semantically individuated. Millians are right to think that content is referential, but wrong if they think that nothing else is needed to explain cognition. Cognitive processing depends not directly on content but on the vehicles of content: concepts and thoughts.

4
The Originalist Theory Defended and Elaborated

This chapter develops the account of originalism sketched in Chapter 3, and compares the view with some rival views. We hope that those who have doubts about originalism will find answers here (see also Chapter 9: "Objections and Replies").

4.1 Words

Chapter 3, section 3.1 mentioned analogies between words and concepts. Like concepts, words are vehicles of representation, are non-eternal continuants, are individuated by their historical origin rather than by semantic or intrinsic properties, and their use is readily propagated through a population. This section defends the analogy and develops it in more detail.

Words have origins.[1] Through time, they change. As they get passed from individual to individual and community to community, their spelling and pronunciation may vary, as mentioned earlier with "color" and "colour", or "lieutenant", as pronounced by an Englishman, and the same word as pronounced by an American. Words can also vary in their reference through time. Their extensions can shrink or grow from those they originally had. An earlier example was the word "meat", and other examples abound. "Place" derives from the Latin *placea* and originally had as its extension broad streets. Today it applies more generally to whole areas. "Pants" was introduced to apply only to men's wide breeches extending from the waist to the ankle. Today, pants can be wide or narrow, short or long, extending from the waist or the hips. "Deer" was originally used for animals generally. Its present extension is much narrower. Likewise for "girl", which originally applied to young people, male or female.

Individuation by origin helps to explain what makes it the case that there are two words "bank". Other candidate individuators, for example spelling, pronunciation, or meaning, seem simply not to match our practice: the same word may change over time in any of these respects. Moreover, words are not bound to a language, for a language can import

---

[1] Millikan (1984: 73) says that words are individuated by their histories; we agree.

words from other languages, as English has done to such rich effect, using a wide range of sources.

A feature that is metaphysically individuative may be hard to know, and may not be our best evidence for sameness or difference. That words are individuated by their origins does not entail that thinkers come to know that words are the same or different by coming to know their origins. We do not appeal to origins in forming the justified belief that "friend" is not the same word as "fiend", nor in forming the justified belief that "faery" is the same word as "fairy". Similarly with concepts. In many cases, it's obvious that concepts are different. In rather rare cases we need to do some historical work. For example, there may be a real question whether the concept HELLENE is the same as, or distinct from, the concept GREEK. To check, we need to find out when the concept or concepts came into existence.[2]

According to Wetzel (2009: 117), the word "goon" derives from an old English dialectical word "gooney", meaning simpleton. This does not settle whether our word "goon" *is* that earlier word, now spelled and pronounced differently, or whether we should say that "goon" is a new word, perhaps shaped by, but distinct from, the earlier "gooney". Individuation in terms of origin helps us understand what we need to know to settle such questions. Was "goon" originally used by someone who was trying to say the word "gooney"?[3] Or was it used by someone who thought they could invent a new word? If the first scenario is historically correct, it suggests we have a single word that has changed its spelling and pronunciation. If the second is closer to the truth, we have reason to say that there are two distinct words in the story.

Uses of a word, events in which it is spoken or written, stand to the words themselves rather as uses of concepts stand to concepts. Words, like concepts, are abstract objects, whereas their uses or tokens are concrete events. Words and concepts are typically shareable, whereas typically just one subject is the agent in an event of using a word or a concept. Both words and concepts invite the same challenge: what makes a use of a word or concept a use of one word or concept rather than another? The answers take the same form in both cases: there are originating acts in which words or concepts are introduced, and these form the basis for subsequent propagation through the linguistic or conceptual community. Non-originating uses are actions that are in some way dependent upon earlier uses, by the same or other users.

Children start "picking up" words at about 12 months, and between 14 and 18 months are said to be able to learn 10 or more words in a day. What is involved in picking up or learning a word? A child needs to be in some way responding to a word she has heard,

---

[2] It seems that the concept GREEK was introduced by the Romans for Greeks they encountered in Italy, who had long thought of themselves as Hellenes.

[3] Kaplan suggests that intending to repeat a word is almost enough to guarantee success. In particular, "the difference in sound or shape or spelling [between source word and a repetition of it], can be just about as great as you would like it to be" (1990: 101). This is probably an exaggeration (as Lepore and Hawthorne (2011) say, a grunt is not a repetition of a word, however it may be intended), but it shows that a high degree of similarity is not necessary.

otherwise she has produced a "made-up" word of her own. One might represent the appropriate response as forming the intention to use the newly encountered word in the way that the source used it. Though this might not be far-fetched for an adult learning a second language, it manifestly over-intellectualizes what is going on in normal cases of a child learning a first language. On the other hand, even for the child, the relationship between source and new usage is not just brutely causal, but is open to influence by reasons. Children accept correction: "No, it's *s*nake, not *n*ake." "Not *e*phelant; *elephant*." The disposition to accept correction constitutes a form of deference to the word-using community, and this deference is crucial for the child's state to count as one in which she has learnt a word.

The upshot of word-learning is a mechanism, within the child, for producing tokens of that word. The word in question is individuated by the source of the learning. If it is the word "elephant" that we are trying to teach an infant by using it ourselves, then, if we succeed, the result will be an "elephant"-reproducing mechanism in the infant. What makes it the word "elephant", rather than another word that we are teaching involves our relation to the historical introduction of that word. So, at longer range, the infant's "elephant"-reproducing mechanism also traces back to the historical origin of the word.

Once a word is acquired, some fact about the child must make it the case that, on some specific occasion on which she uses *a* word in thought or speech, she is using *this* word, the word W, rather than another. She might be using W for something to which it does not apply; she might be mispronouncing it; so application and pronunciation supply at best defeasible evidence. The correct constitutive condition is that the word the child produces on this occasion comes from her W-reproducing mechanism, rather than from any other word-reproducing mechanism. What makes a mechanism one for reproducing one word rather than another is fixed by the facts of word-acquisition, and the corresponding deferential dispositions.

There is a chain of questions and answers. What makes this use of a word a use of W? It comes from a W-reproducing mechanism. What makes this a W-reproducing mechanism? It was formed under the impact of W-learning. What makes the learning event one of W-learning? Facts about the teacher's use, passing through various W-reproducing mechanisms, and leading back ultimately to the event in which W was first introduced.

This is a natural picture to give of the individuation and use of words; an analogous picture applies to concepts. There is a concept-originating event, an act of subject S_1, in which concept C is originated. This generates a C-reproducing mechanism in S_1, which can create copies or tokens of C. Being produced by this mechanism is what makes S_1's later use of a concept a use of C. If S_1 transmits the concept to other thinkers, say S_2, something similar occurs: a C-reproducing mechanism is formed in S_2. The mechanism counts as a C-reproducing one in virtue of having been formed under the impact of S_1's uses of C. If S_2 subsequently uses a concept derived from her C-mechanism, that use is a use of C.

The reality of origination and propagation for words cannot be contested, and it serves as a model for the origination and propagation of concepts.

The nature of words is subject to two complications, which may illuminatingly be compared with concepts. One is that although spoken uses of words are ephemeral (even if the event is recorded, a specific spoken use of a word does not survive the act of speaking), written uses of words—inscriptions—survive the act of writing. The other complication is special to proper names. There is what Kaplan (1990: 108) calls the "generic" name David, the name shared by everyone called David. But then there are the specific names (Kaplan calls them "common currency names"): David Hume is one David, David Kaplan another.

Is there any analog, for concepts, of the difference between spoken and written words? There may be a somewhat similar contrast, that between fleeting uses of concepts, and cases in which a use of a concept is "laid down", given some kind of permanence in belief and memory. We all believe that air is lighter than water, and we all have believed this for some time. There is the abstract thought, that air is lighter than water, that we all share. But how many uses of this thought are there? At least as many as there are subjects who have this belief. But consider just one subject: is it that every time the belief surfaces to the subject's consciousness, the concepts that constitute it have to be used again? Or is it that there is just one use of the thought, to which the subject stands in the belief relation, and that what varies is whether this single use or token of the thought is or is not present to consciousness?

At least some cases are properly described in the latter way. As already emphasized, a thought is a truth-evaluable structure of concepts; it need not be a conscious episode, or an object of awareness. One should distinguish three kinds of belief (or similar propositional attitudes): (i) the purely dispositional kind; (ii) the beliefs that are actually present in the subject but not currently within consciousness;[4] and (iii) conscious occurrent beliefs. A purely dispositional belief is a thought the subject would endorse, were it presented, but which she has not entertained. A belief that is endorsed, but of which the subject is not conscious, seems to us analogous to an inscription of a sentence: at some point the belief was entertained and endorsed, and that very (token) thought somehow persists, justifying us in now ascribing the belief to the subject. That's analogous to an inscription of a word outliving the act of inscribing it.

How are generic and specific proper names related? A generic name is something like a template or blueprint, and its various specific names are typically created by a copy-like application of the template. The generic name itself is not even supposed to have a reference. Consider a publisher of a book of baby names. The names in the list are not supposed to refer to any babies (or anything else.) In the interest of providing her readers with something new, the publisher makes up a name, that is, a generic name, and adds it to

---

[4] This kind could be further divided, according to how easy or how likely conscious access would be. The phrase "implicit belief" is sometimes used for purely dispositional beliefs, and sometimes for beliefs not currently accessed in consciousness.

the list (perhaps with some remarks about the sex or personality it would suit). At that stage, there is no answer to the question what the name refers to (or what it is supposed to refer to). If the generic name appeals to a reader, she might call her baby by that name. The reader has created a specific name from the generic one, by a process of copying, and the specific name, but not the generic one, has reference.

Not all specific names have reference, for example "Vulcan", as used for the planet supposed to be responsible for the perturbation in the orbit of Mercury. The generic name gave rise to other specific names, some with reference ("Vulcan" is the name of a fiery spaniel of our acquaintance), and some with no reference ("Vulcan" is the name of the divine metal-worker of Roman mythology). The specific names that lack reference are nonetheless used under the supposition or pretence that they refer. This distinguishes generic names from specific ones.

We need to recognize both specific and generic names, since a generic name can exist when no corresponding specific name exists, and a specific name can exist when no corresponding generic name exists. The first case is exemplified by the publisher of a book of baby names, two paragraphs back. For the second case, imagine that a parent seeks a totally new name for his child, and hits upon "Cranforthe". No one has ever been called by that name before. There is at that point only the specific name and no generic name; there has been no copying. So a specific name exists with no corresponding generic one.

Both generic and specific names are individuated by their origins, and not by spelling or pronunciation. The same generic name can be spelled "Anne" or "Ann", and there is more than one common pronunciation of the name "Raphael". A specific name may come first, and then be copied, creating the more abstract generic name. For example, after some years, someone else might "borrow" the name "Cranforthe" for her child; the practice of so naming children might become widespread. The first act of copying, in which the name is consciously applied to something other than its original bearer, creates a generic name "Cranforthe". Or a generic name could come first, brought into existence by an intentional act, as we envisaged with the publisher of a book of baby names, with many specific names subsequently copied from it. What makes an introduction of a specific name a use of a given generic name is the intention of the introducer, an intention to copy that generic name. No doubt there are many specific names "David" which now have no currency, but the generic name is alive and well.

Everyone agrees that there are many people called by the one name "David", so everyone accepts generic names. Do we also need to recognize specific names? Could we not instead speak of uses of generic names? The fact that there can be specific names with no corresponding generic name, and conversely, suggests a negative answer. So does the fact that David Kaplan's name "David", that very name itself, refers to something different from what David Hume's name "David" refers to. And, finally, so does the fact that there are no doubt plenty of eighteenth-century Davids whose first name is not now remembered by anyone.

Indexical concepts invite a distinction similar to the one between generic and specific names. The generic first-person concept-template has no referent and is not supposed to have one. That's why we say that a concept-template is not really a concept; likewise there's a sense in which a generic name is not really a name, for there's nothing it names or is supposed to name. The first-person concept-template is available to be copied in the course of creating specific first-person concepts, which each person does for him or her self, and each one of which does have a reference. (Indeed, if the creative act follows the template, it cannot fail to have a reference.) Likewise, the generic name "David" is available to be copied in the course of creating specific names "David".

Unlike generic proper names, indexical concept-templates come with instructions for using the specific concepts formed in their likeness. Any specific concept I is to be used for the subject who thinks the concept. Any specific concept *you* is to be used for someone or something the subject using the concept is addressing in thought or speech. The concept-templates encapsulate the information that corresponds to the "character" (in Kaplan's (1977) sense) of indexical expressions. Using a specific indexical concept requires sensitivity to the character of the corresponding concept-template.

4.2 Concepts are Non-eternal Abstract Continuants

Thoughts are structures of concepts, so if one can say what thoughts are one is well on the way to saying what concepts are. Thoughts are abstract things that can be evaluated as true or false, can be believed or doubted, stand in logical relations, can be shared by different thinkers and can typically be expressed by indicative sentences in language.

Thought is productive in that there is no upper limit to our thoughts, our finite natures notwithstanding. It is systematic in that there are systematic connections among the thoughts available to a thinker. Anyone who can think that John loves Mary can think that Mary loves John. Anyone who can think that John is happy and that Mary is tall can think that Mary is happy and John is tall (Evans 1982). Constituent structure explains the productivity and systematicity of thought (Fodor 1987): thoughts are composed of constituents capable of being rearranged. These constituents are concepts.

Concepts have representational properties, properties that contribute to the truth conditions of thoughts they constitute, but according to originalism they are not individuated by these properties. They are individuated by their historical origin. In this section, we consider the general metaphysical character of concepts, and how things with that character can be created.

Some abstract things are eternal, for example numbers (if there are such things). Many abstract things have clear starting dates, including marriages, pension plans and cocktail recipes. These are non-eternal abstract continuants, and this is the category to which concepts belong.

Things count as abstract if they lack spatial position and have no direct causal powers. Weddings take place in specific locations, but the marriages the weddings initiate have no spatial location (unless we choose to stipulate one, for example the sum of the regions occupied by the spouses at a time). Likewise, concepts have no spatial position (unless we choose to stipulate one, for example the sum of the regions occupied by the heads of users of the concept at a time). Marriages do not have direct causal powers. Being married can make a causal difference in various ways, but it does so through the medium of thoughts about marriage, or conventions governing rights and duties of married people. Likewise, concepts have no direct causal powers. They make a difference in the world only thanks to being exercised or used by thinkers.

Concepts are continuants because they undergo changes, even after coming into being. For example, they are used, perhaps more or less widely at different times, they may come under discussion or go out of fashion, or become associated with distinctive opinions, or play an essential role in a scientific advance. Further, they may change in their semantic properties (see section 4.3 below).

Uses of concepts are their concrete manifestations. Similarly, triplets are a concrete manifestation of the number three, Mr and Mrs Smith are a concrete manifestation of marriage, and this sentence (the one on the page before you, made up of the specific droplets of ink—or pixels—in your copy of this book) contains a concrete manifestation of the abstract word "sentence".

The details of the relation between a use and a concept are not straightforward (on our theory or any other). Although "use" comes from an active word, not all uses of concepts are active, at least in the usual ways activity is understood. In recognition, a suitable familiar concept wells up; it may not be actively sought. In perception, demonstrative concepts are introduced, but the phenomenology is typically passive rather than active.

Not all uses of concepts can be regarded as intentional in a straightforward way, even when the concept is used as part of an undeniably intentional activity. Suppose two people are trying to find a time to meet for coffee and one proposes noon next day. Making the proposal is uncontroversially an intentional act. But the only natural way to characterize the intention is as the intention to propose noon next day for meeting. We neither need nor should attribute an intention to use the concept NOON. Having that intention, in anything like the normal way, would involve having a higher-order concept, THE CONCEPT NOON, in order to think a thought on the lines: I'll apply the concept NOON. No theory should require that using a concept requires using a concept that refers to it. There's the manifest threat of regress; and even if this could be stopped at an early level, we should not build into a theory of concepts that only subjects who possess higher-order concepts can use any concepts at all. So we should simply accept that using a concept as part of an intentional act may not itself be an intentional act, just as moving an arm muscle as part of the intentional act of lifting a glass may not itself be an intentional act. Not everything we do when acting intentionally is done intentionally.

We need to take a further step in the same direction. In our example, the subject deliberately proposed that they meet at noon. This is a thought whose production can be regarded as intentional. Some thoughts, however, simply well up: as in perception, the phenomenology is passive. Since thoughts are structures of concepts, the welling up of a thought is the welling up of concepts. These cases count as uses of concepts, even though the concepts are not exercised as part of an intentional action.

To create a concept is to create a non-eternal abstract thing. Differences among kinds of non-eternal abstracta lead to differences among the kinds of creative act. Creating concepts is not like creating pension plans. To create a pension plan, one first needs to form a concept of the plan to be created, then fill in details, and then somehow implement it—that is, make it available for purchase. This follows a standard pattern for creation in general, for example, creating a table. The creative act is governed by an intention involving a concept for that which is to be created: I visualize or in some other way mentally represent the table I wish to create, and this contentful state guides the creative process. We cannot apply this model to concepts, for that would involve supposing that creating a concept requires a prior higher-order concept for the concept to be created, and that both threatens regress and over-intellectualizes the activity. If we apply to concepts some standard features of creation, we become trapped in circularity. To create a table my action needs to be guided by a mental state involving the concept TABLE. It seems impossible to have the higher-order concept THE CONCEPT TABLE without having the concept TABLE. If we model creating the concept TABLE on creating tables, we would have to say that it is guided by a state involving the concept THE CONCEPT TABLE. If being in this state requires possession of the concept TABLE, we cannot begin to create the concept TABLE without already possessing it. Hence we cannot create the concept at all.

Here are three (possibly overlapping) coherent ways in which a concept can be created, ways not threatened by circularity.

Concept creation is at its most transparent when there is a fully intentional act in which a subject believes there are things of a certain kind, and intends these things to be the referent of a newly forged concept. The content of the intention does not involve the concept to be created. To recall an example from Chapter 3: Gell-Mann believed that there were small things involved in the causation of certain observable phenomena. "Let's call them 'quarks'." Thereby, the concept QUARK was created.

In an overt case of this kind, the referent of the concept is introduced within the scope of the belief, so we can use this pattern to allow for cases in which a concept is, but is not intended to be, empty. Georg Stahl believed that all flammable materials contain an element without mass that is liberated upon burning. For this supposed element he created the concept PHLOGISTON. But there is no such thing.[5]

---

[5] It is difficult to say why the verdict is that there is no such thing as phlogiston, rather than that phlogiston is something involved in combustion, oxygen, perhaps, or hydrogen. Why not say that Stahl had hit upon oxygen's role in combustion, but had mistaken its properties (it is consumed rather than liberated, and has small but non-zero mass)? Discussing this classic problem would take us too far afield, though some remarks in section 4.3 of this chapter are relevant.

An object can come before the mind by being attended to, even without being brought under a concept. Suppose on a walk someone notices a tree and thinks something like: when I see *that* coming back, I should turn left. In thinking this thought, she creates a demonstrative concept for the noticed tree. The method of creation is familiar and routine, but the concept introduced is new, if it meets the conditions of an originating use: there is no deference to prior uses and no accumulation of earlier information. These perceptual-demonstrative concepts are very numerous, possibly outnumbering all others. They are typically not shared and are of short duration.

Running words in a public language through one's head is not the only way to introduce or use a concept. Language-less creatures can have concepts. Naturally, we can give full descriptions of concept creation only for cases in which the creative act is verbally expressible.

Infants are prime examples of language-less users of concepts. The evidence for their possession of concepts comes from their non-linguistic behavior, which can yield detailed clues. For example, Susan Carey says that a child's concept OBJECT involves "criteria for individual and numerical identity... [these] are implicated in the computations that govern the opening and closing of object-files, the computations that determine whether a given object is the same one or a different one from one seen previously" (Carey 2009: 264). Typical infant concepts are created through natural development, not through any process it would be appropriate to call learning. As far as we know, no one has anything of interest to say about the detailed nature of the process of concept creation (as opposed to the huge body of work on the nature and reference of infant concepts). But few doubt that infants create concepts in the absence of language.[6]

The main source of the acquisition of public concepts is not creation but acquisition by immersion in a concept-using practice. This is addressed in section 4.10.

4.3 Fission and Fusion

Originalists hold that each concept has just one origin. This section reviews some putative counterexamples. One kind of case proposes concepts with multiple origins, another proposes a single origin for many concepts. If Leibniz and Newton can both be credited with introducing the concept INTEGRATION, this is a putative example of multiple origins for a single concept. If Newton's introduction of the concept MASS gave rise to the concepts of both RELATIVISTIC MASS and INERTIAL MASS, this is a putative example of a single origin for more than one concept.

---

[6] Extreme nativists, holding that all atomic concepts are innate, may object to the form of words in the text, but they are on board with the spirit of the remark. They have to allow that, in the course of normal development, innate concepts are "triggered" or "activated" at different times. From our point of view, there is little to choose between the task of explaining activation and that of explaining creation. We accept Fodor's description of the issue: "the problem is to explain how a creature's innate endowment (whether it is described in neurological or intentional terms) contributes to the acquisition of its conceptual repertoire" (2008: 145).

One resource available to originalists is to allow fission and fusion for concepts. Since concepts are continuants, they are in principle subject to fission and fusion. However, fission and fusion are not straightforward, even in the apparently simplest cases, so we first review this general point.

A simple case of fission: an amoeba divides, resulting in two amoebas. It seems odd to say that the original amoeba, by dividing, ceased to exist. But if it survived, it cannot have survived as both the new amoebas (for they are distinct) and it's arbitrary to choose just one of the new amoebas as the survivor. There is a temptation to think something contradictory: that the survivors are identical with their progenitor. On every account, this temptation must be resisted. There is more than one way to do so. For amoebas and concepts we think the right thing to say is that the source amoeba or concept ceases to exist. At the moment of division, one entity goes out of existence and two new entities come into being. Rather than think of conceptual fission as requiring the survival (as two?) of the original concept, it is better to do justice to the role of the original concept by saying it gives rise to some of the features of the new concepts. Features of the concepts RELATIVISTIC MASS and INERTIAL MASS were shaped by the predecessor undifferentiated concept MASS; but there are three concepts in this story, and three originating uses.

The point can be made in terms of a familiar terminology: call a "conception" of X a collection of significant beliefs concerning X. The Newtonian conception of mass is similar in many ways to the post-Newtonian conception of relativistic mass, and also, in many ways, to the post-Newtonian conception of inertial mass. But even sameness of conception, let alone similarity, does not ensure sameness of concept. Tim's conception of water is the same as Tom's conception of twater, but they use different concepts to think about these different things.

There may still seem to be a problem, for division sounds like a single act, yet two concepts result. That makes it seem as if there are distinct concepts with a common origin, contrary to originalism.

This might be a problem if one were trying to develop an originalist theory of amoeba, but in the case of concepts it is illusory. There is no single act of conceptual division. The two new concepts, as in the example of mass, originate in different thoughts and sayings, as ingredients in different theories. For concepts, there is no detailed analog of cell division, or of the Neolithic division of a stone to make two flints in a single act.

Fusion occurs rather rarely among natural continuants. Putative examples of conceptual fusion might be described by our opponents as cases in which a single concept was created on distinct occasions, contrary to originalism. As mentioned earlier, some people take Gell-Mann and Zweig to have created the concept QUARK independently, though it was Gell-Mann's word for the concept that became prevalent (Zweig's was "aces"). Likewise, there is a view according to which the concept INTEGRATION was introduced independently by Newton and by Leibniz. According to originalism, these ways of describing what happened must be incorrect, since concepts are individuated by their origin.

One option for originalists is to insist that there really is such a phenomenon as conceptual fusion, with a metaphysical structure similar to fission. Just as the fission of a into b and c involves three distinct things, one of which (a) goes out of existence at the moment the other two come into existence, one can analogously describe the fusion of a and b into c as involving three distinct things, two of which (a and b) go out of existence as the third comes into existence. This provides a picture consistent with originalism, since the Gell-Mann–Zweig concept QUARK, and the Newton–Leibniz concept INTEGRATION, both have origins distinct from their precursors: the later concepts originated in an event of fusion, which was not so for their precursors.

This is as a perfectly coherent description, though we cannot vouch for its historical accuracy. Fusion requires that there be no supplanting of one concept by another, marked by deferential preference for one source rather than another. On the contrary, the chain of deference must not run back beyond the fusion point. In a clear case, this might take the form of a joint paper introducing a concept. The paper would be the originating act with respect to the new concept, and would ideally exploit the two old concepts ("though we continue to use Gell-Mann's word 'quark', we stress that the present paper introduces a new concept, distinguishable from the concepts the authors previously used").

We suspect, however, that it is more historically accurate to say that deference to Gell-Mann trumps deference to Zweig. If so, the right thing to say is that there is a single concept QUARK introduced by Gell-Mann. Zweig introduced a distinct concept, the concept ACES. His conception of aces was very similar to Gell-Mann's conception of quarks. But Gell-Mann interacted with more people, was more widely cited, and won the Nobel prize, so it was his concept QUARK, rather than Zweig's concept ACES, that become prevalent. For all we know, a story with this structure might be the right one for Newton, Leibniz and the concept INTEGRATION.

Other examples of putative multiple origins are more plausibly described in terms of fusion. Suppose a comet is briefly visible over a large city. Many inhabitants, seeing it out of their window, introduce a concept for it. Next day, many inhabitants use their newly minted concept to think about the comet observed the previous evening, and to exchange news and views concerning it.[7] The acts of communication may initiate a process of fusion. After a while, everyone defers to everyone else in using a concept for the comet, and not just to their own idiosyncratic past uses. From many concepts, a single concept is forged, and this is made possible and seamless in part thanks to the similar conceptions associated with the input concepts.[8]

---

[7] Thanks to Brian Miller for the example.

[8] There is also a coherent alternative description: perhaps in a series of interactions between pairs of speakers, one speaker in each pair defers to the other. Then it could be that the concept of a single speaker dominates the others, and becomes the sole surviving concept for the comet.

4.4 Reference: Fixing and Preserving

Originalism as such does not entail a view about the fixation of reference. However, it would be natural to start with a fundamentally originalist view on that issue too. In its simplest form, this would say that the reference of a concept is *fixed* at its origin and then *preserved* by the same mechanisms that preserve the identity of the concept.[9] This contrasts with views (like Fodor's) which make reference at a time depend on nomological relations between the concept and the referent at that time. The simple view would need only a single relation of descent, and it would do double-duty: it would fix which concept was being used and would fix the referent of the concept in that use.

The double-duty view is open to challenges. We have already mentioned the concept MEAT, which seems to have changed its referent despite causal continuities in its use that suffice to preserve the identity of the concept. We will also revisit an application to concepts of Evans's "Madagascar" counterexample to causal theories of reference-preservation for names. The upshot is that though reference is fixed at a concept's origin, and original reference is typically preserved, in some cases the original reference changes over the course of time.

We'll start with questions about reference-fixing before considering preservation. There are some relatively unproblematic cases, like explicit intentional introductions (exemplified by Gell-Mann's QUARK). In these cases, the referent is typically fixed by the intentions of the concept-creator, intentions whose content has no need to use the concept to be created. (There are problems about cases in which these intentions cannot all be satisfied; some such cases are ones in which the concept lacks a referent.) However, these cases are relatively rare. We need also to consider perceptual cases and cases in infant development.

Perceptual cases are problematic because someone presented with a tree is thereby presented with an individual tree, with an oak tree (let's suppose), with the kind *tree*, the species *oak*, the family *red oak*, patches of light and shade, and a whole range of properties (being a tree, being fun to climb, being a source of lumber, and so on—and we've not even touched gavagai-like considerations). Hence we cannot say that the referent of a concept introduced in response to something presented perceptually is just that which is presented, since there is never just one thing presented.

As mentioned earlier, a subject can attend to an object in perception without bringing it under a concept. Hence attention can be appealed to without circularity in explaining the creation of concepts. In this capacity, it makes some contribution to narrowing the range of potential referents. Attending to an individual tree is one thing, attending to the species is

---

[9] Both the original fixing of reference and its preservation need to be distinguished from other questions, for example: what does it take for a subject to be a user of a specific concept (with a given reference)? What does it take for a subject to know the reference or content of a concept she uses?

another. Suppose a subject attends to an individual tree and on this basis introduces a demonstrative concept for it. This is a case in which attention seems well adapted to reduce indeterminacy of reference. Possession of a concept for an individual tree could play a role in the course of introducing the concept OAK. Presented in the admittedly over-intellectualized way suggested by Putnam (1975), one could intend to create a concept whose referent would be the species of which *that* is an instance. In a picture of this kind, attention is the basis of perceptual concept formation, and can generate concepts that can be used in creating more sophisticated concepts.

Background knowledge can affect the initial fixing of conceptual reference. For one thing, background knowledge can shape attention. If you know there's a prowler at large, your attention to small sounds may be very different from the attention of someone in blissful ignorance. To move to a different aspect, it would be hard to understand how a creature could introduce a concept whose referent was a botanical species unless the creature was sensitive to botanically relevant features of things, a sensitivity in some sense constituting background knowledge. These are issues for detailed empirical investigation, and present no conflict with originalism.[10]

These remarks are intended to encourage optimism about reference-fixation for concepts, but obviously they fall way short of a full treatment. The problem is not specific to originalism; nor is the problem of reference-preservation, about which we now make some remarks.

Most public concepts have their referent before we acquire them. In acquiring them, we aim to use them with just the reference they already have in our community; this is part of what we understand by deference. Deference can be modeled (rather over-intellectually) as the recognition that others already use a concept, together with the desire to use the very concept they use, with the very reference it has in their uses. It does not require the notion of an expert, nor does one need to think of "correct use" as use to form a true thought (though that is often the case), as opposed to use that is genuinely a use of the right concept. This picture makes very appealing the idea that conceptual reference is preserved by some kind of causal process relating uses of concepts, since change of reference would correspond to failure of an intention. Uses of a concept are bound together by a relation involving deference and the bringing forward of accumulated information. Whatever the details, the intentions of users play a critical part. New users intend to preserve the reference the concept had in the thoughts of others; old users intend to preserve the reference the concept had in their own earlier thoughts as well as the thoughts of others. If these intentions are not satisfied, it seems that some kind of significant failure has occurred.

---

[10] The kind of investigation we have in mind is exemplified by Murphy (2002, esp. ch. 6), and the work described by Margolis ((1998): see in particular the hypotheses he discusses, from Markman and Hutchinson (1984) and Landau (1994), concerning the dispositions that need to be postulated in order to explain concept-acquisition by infants).

This intuition is challenged by cases of apparent reference shift. As mentioned earlier, the concept MEAT was once used for anything edible, but is now used only for flesh.[11] It's hard to point to any error. It's also hard to imagine that there was any intentional refixing of the referent. The change seems to have been gradual, and many uses would fail to manifest the change and would permit cross-purposes.[12] Any theory of reference (linguistic or conceptual) needs to explain how the change came about, and why we are not all now mistaken about the reference of the concept MEAT.

There certainly are cases in which we are happier to say that a new concept has been introduced, and these may differ in apparently small respects from cases we prefer to describe in terms of a shift of reference. One version of how the island of Madagascar came to be thought of using the concept MADAGASCAR goes as follows.

> Marco Polo wrote in his notebooks about Mogadishu, on the African mainland, using the word "Madeigascar" and calling it an island of untold wealth. On the basis of Marco Polo's notebooks, Italian map-makers assigned the name "Madagascar" to the island we now call by that name. In doing so, they reasoned as follows: he's very insistent that the place for which he is using this word is an island. The only large island in that part of the world is this one (they demonstrate Madagascar on their map). So this is what he must have meant.

In this case, it seems best to treat either Marco Polo or the map-makers as having introduced a new concept, with Madagascar as its referent. The alternative would be to say that there was a single concept which once referred to Mogadishu and subsequently came to refer to Madagascar. This does not seem appealing for the version just given, but is more plausible if we change the example as follows:

> Marco Polo heard some locals using the word "Madagascar" (or some similar word), and was thereby introduced to a concept. He had appropriate deferential intentions: his plan was to use the concept in the way the locals did. He was confused about its referent: the locals used it to refer to Mogadishu, the town on the mainland, whereas he thought they used it to refer to the island Madagascar (hundreds of miles away). Marco Polo's mistaken usage of the concept became standardized, and the usage of the locals had negligible later effects.

In this case, it seems more appropriate to say that the original concept MADAGASCAR changed its referent. How should the contrast be explained?

Reference is a highly theoretical property of concepts, involving some kind of abstraction from thinkers'-reference.[13] At a first approximation, conceptual reference is standardized or conven-

---

[11] In addition to animals, nuts have flesh, but things like spinach and bread do not.

[12] The *OED* cites the following (from Shakespeare's *Comedy of Errors*) as an early use of "meat" specifically for animal flesh: *Dromio of Syracuse:* "I thinke the meat wants that I haue. *Antipholus of Syracuse:* What's that? *Dromio:* Basting." Even though it's only animal flesh for which basting is appropriate, the quotation is consistent with "meat" referring to all food, the specific kind in question being made plain by the context. (Replacing "meat" by "food" leaves the literal content of the exchange unaffected—though not of course the louche innuendoes.)

[13] We here exploit an analog of Kripke's (1977) distinction between speaker's reference and semantic reference. The claim in the text corresponds to Wittgenstein's claim that there could be no "private lan-

tionalized thinkers'-reference. Nowadays, the standard thinkers'-reference of the concept MEAT restricts it to flesh. It would clearly be wrong to say that those of us who now believe that spinach is not meat are mistaken. The standard thinkers'-referent of the concept MEAT excludes spinach.

This gives us one part of the case for a concept having changed its referent. The other part is the case for thinking that our concept MEAT is the same as the earlier concept MEAT. The basis for this claim is simply the smooth history, the concept being handed on in ways that unquestionably make new users count as users of the concept, even if mistakes were made about its referent.

By contrast, in the first Madagascar example, there is a manifest discontinuity. Marco Polo is not credited with an attempt to acquire, and preserve the reference of, an existing concept. His use of the word "Madeigascar" has no more significant connection with Mogadishu than does the use of "John" for a boy in honor of his grandfather. The mapmakers were not trying to conform to a previous local usage, but were deferring only to Marco Polo, trying to give a charitable account of his thoughts. They were not open to accumulating information from previous uses other than Marco Polo's. They would not have cared if they had known that Marco Polo's word "Madeigascar" had a public use to refer to Mogadishu in a language of which they were ignorant. This makes their uses not belong to the use-tree of the Arabic users of the concept.

The world plays a role in the preservation of a concept's reference, as Millikan has stressed (2000, 2011). Successful concepts manage to refer to things which are themselves stable (stable clusters of properties or stable individuals), and this makes them useful in inductive thinking, a utility that contributes to their survival.

Given that thoughts are structures of concepts, allowing that a concept can change its reference entails allowing that a thought can change its truth condition. A fifteenth-century person who thinks that bread is meat thinks something true, whereas a twenty-first-century thinker of that very thought thinks something false. Here "that very thought" refers to a thought-abstraction, not to a thought token. There is nothing problematic about saying that distinct uses or tokens of the same abstract thought may differ in truth value.[14]

4.5 Information, Composition

Concepts individuated in the originalist way can explain features of cognition without having to attribute to them anything like "cognitive content" (contrast Prinz 2002, ch. 10). Frege-style cases are to be explained simply in terms of difference of concept, not in terms of the possession by the different concepts of different semantic properties.

---

guage"—no system of representation without some standardization or conventionalization of reference. It does not take several speakers or thinkers to make a standard: Robinson Crusoe could do it.

[14] Some complications relating to what makes ascriptions of beliefs true are discussed in Chapter 6.

The main idea is that in thinking a thought containing distinct concepts with the same content, one may be in no position to come to know that the different concepts have the same content. Likewise, in thinking distinct but isomorphic thoughts (for example, that Hesperus is visible, that Phosphorus is visible), one may not be in a position to know that their content is the same, and so may take different attitudes towards them, taking one to be true and the other false. Since there may be nothing irrational about ignorance of sameness of content, there may be nothing irrational about taking different attitudes.[15]

Fregean arguments from the usual data only entail that a difference is needed. They do not entail that a difference of content is needed, or that any semantic difference is needed. According to originalism, difference of concept is enough.

Frege himself seems to have been aware that his argument for sense, as a semantic property additional to reference, was non-demonstrative,[16] for he concludes his first reflections with the words "It is *natural*, now, to think of there being connected with a sign..., besides that which the sign designates..., also what I should like to call the *sense* of the sign..." (1892: 158; our emphasis on "natural"). More recent thinkers have been less cautious, for example:

"Sally believes that Charles Dodgson is a logician" and "Sally believes that Lewis Carroll is a logician" can differ in truth value, even though "Carroll" and Dodgson" corefer. If reference exhausted the content of these terms, these sentences would have the same truth value. (Prinz 2002: 6)

Applying the same reasoning to conceptual as opposed to linguistic content, Prinz speaks of the "Fregean insight" that "conceptual content...cannot be exhausted by reference" (Prinz 2002: 6; his more detailed discussion of "cognitive content"—his term for the Fregean sense of concepts—starts on p. 263).

The arguments have a missing premise, that the relevant features of sentences or thoughts are determined by their content alone.[17] Prinz does not state, let alone discuss, this premise. We now show how and why we reject it.

The premise might seem no less truistic than some principle of compositionality. Should not the content of thoughts be determined wholly by the content of the concepts that constitute them? If so, we would be on the way to supplying the missing premise. However, the content of thoughts is not determined wholly by the content of the constitutive concepts. We gave a clear example in Chapter 3. The following thoughts differ in truth value, and so in content, despite being isomorphs:

---

[15] This claim may be challenged by those who believe in the "transparency of mental content". Such views are discussed in Chapter 5.

[16] Fodor (2008: 56) puts the point clearly: "Frege cases show that there must be something more to the individuation of concepts than what they refer to. But it doesn't follow that the relevant something more is the concept's sense or even that it is a parameter of the concept's content." The "relevant features" include truth conditions, and also, for example, the way a thought can affect action. Believing that Hesperus is visible only in the evening may lead to different behavior from believing that Phosphorus is visible only in the evening.

[17] Millikan (2000: 132) makes what we regard as a similar diagnosis, though in very different words (directed at Frege): "One needs an argument that different movements of the mind always correspond to semantic differences."

The thought that Greeks are Greeks is exactly as informative as the thought that Greeks are Greeks.
The thought that Greeks are Greeks is exactly as informative as the thought that Greeks are Hellenes.

Although conceptual content plays a part in determining thought content, sometimes the concepts themselves also play a part, and that is what the examples reveal. Given that a thought is a structure of concepts, there have to be properties of thoughts that reflect the nature of the thoughts themselves, not merely their content. In the example, thoughts are referred to, and truth or falsity of the whole depends on the nature of what is referred to. All that's needed to achieve this position is the truism that properties of what is referred to may affect truth, together with the originalist view that there's more to a thought (a structure of concepts) than its content (a set of worlds).

Originalism is inconsistent with a certain principle of compositionality, according to which the contents of constituents determine the contents of containing complexes "all the way up". This conception of compositionality for content would lead to an unrestricted substitution principle: concepts that agree in content can be everywhere substituted without changing the content of any whole containing them. The Greeks–Hellenes thoughts displayed above differ in content: the first is true and the second is false, so the actual world belongs to the content of the first but not to the content of the second. Yet the second results from the first by replacing one concept by another with the same content. So unrestricted substitution fails, and hence so does any principle of compositionality that supports unrestricted substitution.

However, thoughts satisfy principles of compositionality that are sufficient to explain the productivity and systematicity of thought. The content of a thought is fixed by the concepts the thought contains, together with their content. This allows for an operator like IT IS INFORMATIVE THAT to be sensitive not just to the *content* of the thought to which it is applied (this is just a set of worlds, and an operator of this kind does not intelligibly apply to such a thing), but also to the *identity* of the thought itself. For the thought that Hesperus is Hesperus, the result of applying the concept IT IS INFORMATIVE THAT is a thought that is normally false, since the same concept features on each side of the embedded identity. Applied to the thought that Hesperus is Phosphorus, the result is a thought that can be true, since different concepts feature on each side of the embedded identity.

From an originalist perspective, the so-called "paradox of analysis" is no paradox. One formulation of the paradox is as follows:

if the analysandum and the analysans have the same meaning, the analysis is trivial, but . . . if they do not have the same meaning, the analysis is incorrect. (Langford 1949: 211)

The move from sameness of meaning to triviality is illegitimate. One can grasp distinct concepts with the same content and yet not know they have the same content. Hence an analysis of the one concept in terms of the other (for example, of the concept HELLENES in terms of the concept GREEKS) can be informative. The point does not depend upon our coarse-grained conception of content. However fine-grained you take content to be, there is no sound inference from "S knows the content of c1, S knows the content of c2, the content of c1 is the same as the content of c2" to "S knows (or is in a position to know) that the content of c1 is the same as the content of c2". This is discussed in more detail in Chapter 5.

In practice, analyses usually analyze a simple concept in terms of a complex of concepts (e.g. knowledge is justified true belief, a number is a set of equinumerous sets). No complex concept is the same as any simple concept. In this case it is especially clear that one can know the content of the simple concept, know the content of the complex, yet fail to know that they have the same content even if they in fact do.

Conceptual difference explains not only difference in thoughts and their properties (their informativeness, whether people think them, and so on), but also differences in actions. Compare two subjects whose mental states coincide except that one wishes to see Hesperus whereas the other wishes to see Phosphorus. Neither knows that Hesperus is Phosphorus. We agree with conventional views that this can lead to a difference in behavior: one may set up her telescope at dusk, the other at dawn. The difference in behavior is explained by the different desires, and the fact that the desires are different is explained by the fact that the concept HESPERUS is different from the concept PHOSPHORUS. There is, of course, more to explain: why does the one who wants to see Hesperus set up her telescope in the evening? Fregean theorists say that it's because the concept HESPERUS has as part of its content (perhaps its "cognitive content") being the evening star. By contrast we adopt a simpler explanation: our subjects believe that Hesperus is visible only in the evening. This belief combines well with the desire to see Hesperus, delivering an explanation of the subject's setting up her telescope in the evening. Our explanation is simpler and more readily generalizable than the Fregean explanation. Why does the subject point her telescope in just that direction? Because she believes that's where Hesperus is. Evidently the current precise location of Hesperus can't be sensibly regarded as part of the content of the concept HESPERUS. Furthermore, Fregeans have no distinctive explanation of why someone who knows the identity and wishes to see Hesperus should set up her telescope in the morning. By contrast, for us the pattern is the same as before: she believes that Hesperus is visible in the morning.

Some theorists, though not Frege himself, appeal to a more fine-grained notion of content to explain similarities in behavior, even for concepts that do not share their reference. For example, Prinz (2002: 8) infers from the fact that Tim believes the same things about water as Tom believes about twater, that the concept WATER has the same "cognitive content" as the concept TWATER. But nothing more follows than that the two subjects believe the same things about the different substances. Their beliefs could easily diverge (e.g. Tim might start believing gin was nicer than water without Tom believing that gin was nicer than twater), without affecting any semantic properties of their concepts. We see nothing but harm in confusing similarity in beliefs about something with similarity in the semantic properties of the concepts used. The confusion resembles that between concept and conception.

Originalists can explain Fregean data about informativeness, propositional attitudes, and actions without appealing to conceptual content, but just to relations of sameness and difference among concepts. Moreover, as we show in the next section, Fregean attempts to respond to Fregean data are doomed to fail.

4.6 Mates Cases and the Demise of Two-level Fregean Semantics

There is a kind of Frege case that two-level Fregeans cannot explain, though originalists can. Hence these Fregean theories are not viable rivals to originalism. By a "two-level" Fregean theory we mean one that has just two semantic distinctions: sense and reference. This was not Frege's own view, for he envisaged a hierarchy of distinct senses: indirect sense, indirect indirect sense, and so on. We call these "multi-level" Fregeans views, and discuss them in the next section of this chapter.

An argument derived from Benson Mates (1952) has as its conclusion that no two expressions have the same sense. The upshot would be that there is difference of sense just where there is difference of expression. In some ways, this view would resemble our own: the relevant differences, whether between expressions or concepts, need not be individuated semantically or epistemically. But the position does not conform to Fregean principles about sense. In this section, we develop the Mates-based argument against Frege, and show how originalism handles the cases smoothly.[18]

We start with two principles that are plausibly constitutive of Fregean sense:

(P1) Sentences with the same sense have the same truth value.
(P2) If sentence s1 results from sentence s2 by replacing an expression used in s1 by one with the same sense, s1 and s2 have the same sense.[19]

(P1) is simply an application of the idea that sense determines reference. (P2) is the idea that senses are compositional. Only theorists who have already given up two-level Fregeanism would consider abandoning these principles.

The argument schema begins with a supposition for reductio:

1. Suppose distinct expressions e1 and e2 have the same sense.
2. Take an arbitrary sentence s1 containing e1 (if e1 is a sentence, s1 can be e1 itself). Let s2 be the result of replacing an occurrence of e1 in s1 by e2.
3. By (P2), the sentences in each pair {a,b}, {c,d}, {e,f} below have the same sense:
   (a) s1.

---

[18] We find that Fine (2007: 129–31) uses Mates' argument to draw what we take to be a somewhat similar conclusion: "The Fregean has been hoisted by his own petard."

[19] This is the premise that multi-level Fregeans will find unsatisfactory: sense needs to be relativized to linguistic context.

(b) s2.
(c) Whoever believes that s1 believes that s1.
(d) Whoever believes that s1 believes that s2.
(e) Nobody doubts that whoever believes that s1 believes that s1.
(f) Nobody doubts that whoever believes that s1 believes that s2.
4. (3e) is true.
5. So, by (P1), (3f) is true.
6. But (3f) is false.
7. The blame for the contradiction is to be placed on (1), which accordingly must be rejected quite generally: no distinct expressions have the same sense.

The validity of the argument is not open to question. Two-level Fregeans cannot challenge (P1) or (P2), for these principles are constitutive of sense as they conceive it. Somewhat ironically, Fregeans and Millians might stand shoulder to shoulder in denying that there is a genuine difference of truth value between (3e) and (3f). Such a denial, however, is highly implausible, as becomes vivid when we replace these schemata by the actual examples Mates used:

(e) Nobody doubts that whoever believes that all Greeks are Greeks believes that all Greeks are Greeks.
(f) Nobody doubts that whoever believes that all Greeks are Greeks believes that all Greeks are Hellenes.

Mates offers "Greeks" and "Hellenes" as examples of synonyms, but invites doubters to select any other pair, claiming that there will still be discrepancies of truth value for the analogs of (e) and (f).

It's a consequence of both Millian and Fregean theories that (e) and (f) do not differ in truth value. Since it seems to us clear that they do differ in truth value, we take this consequence to count against the theories. In contrast, originalism has a straightforward way to accommodate the intuitive judgment of difference of truth value. The concept GREEK is distinct from the concept HELLENE, thanks to having a different and more recent origin: the Illyrians introduced the concept GREEK for Greeks they encountered in Italy, but at that point the Greeks already thought of themselves as Hellenes (using a much older concept). Hence the thought that Greeks are Greeks is distinct from the thought that Greeks are Hellenes. Hence it is possible for the thoughts to have different properties, including the properties needed to verify (e) and falsify (f).

By making sameness or difference of sense a semantic or epistemological feature, the Fregean project is threatened by circularity. Fregeans want to say that the sense of "Hesperus" differs from the sense of "Phosphorus" *because* one could rationally accept the understood sentence "Hesperus is Hesperus", without accepting the understood sentence "Hesperus is Phosphorus". These epistemological differences are constitutive of sense. But then they also want to say that one can coherently have the one belief without the other *because* the senses are different. The explanation short-circuits. For originalists, by contrast, sameness and difference among concepts is not constituted by semantic or epistemic facts, but by historical facts. Concepts thus individuated stand ready to provide genuine explanations of the semantic and epistemic data.

Mates cases highlight the impossibility of providing a suitable criterion for sameness of Fregean sense. Ironically, even differences of informativeness elude adequate description in Fregean terms, for thoughts with the structure that x = x will differ in informativeness from ones of the structure that x = y no matter how intimately related are the expressions that introduce the concept x and the concept y; even if the relation is as intimate as sameness of Fregean sense.

Here's a standard way to characterize sameness of Fregean sense:

(F) For all words w, w', if w has the same sense as w' then for every sentence S, S', if S' duplicates S except for having an occurrence of the simple word w' where S has the simple word w, then, at any time, competent rational speakers of the language who have attitudes of acceptance or rejection to each of S and S' have the same attitude to both at that time.

The idea conforms to Fregean views: sameness of sense prevents difference of attitude among competent rational users. To check that "Hesperus" and "Phosphorus" come out as different in sense, consider that "The ancient astronomers believed that Hesperus is Hesperus" and "The ancient astronomers believed that Hesperus is Phosphorus" are related as S and S', with "Hesperus" as w and "Phosphorus" as w'. But plenty of competent users (all of us who have not been led astray by the lure of Millianism) take different attitudes to them, accepting the first and rejecting the second.

To be sure of revealing difference of sense it's safest to use a hyperintensional embedding, as we did in the previous paragraph. For it may be that we and you, so deeply and professionally familiar with the identity of Hesperus and Phosphorus, have no attitude or the same attitude to every pair in which these expressions occur unembedded.

(F) delivers Mates' result that no distinct expressions have the same sense. We know of a rational person, Pablo, who understands both "Greeks" and "Hellenes" and knows they have the same sense, but believes that some people—the dullards—understand them without knowing they have the same sense. For this to be possible, we ourselves do not have to reject transparency (the view that someone who understands a pair of expressions with the same sense thereby knows they have the same sense); it is enough that Pablo, a possibly seriously misled philosopher, does so. Pablo accepts "The dullards believe that Greeks are Greeks" but rejects "The dullards believe that Greeks are Hellenes". The Fregean criterion delivers that "Hellenes" and "Greeks" differ in sense, which contradicts the assumption that Pablo knows they have the same sense. This provides a Mates-like recipe for undermining any alleged sameness of sense.

Fregeans are right to draw attention to the Fregean data, but they did not go far enough. Mates cases are essentially similar, yet cannot be explained in two-level Fregean terms. Millians are mistaken because they do not take the Fregean data seriously and at face value. By contrast, originalism does justice to Fregean data in a very simple way, and a way that accords with straightforward views about the nature of thought. Cognitive processing depends on its vehicles, concepts and thoughts, not just on their content, and Mates cases make this dramatically plain.[20]

4.7 Multi-level Fregeanism

Frege himself held that an expression's sense is a function of its linguistic context. In an ordinary, unembedded, context, the sense of "Hesperus" may be given by the description "the evening star"; this is its "customary" sense. Its reference is Venus. However, "in indirect speech one talks about the sense, e.g., of another person's remarks" (Frege 1892: 159). Frege took this to mean that in reporting propositional attitudes, one is referring to thoughts.

Thoughts for Frege are structures of senses, and they have a truth value as their reference. If we are to "talk about" a thought, we need to refer to senses, so our words need to have senses as their reference. In ascribing a propositional attitude, for example

1. John believes that Hesperus is visible

we refer to the thought that Hesperus is visible.[21] This thought has as its reference a truth value, but in the context this truth value is irrelevant. What matters is the thought itself, not its reference. So in this context the word "Hesperus" does not have its customary reference (Venus); rather it refers to its customary sense, the sense that is a constituent of the thought that Hesperus is visible. In this context, its "indirect" sense is distinct from, since it refers to, its customary sense, given that expressions differing in reference must also differ in sense. The word "Hesperus" has its reference and two distinct senses: its customary sense, given by "the evening star", and its indirect sense, which is a sense whose reference is the customary sense of "Hesperus", a way of thinking about the customary sense of "Hesperus". There are three semantic levels: reference, customary sense, indirect sense. We should not rush to reject this picture, for we must all agree that, if there are senses, there must be ways of thinking about them, and so there must be senses whose referents are other senses.

On this version of Fregeanism, the hierarchy does not stop there. A deeper embedding will trigger a higher-level sense, one whose reference is the (lowest-level) indirect sense. For example, in

2. Sally wonders whether John believes that Hesperus is visible

---

[20] In this discussion, we assume that the concept HELLENE is distinct from the concept GREEK. We allow that we might be mistaken on this point, and in Chapter 7 we discuss an attempt to construct specially hard Mates cases on the supposition that there is just a single concept.

[21] Though attributions of propositional attitudes are one conspicuous case in which we "talk about" thoughts there are many others, for example phrases of the form "the thought that...", sentences prefixed by "It is apriori that...", and so on.

we are introduced to the sense that was the object of Sally's wondering, that is, the sense of "John believes that Hesperus is visible". "John" therefore needs to have its indirect rather than its customary sense. The situation with "Hesperus" is more exotic: what is needed is a sense fit to refer to the sense that "Hesperus" has as it occurs in (1); that is, a sense fit to refer to the indirect sense of "Hesperus". This must be distinct from, since differing in reference from, the indirect sense: we could refer to it as the indirect^2 sense. Since there is no upper limit to the number of embeddings of this kind, there is no upper limit to the value of the superscript—that is, to the number of distinct indirect senses.

From the perspective of this multi-level Fregeanism, principle (P2) from the previous section, repeated here,

> (P2) If sentence s1 results from sentence s2 by replacing an expression used in s1 by one with the same sense, s1 and s2 have the same sense

will be regarded as at best misleading, for it suggests that the sense of an expression or sentence does not vary with linguistic context. A more appropriate formulation would be on these lines:

> If sentence s1 results from sentence s2 by replacing an expression used in s1 by one which, in that linguistic context, has the same sense, s1 and s2 have the same sense.

From the fact that two expressions have the same customary sense it does not follow that they have the same indirect sense. If they do not, substitution will preserve sense in unembedded contexts, but may not in embedded ones.

Applied to Mates cases, the multi-level Fregean response goes like this: agreed, "Greeks" and "Hellenes" have the same customary sense. However, they may differ in indirect^n sense, for some n. If this is so for n = 2, then the following will differ in sense:

> Some people doubt whether everyone who believes that Greeks are Greeks believes that Greeks are Greeks.
> Some people doubt whether everyone who believes that Greeks are Greeks believes that Greeks are Hellenes.

Since, by hypothesis, the indirect^2 sense of "Hellenes" differs from the indirect^2 sense of "Greeks", and since the occurrence of "Hellenes" and the matching occurrence of "Greeks" are doubly embedded, ensuring a sense raised to level 2, the general semantic principles ensure that the substitution will not preserve sense, and so there is no guarantee that it will preserve truth value; which indeed it does not.

One attractive feature of the view is that it gives an explanation of why deeper embeddings may increase the persuasiveness of Mates cases: the higher the value of n, the more likely that expressions that agree on customary sense should disagree on indirect^n sense.

However, the view faces difficulties. How are we to explain mastery of the endless hierarchy of senses associated with every expression? A natural thought is that there is a function from any sense to a way of thinking of that sense; that is, a function from a sense at one level to a sense one level up. Put more intuitively, there would be a single method of canonically thinking about a sense, which a subject can apply to any sense she grasps. (We hold to a similar principle for concepts: for many people, there is no difficulty in principle in moving from use of a concept C to use of a concept THE CONCEPT C, whatever C may be.) Appealing as this natural solution is, it is unavailable in the context, for it would ensure that expressions that agree in customary sense also agree at every higher level of sense. The function that delivers a higher-level sense from a lower-level one will deliver the same higher-level sense for expressions that agree in lower-level sense. That's what it means to be a *function* from senses to senses.

Dummett (1973: 267–8), responding to worries similar to ours, has suggested that Frege's hierarchy of senses should be nipped in the bud. The sense/reference distinction holds only in the unembedded case. Indirect reference is indeed to customary sense, but there is no distinction between indirect reference and indirect sense. Any sense can either feature in its customary way, introducing its reference, or else in a self-referential way, when it introduces itself. This evidently avoids some problems; but it returns Fregeanism to the two-level kind that, as we argued in the previous section, is refuted by Mates cases.

The conclusion is that both two-level and multi-level versions of Fregeanism have fatal problems; problems that do not arise for originalism.[22]

4.8 Knowledge and Conceptual Mastery

According to a long tradition, for every concept there are some facts expressible using the concept which any user of the concept needs to believe. Since the knowledge is delivered just by understanding, it counts as apriori (at least relative to the understanding). According to originalism, this traditional view is incorrect,[23] and is a fecund source of mistaken philosophy. It's a view that underlies the descriptivist theory attacked by Kripke (1972/1980); in our opinion, the main thrust of Kripke's attack has not been refuted. The main point is that for very many concepts, users may diverge in just about any of the beliefs that involve it. Hence there cannot be beliefs which any user of such a concept must possess.

In its simplest form, the view we oppose would distinguish between analytic and synthetic thoughts. An analytic thought is "true in virtue of meaning"; hence (the standard view holds) anyone who understands the thought is in a position to know that it's true. Grasp of a concept is to be equated with knowledge of all the analytic thoughts expressible with the concept, along with the other concepts a subject grasps. Perhaps it is "true in

---

[22] The standard objection to Fregean accounts of attributions of propositional attitudes is that the difference between customary reference and indirect reference prevents intuitively accurate attributions. Intuitively, an attributor should refer to what the person to whom she is attributing the attitude refers, which may not be a sense. In a catch phrase, Fregean views are inconsistent with "semantic innocence". We discuss this issue in Chapter 6.

[23] We find Fodor in agreement: "what concepts you have is conceptually and metaphysically independent of what epistemic capacities you have" (Fodor 1998: 6).

virtue of meaning" that bachelors are unmarried. If so, this is a thought that everyone who understands it knows, and knows apriori. Let's call this the "traditional" view.

Few philosophers would subscribe to the traditional view nowadays, if stated as we have in the previous paragraph.[24] Yet similar views are quite widespread. Various kinds of theorist (two-dimensionalists, narrow content or dual component theorists, functional role theorists) see concepts as differing when they differ in how uses of the concept are controlled by information the subject possesses, and similar when controlled by the same information. This comes close to the traditional view. In particular, the related information is sometimes classified in terms of "criteria" for applying the concept.[25]

A familiar example is that although the "intentional" content of the concept GOLD is the element Au, the "cognitive content" consists in the various properties (criteria) by which we identify it, traditionally listed as shiny, yellow, and malleable.[26] We ourselves have never put malleability to use in identifying gold, and yellowness is neither necessary nor sufficient, even in the actual world, so we find it hard to take the claim seriously. The concept GOLD can coherently be used in speculations like: if the laws of physics had differed in certain ways, gold would not be malleable (yellow, shiny, or whatever). The features proposed are contingent and not necessarily known to users of the concept; originalists find no place for them in a theory of concepts.

Another familiar example. It is often said that the concept WATER has a content according to which it is the clear, drinkable liquid that falls from the sky and fills the lakes and oceans. As any seafarer knows, the liquid that fills the oceans is not drinkable and is frequently not clear. Hence it can't be right to link a grasp of the concept WATER with apriori (or even aposteriori) knowledge that it is drinkable.[27]

Examples of concepts whose correct use must be controlled by the right information might be easier to find in the logical, rather than empirical, domain. Perhaps one understands the concept AND only if one knows that if a conjunction is true, so are the conjuncts, and if two thoughts are true, so is their conjunction. But suppose a subject who appears to possess a concept of conjunction thinks this is not quite right: order can make a difference ("She got married and had a baby" versus "She had a baby and got married"), whereas the

---

[24] We detect its residue in Burge's use of the notion of "partial understanding". He says that someone who does not know that sofas are articles of furniture has only a partial understanding of the word "sofa", or of the concept SOFA. One explanation of why Burge says this, rather than merely that the subject is ignorant of some familiar facts about sofas, would be that he thinks that it's analytic that sofas are articles of furniture, so failing to know this evinces lack of full understanding.

[25] Fodor (1998: 124) also attacks views of this kind, which he characterizes as "cognitivist": "a cognitivist account of concept *possession*; an account of concept possession according to which having a concept is *knowing something*."

[26] The list comes from Locke, and is approvingly taken up by Prinz (2002: 278). Prinz is aware of the problem mentioned in this paragraph, and responds that the relevant aspect of conceptual content "must be determined by counterfactuals in which proxytypes remain fixed," where proxytypes are "successors to Frege's sense" (2002: 281–2), constituting the "cognitive contents" of our concepts. This sounds like stipulating that the Lockean view is correct.

[27] In Chapter 2, section 2.4 we considered a more radical kind of mistake about water (it is really pink and granular).

conditions just stated preclude this.[28] That appears to be a mistake *about conjunction*, and so a mistake on the part of one who uses the concept AND. On the alternative view, according to which the subject lacks the concept AND, having either no relevant concept or a distinct one, there is no mistake at all.

The view (or class of views) we are attacking has the form: for every concept, C, there is some body of information such that anyone who grasps C must know or believe this information holds of Cs. The problem is simply that it's hard to find any information that fits the bill. However, there is a different though related theory, one that links grasp of a concept not to associated criteria, but simply to the ability to apply it correctly (an ability that may or may not be mediated by criteria). The underlying idea might be that using a concept requires knowledge of its content, and this knowledge consists in suitable dispositions to apply it correctly. Initial formulations might be on these lines:

1. Correct use of a nominative concept requires a disposition to apply it, under favorable circumstances, to the object to which it refers.
2. Correct use of a predicative concept requires a disposition to apply it, under favorable circumstances, to objects that possess the property to which it refers.

It's easy to see that (1) and (2) can't be right as stated. First, consider nonatomic nominative concepts, like the concept THE PRESENT KING OF FRANCE. There is no object to which it refers, so someone who grasps the concept cannot in fact apply it to the object to which it refers. Nor need a subject be counterfactually disposed to apply it to the referent, were there to be one. A thinker who counts as being able to use the concept, thanks to an appreciation of its structure and parts, might have no use at all for it, or might falsely (as we are supposing) believe that there is no such king. In either case, the user of the concept would have no disposition to apply it to anything.

A first modification restricts (1) and (2) to atomic concepts. The empty case remains problematic. It's unclear that Leverrier was disposed to apply the concept VULCAN to anything; but if he had had such a disposition it would have been a manifestation of error, and so not a basis for knowledge of how to use a concept. The concept VULCAN has no content, so mastering it cannot require knowledge of content. On some views about properties, the same can be said for the concept PHLOGISTON.

Specific indexical concepts might seem good candidates for requiring a link between possession of a concept and knowledge relating to its content. Suppose a thinker introduces a new specific indexical concept THAT. Is not its referent, and so its content, determined by the thinker's intentions? And must not the thinker know what these intentions are, and so know the concept's content? Thinkers may (by some standards) know what they are intending to refer to, and succeed in referring to it, without knowing (by some standards) what they are referring to. In a phonetic identity parade, we are asked to identify our attacker by his voice (the attack took place in the dark, and the police are

---

[28] We ourselves are inclined towards this view (to which update semantics are sensitive). But the example treats it as a mistaken view.

anxious to ensure we are not prejudiced by visual features of the suspects). The two candidates are asked to say something, while hidden from us by a screen. We recognize the voice of the speaker on our left, and proclaim "That's the man!" Before the curtain is lifted, the men switch places. We know we intended to refer to the attacker (and we did so), but we do not know we in fact referred to the man now sitting on the right. While knowing our intentions, and fulfilling them successfully, we mistake the content of a concept we introduced; a mistake that might lead to an innocent person being found guilty.

The empty case remains problematic, since a concept with no content can be used even though there is no content to be known. It may be part of the user's intention that there be no referent, as when a parent in a game asks a child to guess what *that* is, holding out a closed fist the parent knows to contain nothing. (The parent may continue: is that a sweet? and so on, making plain that a usable concept has been introduced.)

It is not essential to originalism that the ability to use an atomic concept *never* requires knowledge of content; but, setting aside indexicality, as discussed in Chapter 3, we find it hard to discover plausible everyday examples of cases in which such knowledge IS required, and there are plenty of cases in which it manifestly is not.

Even though knowledge of content is typically not required in order to use an atomic concept, thinkers often do know the contents of their concepts. To know the content of a given concept is to know *what* the content of the concept is, and this in turn is to be able to give a non-accidentally correct answer to the indirect question introduced by "what". However, we should not require that typical subjects possess the concept CONTENT, for that is a technical notion that thinkers who have relevant knowledge may lack. Hence we should not rely on thinkers to have a good answer to a question conceptualized using the concept CONTENT, even though we intuitively wish to credit them with some suitably related knowledge.

One way to meet this difficulty is to suggest that a thinker, in order to know what the content of the concept HESPERUS is, needs to know simply that the concept HESPERUS refers to Hesperus. Here we use, and require the knowing subject to use, the non-technical notion of reference, a notion on the basis of which the more general and technical notion of content was introduced. This makes the knowledge requirement less demanding, but it is still too demanding. Thinkers can use concepts without having the concept REFERENCE (young children are examples of such thinkers).

Another way to meet the difficulty is to say that a thinker counts as knowing the content of a concept if she is disposed to use it of things to which it applies. Because of empty concepts (among other reasons), this could at best be a sufficient, and not a necessary condition. It has the advantage of not requiring those who know the content of their concepts to have any semantic concepts.

The two approaches correspond to two ways of thinking of knowledge of content. On the first approach, it is something theoretical, manifest in knowledge of facts linking concepts and the world, and so available only to possessors of semantic concepts. On the second approach, it is more behavioral, inferred from a kind of practical ability. The approaches are not in conflict: one could develop each to provide accounts of both theoretical and practical knowledge of content. As noted, neither account provides a necessary condition for what it is to possess a concept, and both accounts should be thought of as evidential rather than constitutive.

In the case of some concepts, some specific knowledge is required, though it is not well described as knowledge of content. These are the indexical concepts, as mentioned in Chapter 3. Indexical concepts are copied from templates that impose more or less specific requirements on the use of the concepts they shape. For example, a specific concept I must be used to refer to the subject, and a specific concept *you* must be used to refer to the addressee. Knowledge of character (in Kaplan's sense) is required for the use of indexical concepts.

A way to highlight the difference between originalism and more familiar approaches is this: we have no room for a notion of the "correct" use of a concept (unless this means using a concept in a true judgment). More familiar views can raise questions about whether, given that a concept is used, it is used "correctly", meaning by this: used in conformity with the normative demands made by the concept, demands that must be met even in making a false judgment. These demands are supposed to apply to all uses of a concept, even in mere supposition: they are not demands specially related to truth. By contrast, for originalism there is simply the question whether a subject uses or does not use a concept on an occasion. If it is used at all, then it is used "correctly" (as other theorists conceive this). Whether or not it is used in the making of a true judgment is another question.

4.9 Comparison with Fodor

We share many of Jerry Fodor's views: his naturalism, his atomism (the view that many concepts have no conceptual parts, and have their reference independently of the reference of other concepts), and his commitment to a representational theory of mind. We agree that concept possession is not to be explained in terms of knowledge. We also agree with him that language expresses thought, and that understanding a language is knowing what thoughts its sentences express (Fodor 1998: 9).

More specifically, we agree with him that Frege cases can be explained without appeal to semantics that go beyond reference (Fodor 2008: 56). We agree that beliefs with the same content may differ in their causal powers (2008: 68), for beliefs are thoughts, thoughts are structures of concepts, and different structures of concepts may have different cognitive value and different causal powers, even if they have the same content.

Nonetheless, there remain significant disagreements. His position contains weaknesses which can be remedied by adopting an originalist perspective. One concerns the individuation of concepts; another the way in which the content of concepts is fixed; a third is an overlooked possibility for concept learning.

For Fodor, concepts are individuated "syntactically," where this is explained as follows:

Tokens of primitive Mentalese formulas are of different types when they differ in the (presumably physical) properties to which mental processes are sensitive. (2008: 79)

He offers an analogy with the shapes of letters, for which (presumably) *being the same shape as* is not some simple geometric property, for no such property could explain how tokens of the letter "a" can differ from font to font and from print to various handwritten versions. The *same shape* property for letters is presumably in part determined by what the human visual system, in good conditions, treats as the same letter (though this explanation raises the specter of circularity). Fodor holds something similar for atomic Mentalese concepts, for he says that mental processes can't be mistaken "across the board" about what type a basic Mentalese token belongs to.

Fodor's position contrasts with originalism in two dimensions. For originalists, a token or use of a concept is a use of whatever concept stands at the origin of the R-linked chain of uses to which this use belongs. Uses of different concepts belong to different chains of use, and so are related to different other uses. There is no built-in requirement of consistency of causal properties across distinct uses of the same concept. The question whether a subject (or a subject's cognitive mechanisms) could be "mistaken" about the concept to which a use belongs is not one that normally arises. A subject could have a mistaken belief on this matter only if she had a belief; and having such a metaconceptual belief requires a degree of sophistication the typical concept-user does not possess.

The originalist view seems superior, in part because different uses of the same concept might have very different causal powers. This is conspicuous when the uses are by different subjects. If John sees a wildebeest running towards Jill, his use of the concept WILDEBEEST may be associated with very different behavioral consequences from Jill's use of that same concept.[29] The same story can easily be modified to a single subject case. The day on which John saw a wildebeest bearing down on a fellow hiker, his use of the concept WILDEBEEST had very different causal consequences from his use of it the next day, when he saw a wildebeest bearing down on him.

In all the cases, the concept WILDEBEEST is used to think of wildebeests. But this common consequence of the different tokens cannot individuate the type to which the tokens belong, since the concept GNU can also be used to think about wildebeests, though it was not used in the examples.

Fodor takes up some of these issues when moving outwards from individual thought to public concepts, allowing that minds that use the same concepts may be neurologically dissimilar (2008: 89). The right response, he suggests, is to endorse functionalism all the way down: about the relationship between intentional psychology (psychology that makes use of the ascription of intentional states to subjects) and computation, and about the relationship between computation and the various actual and possible physical implementations of given computational processes (2008: 90). The idea is to allow that silicon brains

---

[29] Here we develop an example given by Perry (1979).

may engage in the *same* computations as our brains; and that creatures that compute differently may nonetheless think the same.[30]

Subjects can wrongly think that two uses are uses of different concepts when they are uses of the same concept. This lies at the heart of our response to Paderewski cases (discussed in Chapter 7), and is a possibility excluded within Fodor's theory.

Another main disagreement with Fodor concerns the fixing of reference. For Fodor, the reference of a concept at a time is fixed by facts concerning asymmetric causal dependence at that time. In Mickey Mouse version: at any time at which the concept DOG refers to dogs, instances of dogs cause tokens of the concept DOG. One obvious difficulty is that someone who has learned a concept may become very bad at recognizing instances of it, however nicely they are presented. But they may still use the concept, if only to think falsely, of a dog in plain view, that it is not a dog. According to originalism, by contrast, reference may be fixed by facts that have little to do with an individual thinker. She may come to use the concept by learning it from others, complete with its referent, but with no guarantee that she will stand in any further relation to the referent. Another obvious difficulty with the asymmetric dependence view is that it has nothing to say about empty concepts.

A related disagreement with Fodor concerns concept learning. Fodor says he can think of no other way that a concept could be learned than by inductive reasoning that involves the use (and not just mention) of the target concept; and since this presupposes that the concept is possessed before the learning process can get started, the right conclusion is that concepts cannot be learned. By contrast, according to originalism, most of our stable public concepts are learned from others, by a process of immersion and deference. We aim to use the very concept they used, when they said or thought something. That intention does not require one already to use the concept: it can be referred to without being used. This takes some wind out of Fodor's attraction to nativism.

4.10 Comparison with Millikan

In one important respect, the originalist perspective coincides with Ruth Millikan's: we and she agree that Fregean data are to be explained by appeal to sameness and difference in vehicles of content, rather than sameness and difference in content.[31] However, there are many differences.

For example, Millikan defines concepts so that they are never shared:

a concept is an individual thing—an individual ability that comes into existence at a time or over a time and goes out of existence at or over another time and that belongs to an individual person or animal. I have concepts and you have completely other concepts, though many of them may be concepts be of the same things. (2011: 6)

In earlier work, she is happy to regard concepts as abilities (2000: 2), though as abilities they can in a sense be shared. We do not deny that there may be a notion of interest to

---

[30] This puts pressure on his claim already quoted that concept-types are defined in terms of physical properties.
[31] Millikan (1984, chs 9, 12; 1993, ch. 14; 2000, ch. 6; 2004, ch. 7; 2005, ch. 3).

psychology that is essentially subject-bound or essentially involves abilities. But the originalist account of concepts starts with thoughts, regarded as potentially shareable. This makes concepts also potentially shareable (and indeed very often shared), and it allows for concept-sharing that is not explained in terms of ability-sharing.

Unlike originalists, Millikan is tempted to require that every concept have a referent: "it is easy to see how a person might seem to herself to have a concept that was not in fact of anything, hence that was not, strictly speaking, a concept at all" (2011: 136). She is also tempted in the other direction, in the same paper: "just as something designed to open cans is a can opener even if it is too dull or too badly made actually to open cans, perhaps it is sensible to consider a concept that is badly made, hence fails, to still be a concept"(2011: 141). Although there may be some terminological issue here, not worthy of discussion, there is also something definitely not merely terminological. According to originalism, what Millikan calls "failed concepts"—ones that fail to have a referent, even though intended to have one—can successfully be used to think. Even if the resulting thoughts are not true,[32] they succeed in being thoughts, and this success is crucial to understanding how certain kinds of mistakes and progress are made.

A potentially more radical difference between Millikan's view and originalism is that originalists might be thought to hold to what she calls a "sentence model" of thought (e.g. 2000: 161). She takes it that on this view different tokens of the same concept will count as tokens of the same in virtue of sharing a "shape" (2000: 162), where this marks a blank for some yet to be specified intrinsic property of a token or use.[33] This shows that her sentence model is not an originalist view (despite the fact that originalists do indeed think of concepts as like words, and thoughts as like sentences). Moreover, she argues that, for mental words, to be treated as having the same referent is to be treated as the same symbol:

What effect are we to imagine mental *Cicero* = *Tully* to have, if not, precisely, that it changes the mind's dispositions to mental typing [assigning concept-tokens to concept-types]? Henceforth, mental *Cicero* and mental *Tully* will behave as representational equals. They become the same mental word... (Millikan 2000: 167)

We disagree. For originalists, what makes two uses uses of the same concept is their belonging to a single use-tree, where this is fixed by relational properties of uses—and so not by their "shapes", which are intrinsic properties. Believing that Cicero is Tully leaves the distinct uses as uses of distinct concepts, concepts with different origins. (There is more to be said about the special case of learning identity truths: see Chapter 7 below.) This is as it should be, since even if we know full well that Hesperus is Phosphorus, we need to distinguish the ancients believing that Hesperus is Hesperus from their believing that Hesperus is Phosphorus. We cannot do this if the concepts HESPERUS and PHOSPHORUS "behave as representational equals".

---

[32] Some significant thoughts involving empty concepts are true. To explain Leverrier's behavior, we need to know truths concerning the beliefs he held that contain the concept VULCAN.

[33] She stresses, as we have done earlier in this chapter, that letters and words are not individuated by their shape in any ordinary sense: widely divergent shapes, geometrically considered, may token the same letter or word.

Millikan suggests that the crucial error is the belief (which we hold, and which she says we share with Frege) that "how a thought *functions* has no effect on its content" (2000: 168). She says that this entails that "thoughts are not mental representations":

we cannot suppose that a representation could be a *mental* representation, a representation *for mind*, yet that its representational value was independent of its effect upon mind... (2000: 169)

This consequence would indeed be unwelcome, but it does not follow. On Millikan's view, tokens with the same functional cognitive role are tokens of the same concept. But even those who know that Tully is Cicero need two concepts when they think about the Tully/Cicero thoughts of people who don't realize that Tully is Cicero. If we take this as showing that "mental *Cicero*" and "mental *Tully*" are, even for the knowledgeable, not representational equals (despite what Millikan said in the excerpt just cited), then it's not clear that there will be any extensional disagreement with originalism. But if they are representational equals, as Millikan holds, her theory lacks the resources needed adequately to describe more complex thoughts.

5
Concept Externalism, Originalism and Privileged Access

Originalism is committed to concept externalism: the view that it is metaphysically possible for individuals who are intrinsic duplicates to differ with respect to their concepts. Concept externalism is not the same as semantic externalism for concepts. The latter thesis is that it is metaphysically possible for individuals who are intrinsic duplicates to possess concepts that differ in their contents. According to originalism, concepts are individuated by their origins, not by their contents. Indeed, some concepts lack content altogether. Furthermore, originalism does not entail semantic externalism. Nonetheless, we ourselves accept semantic externalism and many of our remarks in earlier chapters reflect this acceptance or provide reasons for it.

This chapter focuses upon concept externalism and its compatibility with the view that we have privileged knowledge of, or access to, our own conscious mental states, including our own thoughts. Intuitively, we can know which concepts we are exercising in our thoughts and we can know this in a direct and authoritative way, simply by introspection.[1] How can such privileged access obtain if our concepts are fixed by historical facts to which we have no introspective access? Sometimes, it is held further that we have privileged access to sameness and difference in the concepts employed in our thoughts. Again, how can such "privileged access" obtain, if the nature of our thoughts is fixed, in part, by external conditions to which we lack privileged access? That was the Puzzle of the Twins (or at least part of the puzzle).

---

[1] We use "introspection" in what Sydney Shoemaker (1994) calls the broad sense. In the broad sense, one's introspective awareness that one is thinking that p, need not itself be manifested in consciousness by an occurrent thought; in the narrow sense of introspection, it must be. One's introspective awareness that one is thinking that p, is a true belief, formed by introspection, that one is thinking that p. In the narrow sense of introspection, this second-order belief must itself be manifested in consciousness by an occurrent thought. The occurrent thought will be what Burge (1996) aptly calls a "cogito thought". (The occurrent thought that one is now thinking that water is a liquid, the thought that one is now thinking about water, and the thought that one is now thinking are all cogito thoughts.) We often have introspective knowledge of what we are thinking without having cogito thoughts; to count as introspective knowledge, a belief need not itself be manifested in consciousness by an occurrent thought. For instance, one might introspectively know that one is thinking that water is a liquid on occasions in which the only occurrent thought one is having is that water is a liquid. Such cases count as cases of introspection in the broad sense.

In what follows, we call the former thesis of privileged self-knowledge "the privileged access thesis" and the latter thesis "the thesis of introspective knowledge of comparative concepts" (hereafter *IKCC*).[2] We maintain that *IKCC* is false. However, we deny that our arguments against *IKCC* cut any ice against the privileged access thesis; further, there is no difficulty in reconciling the privileged access thesis with concept externalism.

5.1 Formulating IKCC

One way *IKCC* might be formulated, drawing upon some remarks of Falvey and Owens (1994: 109–10), is as follows:

> With respect to any two of his thoughts or beliefs an individual can know apriori via introspection whether or not they exercise the same concepts.[3]

Another way of formulating the thesis is to split it into two parts. Drawing now on some comments of Paul Boghossian (1992: 36), the thesis may be divided up in the following way:

> *Transparency of sameness*: If two of a thinker's token thoughts use the same concepts, then the thinker can know apriori via introspection that they do.
> *Transparency of difference*: If two of a thinker's token thoughts use distinct contents, then the thinker can know apriori that they do.

IKCC, so understood, is easy to refute. Since there is no requirement that the thinker be able to bring the two token thoughts to mind, forgotten tokens are already counterexamples. Let us stipulate, then, that the token thoughts not be forgotten. Still, the token thoughts might exercise concepts that are later misremembered. Suppose, for example, that one is an aging investment banker recalling an auditory linguistic image one chanted to oneself as a child that involved the sounds "I am going to the bank". One might misremember which concept "bank" expressed, believing that one was thinking about a bank in the financial institution sense of "bank", when what one was actually thinking was that one was going to the river bank.

Were the thesis of privileged access taken to include past thoughts as well as present ones, the example just given would refute that thesis too. But no one holds that we have privileged access to our *past* thoughts. When our faculty of introspection is working normally, we know by introspection which concepts we are *now* using in our thought.[4]

---

[2] For us, given the distinction between concept externalism and semantic externalism, the privileged access thesis is not the same as the thesis that we can know directly and authoritatively, via introspection, the *contents* of our conscious thoughts.

[3] Falvey and Owens actually state the thesis with respect to knowledge of sameness and difference of content (as does Boghossian below). This is because, unlike originalists, they individuate concepts by their contents.

[4] It might be replied that when we do know our past thoughts, it is just terminological whether this is to be called introspective knowledge or not. Why not call it "remembered introspective knowledge", where the relevant

Analogously, *IKCC* should be formulated so that what is claimed is that we have direct and authoritative access via introspection to sameness and difference in the concepts involved in our present, occurrent thoughts—access that permits us to know apriori such sameness and difference. Corresponding to the privileged access thesis, then, we have the following comparative thesis:

> *IKCC* When our faculty of introspection is working normally, we can know apriori via introspection with respect to any two present, occurrent thoughts whether they exercise the same or different concepts.[5]

So formulated, it is not obvious that *IKCC* is false. Of course, just how long a time is to count as the present is a question that itself merits discussion; but we shall not attempt to answer it here (no doubt it admits of no precise answer). We assume that the present can be long enough in duration for one to have two thoughts, not just a single thought, and to compare them. Obviously, the period *cannot* be so long that one can *misremember* one of the occurrent thoughts. How long that is is an empirical question.

5.2 IKCC and Switching

We have conscious thoughts not only about our present environment but also about the past. This raises special problems in connection with thought experiments in which subjects are imagined to "switch" between earth and twin-earth.

According to originalism, the concept TWATER, used on twin-earth (and expressed by the twin-earth word "water") is distinct from the concept WATER, used on earth (and expressed by the earth word "water"). Likewise the concept TWIN PAVAROTTI, used on twin-earth (and expressed by the twin-earth word "Pavarotti") is distinct from the concept PAVAROTTI, used on earth (and expressed by the earth word "Pavarotti"). These pairs of concepts have different origins. Moreover, we think that the different concepts have different contents: the content of the concept WATER is water (i.e. H_2O), whereas the content of the concept TWATER is twater (i.e. XYZ). The content of the earth concept PAVAROTTI, is the earth-occupying famous Italian tenor. The content of the twin-earth concept TWIN PAVAROTTI is that person's duplicate on twin-earth.

Now let's imagine a switch. Unknown to him, Paul is transported from earth to twin-earth. He will not notice the switch, since everything on twin-earth is intrinsically exactly like earth. After he has been on twin-earth for a while, deferring to his new concept-using community, it is plausible to hold he counts as a user of the twin-earth concepts, at least in ordinary present tense cases. When Paul on twin-earth thinks a

---

knowledge is both knowledge by introspection and knowledge by memory? In these terms, our point is that introspection alone does not yield such knowledge. Memory is involved and memory lacks any kind of infallibility or even privilege.

[5] We take occurrent thoughts to be conscious episodes. Beliefs manifest themselves in consciousness via such thoughts.

thought he would express by "I like water", it's plausible to regard him as thinking that he likes twater, just as any other twin-earthian does. But what about Paul's thoughts concerning the past? What if Paul says "Pavarotti was a great tenor when I met him twenty years ago" or "I used to drink ten glasses of water a day in my youth"? Should a concept externalist say that the thoughts the utterances express involve the concepts TWIN PAVAROTTI and TWATER, or the concepts PAVAROTTI and WATER? Intuitively, Paul's thoughts are about the earthly individual and liquid. They are caused and sustained by past perceptions that occurred on earth. Intuitively, the memories Paul has on twin-earth are about the entities he encountered on earth, in interactions that caused the memories to be laid down in the first place. Here, it seems, Paul's original earth concepts are now operative.

One might draw the moral that concept externalism is false (and with it originalism), at least if *IKCC* is true (cf. Boghossian 1992: 38–9). This is because, on the inside, it seems to Paul that there is no difference between the relevant thoughts. If, for example, after switching earths, Paul introspects the thought he is disposed to express by the sentence "I used to live in a house by a large body of water" and also the thought he is disposed to express by the sentence "I now live in a house by a large body of water", both of which are occurring in the specious present, he may believe that the same conceptual structure is present in the two cases (apart from tense). By *IKCC*, this introspective belief is knowledge, and so the thoughts are the same. But the concepts cannot be the same, if concept externalism is true. The present tense sentence expresses a thought involving the concept TWATER, whereas the past tense sentence expresses a thought involving the concept WATER. So, concept externalism is false.

This argument can be run in the other direction by assuming concept externalism and concluding that *IKCC* is false. This is the direction of interest to us in this section. However, the argument is not fully successful: the above considerations do not show *by themselves* that once concept externalism is accepted, *IKCC* must go. We have been assuming that Paul exercises two concepts on twin-earth: the concept TWATER, used in present tense and tenseless thoughts, like the thought that drinking a lot of twater is good for you, and the concept WATER, used when thinking about his past. But perhaps this is unjustified. Perhaps Paul uses only the concept TWATER, and not the concept WATER. On this view, when Paul utters the sentence "I used to drink ten glasses of water a day in my youth and I never got sick", he expresses the thought that he used to drink ten glasses of twater a day and he never got sick. This will explain why, for example, Paul takes this to support the thought that drinking a lot of twater is good for you.

If this is correct—if Paul does indeed exercise the concept TWATER in those of his beliefs about the past that he expresses in part using "water"—then, of course, *IKCC* is not threatened. One question is whether this is the right view to take of Paul.

Perhaps it will be replied that the claim that Paul uses the concept TWATER in the relevant beliefs about the past is very counterintuitive; for it has as a consequence that in traveling cases, one's memory leads one astray, that it is clouded or altered by the switch in one's environments. This response seems to us unpersuasive.

Consider the following situation. You see someone, Jones, walking towards you, but Jones is disguised to look just like Smith. You are taken in by the disguise, and you believe of Jones that he is Smith. In this case, you form an inaccurate de re belief, which, in turn, generates some false de dicto beliefs, for example, that you saw Smith today, that Smith was in such-and-such a place, and so on. That inaccurate beliefs are sometimes formed in this way is completely uncontroversial.

For the externalist who takes the position we are considering above, the situation with memory in the traveling case is very similar. After being switched from earth to twin-earth, Paul has memory impressions and images *of* water and *of* events and actions involving water, for example, drinking ten glasses of water (in the de re sense of the term "of", the sense in which Paul can have a belief of or about water without conceptualizing it as water). With the switch to twin-earth, after sufficient time has gone by, Paul's concepts change, and he comes to believe of the liquid in his memory images that it is twater and of certain water-involving historical events that they are twater-involving. So, Paul comes to believe inaccurately *that* there was twater in the lakes he visited in his youth, *that* he used to drink twater, and so on. Still, his memory images and impressions and de re beliefs are firmly tied to the entities, the perception of which caused the memory impressions to be laid down in the first place.

On this account, the intuition that there is something Paul hasn't forgotten in the traveling case is preserved. For on twin-earth, the memory images and impressions Paul conjures up of past events are of events that really occurred. In one sense, then, he hasn't forgotten them. Images and impressions Paul has of them do not disappear; they are retained even in his new setting. What has changed, what has gone wrong, is Paul's conceptualization of those events. He now conceives of them as falling under concepts they do not fall under, e.g., the concept TWATER. That, however, is not counterintuitive, given the nature of the case. Or so it seems to us.

Perhaps it will still be objected that intuitively, one's memory should work in the new setting just as well as it did before. There has been no neurological impairment, indeed no intrinsic neurological change of any sort pertinent to memory. Supposing that certain memories become inaccurate after the switch makes memory defective in traveling cases. And that just isn't plausible.

This reply seems to us to trade on an equivocation on the meaning of "defective". Consider a machine that has been built to detect bombs. In the context in which it is first used—to single out bombs in luggage at airports before the advent of plastic explosives—it works extremely well. But later on, as non-metallic bombs are placed in luggage, it becomes ineffective. The design of the machine is such that in one setting it functions well, but in another setting it fails. In what we call the "design" sense, it becomes defective: it no longer succeeds in doing what it was designed to do. But in another sense, the "hardware" sense, it is not defective: the hardware continues to operate smoothly, there are no mechanical breakdowns in the running of the machine, and given a suitcase with a metallic bomb in it, the machine responds to it effectively just as it did when it was first introduced. In the hardware sense, the machine is *not* defective.

Likewise in the case of memory. Shifting environments does not make memory defective in the hardware sense. The internal physical systems that are relevant to memory continue to work just as they did in the original environment. But shifting environments can make memory defective in the broader design sense. Since the new environment can create mis-memories, on the version of the externalist account we are considering—and indeed must do so, given the appropriate external changes—facts outside the head in the new environment can prevent one from remembering facts one knew at an earlier time, even though physiologically nothing has changed. In such circumstances, memory, considered as a psychological capacity, fails to perform the function for which it was designed: it fails to inform one correctly about facts concerning the past.

Having said all this on behalf of the view that those of Paul's beliefs about the past which he expresses using the term "water" exercise the concept TWATER, we should add that we think that it is perfectly reasonable for the concept externalist to take the opposing line that Paul believes that he used to drink ten glasses of water a day (for example), so long as this is coupled with the further claim that Paul also *mistakenly* believes that this belief exercises the same concept as the concept he expresses by the word "water" in the first sentence he utters ("Drinking water is good for you"). Given these beliefs, the externalist has a natural account of why Paul reasons as he does. For example, she can explain in a straightforward way why Paul *takes* his second remark to support his first.[6] Now, if concept externalism is assumed, *IKCC* must be rejected.

We shall not try to adjudicate between the two accounts of Paul's memory beliefs. But given that there are these two accounts and neither is obviously mistaken, the conclusion we draw is that switching cases, as interpreted by the concept externalist, do not immediately refute *IKCC*. In the next section we turn to other specific and general reasons for questioning *IKCC*.

5.3 The Empirical Implausibility of IKCC

Rudolf believes that cilantro should be used sparingly in his cooking, and he also believes that coriander should be used sparingly in his cooking. However, Rudolf does not realize that cilantro = coriander.[7] When he reflects introspectively upon the thought that cilantro

---

[6] Paul ends up giving bad arguments, but this in no way threatens his rationality. For more on *IKCC* and rationality, see section 5.4.

[7] We set aside the suggestion that "cilantro" refers to the leaves of a certain plant, and "coriander" to the seeds of the same plant. The example is from Falvey and Owens (1994: 110–11).

should be used sparingly and the thought that coriander should be used sparingly, it seems to Rudolph that they are distinct thoughts and thus that the concept CILANTRO is different from the concept CORIANDER. So, by IKCC, Rudolph knows that they are different concepts. However, if originalism is true it could turn out to be the case, even though it is unlikely, that the concepts have a common historical origin and thus that there is really only a single concept. In these circumstances, Rudolph does *not* know by introspection that the concepts are different. So, if originalism is true, IKCC is false.[8]

Is this conclusion tenable? We believe that it is: IKCC is an empirically implausible thesis. We now explain why.

In the external world, we can encounter the same object on two occasions and fail to recognize that it is the same object. Perhaps the object is seen from two different perspectives, or perhaps the appearance of the object has changed without any change in perspective. Consider, for example the case of Hesperus and Phosphorus. Someone might recognize Hesperus in the evening sky and also recognize Phosphorus in the morning sky. Still she might fail to recognize that Hesperus is the same as Phosphorus.

We can also encounter different objects and fail to recognize that they are different. Suppose, for example, that you are seeing a pen on a table before you. As you blink, the pen is removed and replaced by a duplicate. You notice no difference. In such cases, there need be nothing wrong with your perceptual faculty. Yet you fail to recognize the difference.

The fact that this sometimes happens does not show that we do not *typically* know sameness and difference in the things we see. We do. Smith knows that the car he sees in his garage this morning is the same as the car he saw in the garage last night. Jones knows that the coffee cup on her right is the same as the coffee cup she was seeing just before she blinked. Brown knows that the red paint patch he experiences on the wall to his left is different from the red paint patch he experiences on the wall to his right.

Just as we can fail to recognize sameness and difference in external concrete objects so too we can fail to recognize sameness and difference in external properties. Consider, for example, the case of the Müller–Lyer diagram (Figure 1). The length of the left-hand line is

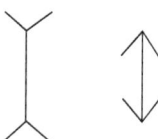

Figure 1

---

[8] The failure of introspection to supply Rudolph with knowledge under the above (unlikely) scenario, in which the concept CORIANDER has the same origin as the concept CILANTRO, does not show that it does not generally supply him with knowledge about sameness and difference of concepts.

the same as the length of the right-hand line but, on the basis of perceptual information alone, we fail to recognize this sameness in length.

Consider also the case of words. As noted earlier, words are non-eternal abstract continuants; and, as with other entities we perceive, mistakes can be made about their sameness and difference. Suppose, for example, you meet two almost identical twins both named "Rafael". You fail to realize that there are two such individuals since you never see them together. Hearing the sentence "Rafael is outside the window," as uttered by one speaker, you naturally assume that the same individual is being referred to by a second speaker who (a moment later) also utters the sentence "Rafael is outside the window". In fact, the speakers, who are more discerning than you, are each referring to a different Rafael. There are, then, two specific individual names with the same spelling, with two different referents. You hear each name but you fail to recognize that the names are different.

The general moral to draw is that nature has equipped us with perceptual faculties that enable us to recognize various entities in our environments and various samenesses and differences among those entities, but mistakes can and do happen even when the faculties are operating smoothly. If introspection is a natural faculty like perception, we would expect it to operate in much the same way. Via introspection, we can usually tell which concepts are operative in our thoughts and we can recognize sameness and difference in these concepts upon many occasions. But mistakes can and do happen. The world can conspire to trip our concept detectors up—and it does so in some of our puzzling scenarios.

Introspection, like perception, is a reliable process or activity. In the case of thoughts and concepts, the process takes as inputs the relevant conceptual structures and delivers as outputs beliefs or judgments as to which thoughts and concepts are present. Reliable processes, upon occasion, go wrong. In the case of "Rafael", you can make a mistake if you are tricked by the sameness or very close similarity in appearance of the two Rafaels. You have mentally associated only one file of information with "Rafael" and so you judge that there is a single name. Had the two Rafaels had different appearances in your experience, you would have had two files of information, each of which was attached to a distinct individual name (with a common spelling). In this case, no mistake about difference would have been made. Of course, had there been (unknown to you) but a single Rafael, whom you encountered in two very different contexts and whose appearance was totally different in those contexts, you might have had two files of information, one mentally associated by you with the name "Rafael", as used in the one context, and the other mentally associated by you with the name "Rafael", as used in the other. In this case, your judgment that there were two distinct individual names, formed on the basis of the existence of the two files, would have been wrong. The process generating that judgment, though generally reliable, would have failed.

In the concept case, we might suppose that associated with each concept is a conception. Introspection uses information in the conception as a quick and easy way of issuing judgments or forming beliefs about concept identity and difference. Such a process usually works, for typically where there is a different conception there is a different referent (even if the referent is not accurately portrayed in the conception) and so a different concept, but upon occasion it goes wrong.

The Cartesian view of the mind has it that mistakes about our own mental lives are impossible. The spotlight of introspection, on this view, shines so brightly that we cannot err with respect to what we are thinking. But how could our inner spotlight deliver such certainty? How could it infallibly prevent us from making mistaken comparisons? If introspection is a natural faculty, the answer surely is that it could not.

IKCC is not committed to the certainty that is part and parcel of the Cartesian picture of the mind, but it is a vestige of that picture. The Cartesian picture has had a powerful grip upon philosophical theorizing about consciousness and only relatively recently have we begun to free ourselves from it. In our view, the same picture still exerts too strong a pull on philosophical thinking about thought. Rejecting *IKCC* is a step along the way to a full, naturalistic, anti-Cartesian account of the mind.

5.4 IKCC and Rationality

One significant worry concerning the rejection of *IKCC* is that it entails that subjects who are patently irrational in their belief formation may nonetheless have to be counted as rational. Consider someone, Samantha, who forms the belief that all snow is white and who also forms the belief that not all snow is white. It is natural to suppose that Samantha, if she has these beliefs at the same time, is irrational. The beliefs she has are contradictory. However, suppose that *IKCC* is given up. Then it might be held that Samantha is absolvable for believing a contradiction, since the contradictory character of her beliefs is inaccessible to apriori reflection. It may seem, then, that if *IKCC* is repudiated, "practically any contradictory belief will be absolvable" (Boghossian 1992: 49). So, even patently irrational subjects will have to be deemed rational. And that clearly is unacceptable.

This conclusion is too hasty. The rejection of *IKCC* is certainly compatible with supposing that some subjects who have contradictory beliefs are irrational. Suppose, for example, that the relevant subjects know that their beliefs are contradictory and yet they do not change anything that they believe. Such persons are irrational and they are not to be held blameless for having contradictory beliefs. In some cases, however, rational subjects may not know that their beliefs are contradictory. Further, in some of these cases, they may be rationally *required* to hold beliefs that are contradictory, and even to believe, falsely, that they are not contradictory. Such subjects are absolvable from blame.

Consider Rachel who hears someone in the coffee shop say to another person, "John Locke was shot". Being an avid follower of the television program *Lost*, Rachel takes the comment to pertain to the character with that name in the show. Later in the day, as she walks into her philosophy class on British empiricism, she overhears a philosophy student say, "John Locke was not shot", and knowing something about the history of British

Empiricism, Rachel mutters to herself, "Of course, he wasn't!" In the case of the second remark she hears, Rachel takes "John Locke" to refer to the famous philosopher. Unknown to her, in both cases, "John Locke" refers to the TV character. In these circumstances, the two utterances (sentence tokens uttered) are contradictory: the one denies what the other asserts. Rachel fails to recognize this fact. She takes the two utterances to be consistent, but she is wrong. Patently, Rachel, in taking this view, is not being *irrational*. To be sure, she has erred. The context of the second utterance leads her to misunderstand to whom the speaker is referring. But Rachel's assessment of the situation does not undercut or threaten her rationality.

What happens in the case of Rachel with respect to the words uttered by others can happen even if there is no misunderstanding. The lesson taught by the example of Paderewski is that in some cases the same concept can be tokened on two occasions without the subject recognizing that it is the same concept. Peter wrongly believes that there are two people called "Paderewski". He may be rational to believe this. He may have been told it on good authority, or have inferred it from something told him by a reliable witness (for example, he might have been told that no politicians have musical talent). Hence he rationally, though falsely, believes that the sentence "Paderewski has musical talent", which he is disposed to utter having heard Paderewski play, does not contradict the sentence "Paderewski does not have musical talent", which he is disposed to utter as he watches Paderewski give a political speech. This is so even if he understands both sentences. What is true for the sentences Peter is disposed to utter is true for his thoughts. Since Peter falsely but rationally believes that the concept he is exercising when he uses the name "Paderewski" in each of the above cases is different, he is rational in believing that the beliefs he expresses in uttering "Paderewski has musical talent" and "Paderewski does not have musical talent" are not contradictory. Indeed, given his false starting point, Peter is rationally *required* to believe that he is not involved in a contradiction, even though he is (see Chapter 7 for further discussion).

Peter's situation is not the usual one; nor is that of Rachel. Typically, mistakes of the above sort do not happen. Typically, our concept detector does what it is supposed to do and we do not err with respect to sameness in our concepts. Rejecting *IKCC* is thus consistent with sensible views about rationality.

Here is a related criticism of that rejection. If we cannot know apriori via introspection that two thoughts are different, then certain inferences that are invalid will seem valid to us. Consider once more Paul, who has been transported from earth to twin-earth. Paul may reason in the following way (Boghossian 1992: 45):

1. Whoever floats on water gets wet.
2. Pavarotti once floated on water.

Therefore,

3. Pavarotti got wet.

Here (1), (2), and (3) are sentences. Paul uses (1) to express his belief that whoever floats on twater gets wet. Paul arguably uses (2) to express his belief that Pavarotti once floated on water, since his memory is rooted in his experiences on earth. From these beliefs, obviously Paul is not entitled to infer the conclusion concerning Pavarotti expressed in (3). But if *IKCC* is false, Paul is in no position to recognize the invalidity of the inference he has drawn. This, it has been held, is unacceptable, for it entails that Paul is not disposed to conform to the principles of logic on an apriori basis and therefore Paul is irrational.

One reaction to this argument is to reject the assumption that Paul uses (2) to express the belief that Pavarotti once floated on water. On this view, given his embedding in the environment on twin-earth, Paul believes that Twin Pavarotti once floated on twater. Believing this, he believes that his argument is of the following form:

For all x, if Fx then Gx
Fa

So,

Ga.

Since this reasoning pattern is valid and Paul believes that it is, he is rational. Of course, the second premise of the argument is false, and thus the argument is unsound, but this does not undermine Paul's rationality.

Another reaction is to grant that Paul uses (2) to express his belief that Pavarotti once floated on water and to accept that Paul is indeed in no position to recognize the invalidity of the inference he has drawn, but to insist that this does not make him irrational. Paul, we may suppose, is like the person who, upon hearing the following argument, takes it to be valid:

All reindeer have four legs.
Rudolph is a reindeer.

So,

Rudolph has four legs.

In reality, the argument is invalid since "Rudolph" in the second premise is used to refer to a reindeer, whereas "Rudolph" in the conclusion is used to refer to a human being. One who hears the argument and assumes that it is valid is not behaving irrationally. Indeed, if the false assumption that the name "Rudolph" is unambiguous is rationally based, rationality *requires* the hearer to draw the conclusion that Rudolph has four legs.

Paul, then, on this view of his situation, is perfectly rational, even though he is mistaken in supposing that the concept he expresses by "water" in the first premise is the same as the concept he expresses by "water" in the conclusion. Assumptions of this sort are generally true, for Paul's kind of traveling does not occur in normal life,[9] and so generally we do not reason invalidly when we take ourselves to be reasoning validly. But there is no apriori guarantee that we are not travelers.

Paul is a bit like the person who is deliberating about what to do. An agent, given his knowledge of the situation he finds himself in, may come to a conclusion about the right course of action—a conclusion that is fully warranted by the information available to him—even though in the circumstances it was the wrong thing to do. Evaluating this person from the moral point of view, we may find no fault with his internal reflections, notwithstanding the fact that there was a bad upshot. Correspondingly, evaluating Paul as a rational subject, we may find no reason for criticism even though in the circumstances he holds bad beliefs and produces bad arguments.

5.5 The Privileged Access Thesis

What consequences does the rejection of *IKCC* have for the privileged access thesis? That thesis may be stated as follows:

(PA) If our faculty of introspection is functioning normally, we can infallibly know by introspection which concepts we are exercising in our thoughts, in a direct and authoritative way.

Suppose you have a thought that you sincerely express in the sentence

4. All gorse bushes are furze bushes.

If (PA) is true, you can know which thought you are having simply by introspection. Suppose it seems to you (as in the typical case) that your thought is that all gorse bushes are furze bushes. Then, assuming that your faculty of introspection is working normally, the privileged access thesis entails that you know that your thought is that all gorse bushes are furze bushes.

Suppose now you have a thought that you sincerely express in the sentence

5. All gorse bushes are gorse bushes.

Given (PA), you know that your thought is that all gorse bushes are gorse bushes. Is the thought you express in (5) the same as or different from the thought you express in (4)? Once *IKCC* is rejected, it must be admitted that introspection, even if the faculty is in working order, is not an infallible source of the answer to this question. For introspection is not infallible when it comes to telling you whether the concept GORSE is the same as (or different from) the concept FURZE. But this in no way threatens (PA). Given privileged access, you do know your thought in each case and you know it on the basis of introspection.

---

[9] Although there is no switching from earth to twin-earth, there is sometimes switching from one linguistic community to another with a change in meaning of words that is not picked up by the traveler, and a corresponding change in concepts (given social externalism of the Burgean sort).

We ourselves do not unqualifiedly endorse the privileged access thesis. As we noted in the last section, if nature can conspire to trip us up with respect to sameness and difference in concepts, then why should it not do so with respect to concepts themselves? Our purpose here is simply to note that the rejection of *IKCC* is compatible with the acceptance of privileged access. Although we do not unqualifiedly endorse the privileged access thesis, we believe we *typically* know which concepts we are exercising in our thoughts by introspection, just as we typically know what we are seeing by means of our faculty of vision. Still, if introspection is a natural faculty of belief formation, we should expect mistakes to occur sometimes, just as they do in perception, even when the faculty is working properly.

It is arguable that introspection never goes wrong in certain special circumstances: when the introspective belief is manifested in a conscious occurrent thought of the type, thinking with this very thought that I am thinking that *p*. The incorrigibility of such cogito thoughts is easily explained: the second-order thought literally includes the first-order one and so error is impossible with respect to the first-order thought state type tokened. This point has been developed by Tyler Burge (1996). However, the impossibility of error with respect to which first-order thought state type is tokened in undergoing a token cogito thought does not entail impossibility of error with respect to sameness and difference in the content involved in undergoing two different token cogito thoughts.

The remaining sections of this chapter are devoted to an examination of the charge that concept externalism (and in particular concept externalism of an originalist sort) is incompatible with privileged access. There are two leading arguments for incompatibilism. We turn first to one that appeals to twin-earth switching cases.[10]

5.6 Privileged Access and Switching Cases

Suppose that Oscar, without his knowledge, has been traveling back and forth between earth and twin-earth. With each move, he stays long enough to acquire the concepts of the locals, but he knows neither that water is H_2O nor that twater is XYZ. When he utters the present tense sentence "Water is a liquid" after a sufficient period on twin-earth, he comes to express the thought that twater is a liquid, just as the members of the indigenous population do. Oscar, however, is unaware that such shifts in his thought and speech occur.

The case has been claimed to present a difficulty for compatibilism: the view that externalism and privileged access are compatible (see Boghossian 1989). Suppose that on a

---

[10] Switching cases were introduced by Burge (1988). He argued that they fail to show that externalism is incompatible with our having privileged access to cogito thoughts. Cogito thoughts are, he pointed out, true by virtue of our thinking them; they are pragmatically necessary. Boghossian (1989) conceded that cogito thoughts are true by virtue of our thinking them, but challenged whether such beliefs count as *knowledge* in switching cases; and he argued, by appeal to switching cases, that externalism is incompatible with privileged access (when introspection is understood in the broad sense). Of his argument, more below. Sections 5.6–5.9 of this chapter draw on material in McLaughlin and Tye (1998a).

particular occasion while residing on earth, Oscar occurrently thinks that water is a liquid. Given his travels, that he is thinking that twater is a liquid is a relevant alternative to his thinking that water is a liquid.[11] The introspective evidence available to Oscar is compatible with its being the case that he is thinking that twater is a liquid; so, his introspective evidence does not exclude that relevant alternative. Thus, Oscar cannot know by introspection that he is thinking that water is a liquid.[12]

Even if this argument is sound, it does not establish that if concept externalism is true, then the privileged access thesis is false.[13] For the privileged access thesis allows that one may be unable to know which concepts one is using in thought, if one's faculty of introspection is not functioning properly. It would, however, be a truly desperate and ad hoc move for compatibilists to respond to the problem by claiming that Oscar's faculty of introspection would be malfunctioning. The response would render the compatibilist position quite implausible. Compatibilists and noncompatibilists alike should agree that switching from residency in the English-speaking environment to residency in the Twin-English-speaking environment and then switching back again would not automatically result in the malfunctioning of introspection.

Given the shared assumption that traveling Oscar's faculty of introspection is functioning properly, the switching argument can be formulated as a reductio ad absurdum of the compatibilist thesis. For given (PA), the assumption that Oscar's faculty of introspection is functioning properly will imply that he is able to know by introspection that he is thinking that water is a liquid. Combining this reasoning with the reasoning stated above a contradiction follows: Oscar can and cannot know by introspection that he is thinking that water is a liquid. Proponents of switching arguments for incompatibilism can thus maintain that, by reductio, we should reject either (PA) or the externalist thesis that implies that Oscar's thoughts shift with his travels.

We shall argue that switching arguments fail to establish incompatibilism.

5.7 Introspective Evidence

Switching arguments assume the following thesis:

The Introspective Evidence Thesis: Introspective knowledge of which concepts we are using in our occurrent thoughts is based on evidence that we can introspect.

---

[11] Here as elsewhere, by "relevant alternative" we mean a possibility that the subject's basis for belief must rule out in order for the subject to possess the knowledge in question. Two classic discussions of this notion are by Fred Dretske (1970) and Alvin Goldman (1976). Discussions of switching cases in which the notion is invoked can be found in Boghossian (1989); Warfield (1992); and Ludlow (1995a and 1995b).

[12] Cf. Boghossian (1989: n.12).

[13] We should add that concept externalism, on its own, does not *entail* that with the switch, Oscar comes to express the concept TWATER by "water" (in his present tense remarks). However, the claim that the locals on twin-earth possess the concept TWATER (and not the concept WATER) is independently very plausible. Given this claim, if Oscar acquires the concepts of the locals, he acquires the concept TWATER.

What introspective evidence is available to someone having an occurrent thought? Proponents of switching arguments often speak of the introspective evidence as qualitative mental states. In Oscar's case, the qualitative mental state is supposed to be common to his occurrently thinking, while on earth, that water is a liquid, and to his occurrently thinking, while on twin-earth, that twater is a liquid.

These philosophers seem to have in mind something along the following lines: one's introspective evidence that one is thinking that p, is that one is having an auditory image with certain qualitative features. What are the qualitative features in question? Presumably, they include imagistic phonological and stress features. Whether they include syntactic features depends on whether the qualitative features are supposed to be intrinsic; for syntactic features are arguably not intrinsic features of the auditory image. But, in any case, let us count syntactic features among the introspectible qualities of the image.

If, as we hold, concepts are individuated by their origins, then, given the introspective evidence thesis, Oscar's thinking that water is a liquid will fail to supervene on the introspective evidence available to him. Further, given this view of what evidence is introspectively available to Oscar, we will be able to describe switching cases: cases in which Oscar switches from one concept-determining condition to another for the type of auditory image in question (i.e., one with the imagistic phonological, stress, and syntactic features in question). Hence, there will be relevant alternative thoughts that switching Oscar's introspective evidence will fail to rule out. Hence, on a relevant alternatives view of knowledge, the privileged access thesis will be false.

Need proponents of privileged access accept that the introspective evidence available to a thinker is compatible with some alternative thoughts? We think not. Consider again the introspective evidence thesis. According to that thesis, introspective knowledge of our occurrent thoughts is based on evidence that we can introspect. One might take the evidence on which introspective beliefs are based to consist in introspective beliefs that provide evidential reasons. Intuitively, however, one's evidence for believing that one is thinking that p, does not consist in further beliefs at all. Intuitively, one has introspective access to certain mental states, and these states are one's evidence for one's introspective beliefs without providing a propositional justification for those beliefs. On this reliabilist view of introspective knowledge, introspective beliefs are warranted because of their causal ancestry, which will include the introspected mental states in question. The introspective evidence thesis enjoys intuitive support, we maintain, on the reliabilist reading of "evidence" and not on the reading that construes evidence as beliefs that are evidential reasons.[14]

It is open to advocates of a reliabilist account of introspection to maintain that the mental states that are a thinker's introspective evidence in such cases are the occurrent

---

[14] Paul Moser (1989: 156–8) draws a distinction between two notions of being based on evidence that is related to the one we are drawing. For a general discussion of theories of the basing relationship, see Keith Allen Korcz (1997).

thoughts the introspective beliefs are about. A proponent of privileged access can thus reject the assumption that Oscar has introspective access to his occurrent thought that water is a liquid only via his introspective access to a qualitative mental state of the sort described earlier. If this view of his introspective evidence is correct, then Oscar's introspective belief that he is thinking that water is a liquid is based on conclusive evidence, namely on his state of occurrently thinking that water is a liquid. His introspective evidence will thus exclude all relevant alternative thoughts since it will exclude all alternative thoughts. On this view of the introspective evidence, proponents of privileged access—whatever their views about concept externalism—can embrace the introspective evidence thesis.

The fact that one's belief that one is thinking that p strongly supervenes on the introspective evidence does not entail that one's belief is self-evident or self-warranting. We happily concede that no belief is self-evident, that is, that no belief is an evidential reason for itself. On the reliabilist view we favor, the occurrent thought that p (and not the belief that one is thinking that p) is one's evidence for the belief that one is thinking that p. The occurrent thought is the evidence for the belief without being an evidential reason for it.

It is beyond the scope of this chapter to defend a full theory of introspective knowledge. Our main concern in the current section has been simply to show that switching arguments do not demonstrate that privileged access is incompatible with concept externalism.

5.8 Privileged Access and McKinsey's Recipe

Michael McKinsey (1991) has described a recipe for arguing that externalist theses are incompatible with privileged access. Suppose an externalist thesis implies that certain thoughts are individuated, at least in part, by environmental factors. Let the thought that p be a thought of the type in question. McKinsey's recipe for trying to show that the externalist thesis is incompatible with privileged access is essentially the following: find some E such that (i) E cannot be known apriori; yet (ii) the externalist thesis implies that it is apriori true that if one is thinking that p, then E. According to McKinsey, if such an E can be found, it can be successfully argued that either one cannot know apriori that one is thinking that p, or it is not apriori true that if one is thinking that p, then E, from which it may be inferred that the version of externalism is incompatible with privileged access.[15]

We shall first consider a version of externalism that Colin McGinn maintains is supported by Putnam's twin-earth thought-experiment (mentioned above). McGinn's

---

[15] In this discussion, introspective knowledge is standardly counted apriori, presumably because it is independent of information from the senses. Although this would trivialize the claim that there is apriori knowledge of contingent truth (cf. Kripke 1972/1980: 56–7), the issue is merely terminological: there are simply weaker and stronger ways of characterizing apriority.

version deserves special attention since it is, we believe, the strongest externalist thesis any externalist has claimed to be supported by that thought-experiment. We shall argue that a McKinsey-type recipe cannot be used to show that McGinn's externalist thesis is incompatible with privileged access. Then, we shall argue the same for the version of externalism that Burge claims is supported by his own twin-earth thought-experiment. Then finally we shall take up McKinsey's recipe in the context of originalism and concept externalism. What we shall try to show is that the responses to McKinsey with respect to McGinn's externalist thesis and with respect to Burge's externalism apply mutatis mutandis to concept externalism of the originalist type.

5.9 McGinn's Externalism

McGinn (1989: 30–6, 47–8) maintains the following thesis:

(M) If the concept K is an atomic, natural kind concept, then one possesses it only if one has causally interacted with instances of K.

He takes this to be a conceptual truth, knowable apriori on the basis of Putnam's twin-earth thought-experiment.[16]

Before considering whether this thesis is subject to a McKinsey-type argument, we should note that McGinn explicitly rejects the stronger thesis that if the concept K is a natural kind concept, then one possesses it only if one has causally interacted with instances of K. McGinn maintains that while the concept H_2O is a natural kind concept, it is not necessary to have causally interacted with any instances of H_2O to possess it. Possession of the concept does not even require that there be any H_2O (McGinn 1989: 35). The concept H_2O is not atomic; for an atomic concept lacks conceptual constituents. The concept H_2O is a descriptive concept, and thus molecular. McGinn asks us to imagine a possible world that contains hydrogen and oxygen, yet no H_2O, since hydrogen and oxygen are scarce and widely separated. A scientist in such a world who has the concepts HYDROGEN, OXYGEN, and BONDING could develop the concept H_2O by theorizing (correctly, let us suppose) that hydrogen can bond with oxygen in the combination H_2O.

While McGinn rejects the stronger thesis in question for the reason just noted, he nevertheless embraces the weaker thesis (M). Atomic natural kind concepts, he maintains (1989: 35), cannot lack an extension. McGinn explicitly claims that the concept WATER is an atomic natural kind concept. Thus, he holds that one cannot think that water is a liquid unless one has causally interacted with water.

How might McKinsey's recipe be used to argue that McGinn's version of externalism is incompatible with privileged access? It might be thought that given (M), and the fact that

---

[16] While we shall defend the compatibility of (M) and privileged access, we do not believe that (M) can be supported by Putnam-type twin-earth thought-experiments alone. We deem (M) of interest, however, because it is, as we noted, the *strongest* externalist thesis that any proponent of externalism has maintained *is* supported by Putnam-type twin-earth thought-experiments.

the concept WATER is an atomic, natural kind concept, it follows that one can know apriori that one is thinking that water is a liquid only if one can know apriori that one has causally interacted with water. It is plainly false that one can know apriori that one has causally interacted with water; indeed, it is plainly false that one can know apriori even that there is water. Hence, either privileged access fails or (M) is false.

This line of reasoning is invalid. It is permissible to infer from (M) that one can know apriori that one has causally interacted with water only if it is assumed further that it is apriori knowable that the concept WATER is an atomic, natural kind concept. We think it is an open question whether it can always be known apriori whether a concept is atomic.[17] But, in any case, on McGinn's intended notion of a natural kind concept, we certainly cannot always or even typically know apriori that a concept is a natural kind concept. For on his notion, the concept K is a natural kind concept only if K is a natural kind; and that some K is a natural kind is typically not something that we can know apriori. In particular, while water is a natural kind, we cannot know that apriori. It is epistemically possible that water might have turned out to be like air, or like jade. We could conceivably discover, for example, that there actually is no single sort of substance to which the concept WATER applies. Indeed, it seems epistemically possible that the concept WATER could turn out to be like the concept PHLOGISTON. That is enormously unlikely, of course, but it is epistemically possible. Thus, even if our concept WATER is indeed an atomic, natural kind concept, we cannot know apriori that it is.

Even if, as McGinn holds, (M) is apriori, it is not apriori knowable that this version of externalism is true of the concept WATER. Twin-earth thought experiments involving the concept WATER rely on the empirical assumption that water is a natural kind. Such thought experiments are not intended to *show* that the concept WATER is a natural kind concept. Rather, they *presuppose* that it is. The point of such thought experiments is to establish a general thesis along the general lines of (M). Consequently, even given the apriority of (M), the fact that we can know apriori that we are thinking that water is a liquid does not imply that we can know apriori that we have causally interacted with water or indeed even that water exists.[18]

The central point parallels one that is often made about so-called object-dependent thoughts. Object-dependent thoughts are ones that involve the exercise of a concept that

---

[17] Suppose, for example, that conceptual activity could be neuro-imaged, and there was strong reason to think that there was a general correspondence between what areas light up and what concepts are being exercised. Suppose also that, when using the concept ARTHRITIS, two areas are found to light up, one of which also lights up when the subject uses the concept TENDONITIS and the other of which also lights up when the subject uses the concept ARTHRODIRA. That would be defeasible evidence that the concept ARTHRITIS was nonatomic for the subject, whatever her own views on the matter.

[18] Boghossian (1997) employs a McKinsey-type argument against a version of externalism like (M), except that it invokes a different notion of a natural kind concept from McGinn's: that of a concept that *aims* to denote a natural kind, whether or not the concept succeeds. Boghossian maintains that one can know apriori whether a concept aims to denote a natural kind. We do not dispute that. However, to our knowledge, no externalist maintains (M), where by a "natural kind concept" is meant a concept that aims to denote a natural kind. Moreover, since a concept that aims to denote a natural kind can fail in its aim, there is nothing to recommend the externalist view in question. For further discussion, see McLaughlin and Tye (1998b).

purports singularity of application and is such that there is in fact some actual (contingent) individual to which the concept singularly applies. Such thoughts are individuated in part by external factors, namely by the existence of the individual in question. Thus, suppose that the thought that Cicero is an orator is an object-dependent thought because the concept CICERO is in fact a singular concept of an actual individual, namely Cicero. Then, in any possible world, w, someone can think that Cicero is an orator in w only if Cicero exists in w. Obviously, one cannot know apriori that Cicero exists; it is epistemically possible that Cicero is a fictional character. It does not follow, however, that one cannot know apriori that one is thinking that Cicero is an orator. What the theory of object-dependent thoughts implies is that if Cicero actually exists, then in any possible world, w, one can think that Cicero is an orator in w only if Cicero exists in w. Since one cannot know apriori that Cicero actually exists one cannot know apriori that there is some actual individual, Cicero, such that one's concept is a concept of that individual. If the thought that Cicero is an orator is an object-dependent thought, then that is an aposteriori fact about it. One can know apriori that one is thinking that Cicero is an orator. What one cannot know apriori is that one's thought that Cicero is an orator is an object-dependent thought; for one cannot know apriori that the concept CICERO succeeds in picking out an actual individual. Similarly, while one can know apriori that one is thinking that water is a liquid, one cannot know apriori that one is having a thought involving a natural kind concept; for one cannot know apriori that the concept WATER succeeds in picking out a natural kind. If (M) is true and the concept WATER is indeed an atomic, natural kind concept, then the thought that water is a liquid is a kind-dependent thought. However, that the thought is a kind-dependent thought is an aposteriori fact about it, not an apriori one.

5.10 Burge's Externalism

The strongest version of externalism that is alleged to follow from Burge's own (1979) twin-earth thought-experiment seems to us to be straightforwardly compatible with privileged access. Burge's thought-experiment is intended to show that the following thesis is a conceptual truth:

(B) If one exercises a deferential concept in thinking that p, then if one is a member of a linguistic community, the deferential concept is individuated partly by socio-environmental factors.

The socio-environmental factors will include the relevant linguistic conventions of the community in question.[19] It seems plausible that one can know apriori whether a concept one possesses is a deferential concept. But even if one can, thesis (B) patently does not

---

[19] Since two intrinsic physical twins can be members of different linguistic communities with relevantly different conventions, or one twin can be a member of a linguistic community and the other not, the following thesis is implied by (B): If one exercises a deferential concept in thinking that p, then the fact that one is thinking that p fails to supervene on intrinsic physical facts about one. Burge's externalism is not restricted to natural kind concepts; it covers any deferential concept.

imply the false thesis that one can know apriori that one is a member of a linguistic community (or that other people exist). The fact that one cannot know apriori that one is a member of a linguistic community (or that other people exist) is straightforwardly compatible with (B) and the assumption in question. McKinsey's recipe cannot be used to show that (B) is incompatible with privileged access.[20]

5.11 Originalist Concept Externalism

As noted at the beginning of this chapter, concept externalism is the thesis that it is metaphysically possible for intrinsic duplicates to differ with respect to the concepts they possess. Originalism is the thesis that atomic concepts are identical if and only if they have the same origin. Originalist concept externalism may be stated as follows:

(OCE) If an atomic concept C has an origin O, then it is metaphysically necessary that C has origin O.

Is (OCE) threatened by McKinsey's recipe? Suppose Oscar is thinking a thought that uses the concept HESPERUS. Then Oscar acquired the concept either by introducing it himself or by joining a practice of using the concept. According to the usual story, the concept was introduced long ago by a Babylonian viewing the evening sky. So, assuming Oscar is not himself an ancient Babylonian, he acquired the concept in the latter way. There is no apriori guarantee, however, that the usual story is correct. For all we know apriori, the concept HESPERUS was introduced by the Romans or by the Illyrians. For all we know apriori, the concept was introduced for the morning star. Indeed, for all we know apriori, the concept HESPERUS is empty. The antecedent of (OCE), then, is not itself an apriori truth even if (OCE) is apriori. So, the consequent of (OCE) is not apriori either. So, McKinsey's recipe cannot be used to show that originalist concept externalism is incompatible with privileged access.

---

[20] Jessica Brown (1995) has argued that Burge is, nonetheless, committed to a version of externalism that satisfies McKinsey's recipe. This charge is made as part of an ad hominem argument against Burge, who explicitly endorses a privileged access thesis. For criticisms of her argument, see McLaughlin and Tye (1998c).

6
The Metaphysics of Thought

The standard or orthodox view of thought is that thinking that p consists in bearing an appropriate psychological relation to the proposition that p, where the proposition that p is picked out by the expression "that p". On this view, the proposition that p is what is thought in thinking that p.[1] Belief and other propositional attitudes differ from thought in the psychological relation the subject bears to the proposition.

Some philosophers (Frege 1892) hold that the relevant psychological relations are direct. Others suppose that the relations are mediated by further relations to an appropriate vehicle of content. On one well-known version of the latter proposal (Fodor 1978), believing that p involves having a sentence tokened in the subject's belief box (individuated functionally) that is itself appropriately semantically related to the proposition that p.

Originalists reject the orthodox view. We deny that thinking (believing, etc.) consists in bearing an appropriate psychological relation to a proposition, be it Russellian or Fregean in nature. Indeed, we deny that thinking (believing, etc.) consists in bearing an appropriate psychological relation to *any* sort of content. This is not because we are eliminativists with respect to thought contents. Our position is that the content of a thought is not to be identified with what is thought; relatedly, we hold that the content of the thought that p is not the referent of "that p" within the expression "the thought that p". And what goes for thought goes for other so-called "propositional attitudes".

The orthodox view has been defended by a variety of philosophical arguments. Later in this chapter we will take up these arguments and offer an evaluation of them. First, we present our positive view of the metaphysics of belief and thought.[2]

6.1 The Metaphysics of Belief and Thought: The Positive Account

The key metaphysical components of our approach are as follows. One who thinks that p stands in an appropriate psychological relation to a conceptual structure. The conceptual structure or thought is a vehicle of representation. As such, it has a representational

---

[1] See, e.g., Burge (1980); Bealer (1998); Schiffer (2003).
[2] Gilbert Ryle (1930) has a nice presentation of arguments for what we are calling "the orthodox view".

content. The content of the thought need not be the same as the content that *p*, however. Nor need the thought to which the thinker is psychologically related be the thought that *p*. Even though one who entertains a thought is in a relational state, of which a thought is a relatum, it does not follow that ascriptions of such states are semantically or syntactically relational, referring to the thought *as a relatum*.

Consider the case of driving. Driving is a relational activity. If you drive, you drive some vehicle or other, a pick-up truck, a car, a motorbike. One who drives is in a relational state or condition or undergoes a relational event. Still, the report of one's driving need not be explicitly relational in form. And even when it is, the entity to which one is related in the report need not be the vehicle one is driving, as when it is said that Tom is driving Jane, for example. We will have more to say about belief and thought ascriptions below.

According to originalism, the content of a thought is a (possibly empty) set of possible worlds, namely the set in which the relevant conceptual structure is true. The content of a thought, unlike the thought having that content, is *unstructured*. There are no individuals or properties or relations that are constituents of thought contents. In the realm of thought content, there are no singular propositions.

The content of a thought is not what is thought. What you think in thinking that $2 + 2 = 4$ is not what you think when you think that Goldbach's Conjecture is true, but on the above view of thought contents, the two thoughts share the same content (the set of all possible worlds), if Goldbach's Conjecture is true. Indeed, there really is no such thing as what is thought, if this is taken to be an entity answering to a singular term of the type "What S thinks" in a true identity statement of the following sort:

What S thinks is that *p*.

This is because expressions of the type "that *p*" are not themselves genuine singular terms in propositional attitude contexts and so, correlatively, sentences of the type "What S thinks is that *p*" are not used to make genuine identity assertions.

In taking this view, we do not deny that expressions of the type "What S thinks (fears, desires)" are grammatically singular terms. Rather, they do not function *as* singular terms, at least as they are typically used. In this respect they are like such terms as "the average family" and "the sake of France". They are also like such a term as "what Ponce de León was searching for". Given that Ponce de León was searching for the fountain of youth, it seems perfectly correct to say that what he was searching for is the fountain of youth. But evidently the latter statement is not an identity statement since there is no fountain of youth.

Turning now to the case of beliefs, we hold correspondingly that there is no such thing as what is believed when it is accurately reported that what is believed is that so-and-so is the case. We do not deny that there are beliefs, however, and these are either explicit or implicit. Explicit beliefs are occurrent or episodic. They may last many years or just a few moments. Explicit beliefs are encoded in truth-evaluable conceptual structures that reside in a functionally discrete compartment in the head. Implicit beliefs are dispositional. If you believe that Napoleon never used the telephone, likely your belief is implicit. It is so since it is something you believe explicitly once you consider the matter, but likely not something you believed explicitly before we brought the example to your attention.

In the case of explicit belief, when we say that you believe that so-and-so, our ascription is true so long as you stand in the appropriate relation (call this "the BEL relation") to a conceptual structure tokened in your belief box. The conceptual structure that is your belief bears a certain complex context-sensitive relation (call this "R") to a conceptual structure that is expressed in the ascription. This relation R may fall short of identity in some cases.

Here is an illustration of the above points. Suppose that you meet us and form the opinion that we are both very tall. The belief you form is an explicit one. The conceptual structure expressed by our use of the sentence "We are both very tall" (call it "S") is not the one encoded in your explicit belief box, since it uses our concept WE, as applied to us, and you cannot exercise that specific concept. What is encoded in your belief box is *another conceptual structure*—perhaps that Sainsbury and Tye are both very tall—and it is R-related to S. It is via the fact that you have in your head, in the relevant functional compartment, a conceptual structure that is R-related to S that you believe that we are both very tall.

When we ascribe to you an implicit belief, you need not stand in the BEL relation to a conceptual structure tokened in your explicit belief box.[3] Here it suffices that you be so related once you consider the relevant issue or question. And as before (mutatis mutandis), in believing that so-and-so, you need not have tokened in your belief box the thought that so-and-so even at the time of reflection.

There remains the pressing task of fleshing out the above passing remarks about belief and thought ascriptions into a more detailed positive account. In this connection, more too needs to be said about the nature of the relation R. These matters are taken up in section 4. Next we examine the main arguments for the orthodox view we reject, and explain why we find them lacking.

6.2 Arguments for the Orthodox View

One well-known argument is simply this: consider some true sentence ascribing a belief, for example,

1. Smith believes that polar bears are being harmed by global warming.

From (1), it is permissible to infer

2. There is something Smith believes.

---

[3] Since you can believe that something is the case without standing in the BEL relation to a conceptual structure tokened in your explicit belief box, BEL is not a relation of believing.

If there are no belief contents, then (2) is false. So, (1) must be false. So, generalizing, if there are no belief contents, then no one believes anything, which is absurd.[4]

A second argument appeals to inferences like these:

3. (a) Smith believes that the US financial situation is worsening.
   (b) Jones believes that the US financial situation is worsening.
   (c) Therefore, Smith and Jones believe the same thing.
4. (a) Smith believes that there is life on Venus.
   (b) That there is life on Venus is Fiona's theory.
   (c) Therefore, Smith believes Fiona's theory.
5. (a) Smith believes that there is life on Venus.
   (b) That there is life on Venus is implausible.
   (c) Smith believes something implausible—to wit, that there is life on Venus.

These are valid inferences.[5] According to advocates of the orthodox view, the hypothesis that contents are things that are believed offers the best explanation of their validity. Thus, in the case of (3), it is held that Smith and Jones believe the same thing only if there is a common content that is both what Smith believes and what Jones believes. In the case of (4), the idea is that there is some content—Fiona's theory—and that is what Smith believes. In the case of (5), it is held that there is a content having the property of being implausible, and this entity—that there is life on Venus—is Smith's belief.

A third argument focuses upon different propositional attitudes. For example, what Smith desires can be the same as what Jones believes. Different propositional attitudes sometimes share common objects. From this, it is inferred that there are common objects for the relevant attitudes.

A final argument seeks to reach the conclusion that contents exist via appeal to the fact that the things people believe have semantic properties. For example, consider the following:

6. What Smith believes is true.
7. What Smith believes entails what Jones believes.

The truth of (6) seems to require that there be an object of Smith's belief to have the property of being true. Similarly, the truth of (7) seems to require that there be an object of Smith's belief and a further object of Jones' belief such that the first has the property of entailing the second.

---

[4] In presenting these arguments, we take them to purport to establish that there are belief (thought) contents, understood as things that are what is believed (thought, etc.), rather than more specifically that there are propositions. We do so, since we wish to show that the arguments do not succeed in establishing the broader thesis never mind the narrower one.

[5] (4) and (5) are taken from Schiffer (2003). For a critical discussion of Schiffer's overall position on the objects of belief (and meaning), see Sainsbury (2005a).

6.3 Evaluating the Orthodox Arguments

Let us begin with some preliminary remarks about ontological commitment. As we speak in ordinary life, the use of "there is" is not always ontologically committing.[6] If Jane is friendly, we may legitimately infer that there is something Jane is—namely, friendly—but evidently there is no such object or entity as friendly. Indeed, the sentence

1. There is (exists) such an object as friendly

is not even well-formed. Here is another example that illustrates this point. Consider the sentence

2. Macbeth hallucinated a dagger.

From (2), one can properly infer the following:

3. Macbeth hallucinated something.
4. Macbeth hallucinated some object.

But (2) does not entail

5. There is (exists) some dagger Macbeth hallucinated.

(5) is false. If there really were some *dagger* Macbeth was hallucinating, he would not be hallucinating at all! Indeed, if there really were any *thing* Macbeth was hallucinating, then he would not be hallucinating. The quantifier phrase "some object" or "some dagger" cannot safely be exported in contexts such as (2) and (4).

Even so, from (2) it does seem permissible to infer

6. There is something Macbeth hallucinated (namely, a dagger).

Our explanation is that in (6), "there is something" is not an object quantifier. It functions in the same way as "there is something" in

7. There is something John is (to wit, unhappy).

Here is one further example. Since Ponce de León was searching for the fountain of youth, he was certainly searching for something. Intuitively, if Ponce de León was searching for something then there is (or was) something he was searching for. But it is not the case that there is (or was) a fountain of youth for which he was searching.

These phenomena can be explained as follows. The "thing" in "something" is not ontologically serious.[7] By contrast, expressions like "object" and "entity" are used in philosophical discourse to mark ontological commitment; and words like "dagger" and "fountain of youth" are used by everyone in that way in extensional contexts. That

---

[6] Compare Azzouni (2010: 17): "Uses of 'there are' needn't presuppose existence".

[7] Moltman (1997) calls such quantifiers "special". One of her telling examples is on these lines. From "Ponce de Leon sought all the fountains of youth" we can infer "Ponce de Leon sought something, namely all the fountains of youth". If "something" were an ordinary object quantifier, it would have to be plural, to match the number of "fountains".

explains the contrast between the true (6) and the false (5). Ontologically non-serious quantifier phrases can be applied with wide scope, as in the move from (2) to (6); but wide-scope application of ontologically serious quantifier phrases is not always truth-preserving, as the pair (2) and (5) show.

The points we have been making may be applied to the case of belief and other propositional attitudes. Thus, consider the first argument in section 2 for the existence of belief contents, understood as things that are what is believed. It is certainly true that if Smith believes that polar bears are being harmed by global warming, then Smith believes something. Indeed, there is (as we ordinarily say) something Smith believes, namely that polar bears are being harmed by global warming. It does not *follow* that there exists an entity that is what Smith believes. The first argument, then, is unsuccessful.

Turning to (3) in section 6.2, we grant that if Smith and Jones believe that the US financial situation is worsening, then they believe the same thing. The initial point we wish to make is merely that it does not follow that there exists an entity Smith and Jones believe. Compare: if two people both desire eternal life, they desire the same thing, but there need not exist any such entity as eternal life (however much they desire it). There is something they both desire, but it is not the case that there is such a thing as eternal life which they both desire.[8]

The advocate of the orthodox view may respond that the validity of the argument in (3) is not intended as a *proof* of the orthodox view. Rather the orthodox view offers the best explanation of the argument's validity. But here we beg to differ. On our account, Smith and Jones share a belief, which itself is a conceptual structure. That entity has a content but is not itself a content. This position is not in any way obviously worse than the orthodox view. Which view is ultimately superior depends on which view offers the best account of the various puzzles of thought.

As for the need (in some cases) for a common object for different propositional attitudes, as urged in the third argument, if the argument is taken to be a proof of the orthodox view then again, in our view, there is a kind of scope error. If what Smith desires is what Jones believes, Smith desires something and Jones believes the very same thing. Further, there is something Smith desires and Jones believes, for this applies an ontologically non-serious quantifier phrase. It does not follow, however, that there is some entity that Smith desires and Jones believes, for that would be to apply in widest scope an ontologically serious quantifier phrase. If you fear eternal damnation and we (in our perverse way) desire it, you and we have different attitudes to the same thing, but again it does not follow that there exists any such state as eternal damnation. The application of

---

[8] Geach (1976: 312) gives a nice example of an invalid argument, which should discourage simple-minded views about the validity of the kinds of inference under discussion: That N.N. assassinated King Charles XII of Sweden was a national disaster; Andersen's thesis is that N.N. assassinated King Charles XII of Sweden. Ergo: Andersen's thesis was a national disaster.

an ontologically non-serious quantifier phrase is acceptable (there is something we fear and you desire); but there is no eternal damnation having the property that you fear it and we desire it.

If the advocate of the orthodox view responds by saying, as before, that the orthodox view offers the best explanation of the argument's validity, we demur. We accept that there really is an entity that is common to both Smith and Jones, namely a certain conceptual structure, a thought. Almost all theorists allow that there are such entities as vehicles of representation, and that's what thoughts are.

Turning now to (4) in section 6.2, essentially the same points can be made once more. That there is life on Venus is Fiona's theory. What Harold believes is Fiona's theory, but it does not follow that there exists a common object for their attitudes. What follows is simply that they bear attitudes to the same thing, where "thing" functions in an ontologically non-serious way. There is something in common to Fiona and Harold's attitudes. But this object is not a content.

In reply to the final argument in section 6.2, we can speak of the semantic properties of what people believe, even though believing is not a relation to a content. What makes it the case that what you believe is true is the fact that your belief is true, where your belief is the vehicle of representation (conceptual structure/thought) to which you are related in having the belief. Similarly, what makes it the case that what Smith believes entails what Jones believes is simply the fact that Smith's belief entails Jones' belief: it is not possible for Smith's belief to be true and Jones' belief to be false.

These points also undercut the appeal to (5) in section 6.2. If Smith believes that there is life on Venus, Smith does indeed believe something implausible (let us grant). Insofar as there is a bearer of the property of being implausible, it is simply Smith's belief (a structure of concepts). That there is life on Venus is implausible (let us agree), but what makes this so is just the fact that the belief that there is life on Venus is an implausible belief.[9]

6.4 Attitude Ascriptions

The view we reject—that ascriptions of belief and other mental states involve relations between subjects and contents—has the virtue of promising to provide a straightforward account of how these ascriptions work semantically. The rejected view involves three elements: (i) the complementing "that" clause is a singular term standing for a content; (ii) the propositional verb, for example, "believes," expresses an ordinary two-place relation; and (iii) its first place is filled by an ordinary noun phrase. This view would parse an ascription like

---

[9] Might there not be implausible things no one has ever believed? Yes; but this is just the analog for beliefs of sentences for language. There are many implausible sentences that have no actual tokenings. Correspondingly, there are many implausible thoughts that have no actual tokens.

1. Galileo believed that the earth moves.

as having the overall logical form "Rab", more fully:

2. Believed (Galileo, that the earth moves).

Since we deny that that-clauses are singular terms, we must repudiate this approach to explaining how ascriptions of beliefs function. What can we offer in its place?

Our positive account of ascription of propositional attitudes draws on some insights we attribute to Davidson's paratactic analysis (1968). Davidson claimed that the logical form of

3. Galileo said that the earth moves.

is

4. Galileo said that. The earth moves.

"That" is to be understood as a demonstrative pronoun, referring forward to the immediately following utterance (that is, to the attributor's utterance of "The earth moves"). The analysis of the logical form is:

5. My next utterance makes me and Galileo samesayers. The earth moves.

The second utterance is typically not asserted, even if the first is. In the analysis, the relation of samesaying is made explicit, and Davidson insists that it is not identity (Galileo spoke in Italian, but the attribution is in English). He also claims that it is not even an equivalence relation, for reasons flowing from the indeterminacy of translation. There could be three utterances, x, y, and z, such that y and z stand in the samesaying relation to x but not to each other.

We remain neutral on, or even reject, some aspects of Davidson's proposal. As applied to propositional attitudes generally, we do not think that reference to an utterance is involved in every ascription of an attitude; an attitude can be ascribed in silent thought, with no utterance.[10] However, we extract the following insights:

(a) When an attitude is ascribed, the attributor, in the complement part of his attribution, puts a thought on display, which is typically not asserted. (If the attribution is simply being thought, rather than uttered, the display is for the benefit of the attributor herself.)
(b) The displayed thought expresses a thought of the attributor, and may draw for its expression on features of the attributor's context (e.g. its time) that are not shared with the subject of whom the attribution is made.

---

[10] We also think that the methodology of logical form, which is crucial to Davidson's approach, requires development in directions very different from Davidson's.

(c) The correctness of the attribution is determined by whether the subject of the attribution is appropriately related to a thought which is in turn appropriately related to the thought that is put on display.
(d) This relation between the thought of the subject of attribution and the thought displayed by the attributor, which we earlier referred to as the R-relation, is not an equivalence relation. Davidson's samesaying is an example of an R-relation.
(e) The R-relation is sensitive to contextual factors.
(f) The R-relation may differ for different verbs of attitude. Thus the R-relation may be more constrained if the verb of ascription is "he said precisely, and in so many words, that..." than if it is merely "he said that...".

Our originalist theory of concepts does not entail these views, but they fit with it in a very natural way. A key source of academic debate concerns the difficulty of giving any general and illuminating conditions under which attitude ascriptions are true. We do not wish to downplay this difficulty, but we claim that our theory provides a helpful way of framing the problems, and an explanation of why they arise.

On our view, Davidson's example, "Galileo said that the earth moves", would be understood as follows. The thought put on display is that the earth moves. The attribution is true iff Galileo expressed in words[11] a thought R-related to that thought. In the case of "Galileo believed that the earth moves", the account is the same except that instead of Galileo expressing in words a thought, the requirement is that Galileo stand in the belief relation to a thought.

Our focus in what follows will be on giving a feel for the different demands that may be placed on the R-relation in different contexts. We can organize the discussion by asking: what are necessary and sufficient conditions on the R-relation for the truth of the ascription? A natural idea is that identity is sufficient: if the subject of the attribution is appropriately related to the very thought displayed in the attribution, surely the attribution is true? This idea is encouraged by the following example:

6. We all (authors and readers of this book) believe that the earth moves.

The thought put on display is that the earth moves, where "moves" is timeless, rather than a genuine present tense. The concepts involved in the displayed thought are shared among most English-speakers (and possibly speakers of other languages as well). In this case, what makes (6) true is that the very thought displayed is present in, and plays a suitable causal role in, the heads of all of us, authors and readers alike. In this case, R can be identity. This serves as a paradigm of an ideal case, in which attribution is made true by the literal sharing of thoughts (i.e. thought-types).[12]

---

[11] If the speech act of saying were the focus of one's interest, one might wish to provide a more nuanced description of this act.

[12] On our version of originalism, there are some qualifications to the claim that if the subject of the attribution stands in the appropriate relation to the very thought displayed in the attribution, the attribution is true. This is because we allow that a concept's content can shift over time. A 15th-century person, Harold, might be belief-

Here's a simple example in which R is not identity. On Wednesday you believe something you would express by the words "It's sunny". The present tense concept in your thought selects some part of Wednesday. If we wish to say on Thursday what it was you believed, an unimpugnably correct attribution is:

7. You believed that it was sunny.

The thought we put on display is one involving a past tense. But your thought, the one that makes our attribution true, does not involve a past tense but only a present tense. The tense concepts differ not only in that one is present and one is past. The present tense concept is more specific, taking one to part of a specific day. The past tense concept is less specific, taking one simply to some time or other preceding the time of the attribution. In this example, the shift in temporal perspective means that it would be impossible correctly to attribute a belief by displaying a thought to which the subject of the attribution was belief-related. R cannot be identity.

Closer reflection on attributions like (7) suggests that the "was" does not represent a self-standing past tense, but rather introduces a time set by the tense of "believed." What (7) requires for its truth is that at some past time, t, you believed at t that it was sunny at t. The time at which the attributed believing occurred needs to be the same as the time involved in the thought believed. The fact remains that the thought displayed in (7) is not a thought that, by being present to your mind on Wednesday, makes (7) true, for the thought present to your mind did not have a constituent corresponding to "at t". Even if the "is" in "is sunny" takes one to the very same time, it does so by a tense concept, not by the kind of concept that can introduce reference to an arbitrary time (t). The situation can be made clearer by considering a modification of (7) in which it begins with "On Wednesday". Then what is required for its truth is that on Wednesday you believed that it was sunny then (i.e., on Wednesday). Once again, that way of referring to a day, by the concept THEN or WEDNESDAY, need not feature in a thought you had on Wednesday that would be enough to make the modified (7) true.

Indexicals, like tenses, call for perspectival adjustment in attitude attribution. Attributors can but occupy the perspective from which they speak and think, but this may not be the perspective of the subjects whose thoughts they are trying to report. Consider an example mentioned earlier

8. Our colleagues believe that we are tall.

---

related to the thought that spinach is meat, and we might display this thought in the 21st-century attribution "Harold believed that spinach is meat". The attribution is certainly misleading, and it's doubtful whether it is true. It's misleading, because it suggests that Harold's thought had the same content as ours, in which case he believed something obviously false, whereas what he believed, at the time he believed it, was true. Hence the best candidate for a sufficient condition is identity of thought and sameness of content. We'll see that there are many cases in which R can be significantly weaker even in true attributions: R need not require identity of thought together with sameness of content. Indeed, we'll see that an attribution can be true even when the thought displayed in the attribution is different from, and different in content from, any thought to which the believer is belief-related.

This attribution is true (where "our" and "we" refer to the authors of this book). What thoughts in the heads of our colleagues, and to which they are related by the belief relation, will make this true? Confident as we are of the truth of (8), we do not have any definitive answer to this question. Perhaps one colleague is belief-related to the thought that Sainsbury and Tye are tall, another to the thought that Tye and Sainsbury are tall, another to the thought that Michael and Mark are tall, another to the thought that the authors of *Seven Puzzles* are tall. All these colleagues contribute to what makes (8) true. Each of their thoughts is R-related to, but distinct from, the one put on display in (8). No R-related thought in the head of a colleague can use the concept WE as we do, so every R-related thought that helps make (8) true is distinct from the one displayed in (8).

In some contexts it may be correct to say that what a certain colleague believes is that the authors of *Seven Puzzles* are tall, even though they do not believe that Sainsbury and Tye are tall. For example, the former would be a correct report of something believed by one who sincerely says: "I've no idea who the authors of *Seven Puzzles* are, but I gather they are tall." It would not be correct to report such a person as believing that Sainsbury and Tye are tall. This is a context in which thoughts R-related to the thought displayed in (8) are not R-related to each other.[13]

In this departure from identity by the R-relation, the thought displayed and the thought in the truth-maker are sub-isomorphic but not isomorphic. Since isomorphism is obviously not sufficient in reporting Hesperus/Phosphorus beliefs, we can conclude that it's neither necessary nor sufficient for the R-relation. Might sub-isomorphism be necessary or sufficient? It can't be sufficient, if the stronger relation of isomorphism is not in general sufficient; but it might be necessary.

One counterexample to this suggestion is already on the table: tense. Sub-isomorphism would require the thought displayed and the thought in the truth-maker to refer to the same time, even if they did so using concepts with different structures. But whereas a present tense does refer to a specific time, the simple past tense does not. Hence the thought put on display in the claim that Sally believed it was sunny is not even sub-isomorphic to the thought to which Sally is belief-related and which makes the claim true.

Might sameness of content be necessary? Here's an example which suggests a negative answer. Suppose you set out to climb K1 but thanks to a navigational error end up, unknowingly, climbing K2. You look up and see that the summit is not too far away. We can correctly report you as believing that you'll make it to the summit of K2, even though you would not accept that account of what you believe, and even though you have not exercised the concept K2. You think you believe that you'll make it to the summit of K1. What matters is finding a belief that will explain your behavior. What we ascribe may well be isomorphic to *a* thought to which you are belief-related, for

---

[13] So, the R-relation is not transitive. Left open is the possibility that for every context, the R-relation is an equivalence relation in that context. We have doubts about this, but will not pursue these here.

example the thought you might express with the words "I'll make it to the summit of *that*". But there is nothing clearly incorrect about reporting your sincere utterance of "I'll make it to the top of K1" as an expression of your belief that you'll make it to the top of K2. In this case the ascription does not even match the referential truth conditions of the utterance, literally understood. One might dismiss this as a case of "loose talk": the report is strictly false, even though acceptable for most purposes. Or one might say that this is implicitly de re (see next section). Or one might allow that it is a strictly correct or true report, for laxer standards obtain in the context. We do not have a strong preference. The main point of the example is to show how the originalist theory makes very plain precisely what the choice involves.

Originalism helps us understand the competing pressures we are under when ascribing propositional attitudes. Ideally, in attributing an attitude, we would like to be able to put on display the very thought that features in the truth-maker for our attribution. Sometimes, perspectival shifts make this impossible. Often, ignorance or considerations of relevance make it appropriate to be less specific than any truth-making thought (more examples of this later). As we'll see shortly, we sometimes have less interest in the nature of the truth-making thoughts than in what these are about, which gives wide license to depart from the concepts occurring in the truth-making thought.

6.5 De Re, De Se, De Dicto

So far we have considered only what are called "de dicto" attributions of attitudes—attributions with a complete thought in the complement. We now turn to "de re" thoughts and de re attributions of thoughts.

On one conception of a de re thought, it concerns an object which is not conceptualized in the thought.[14] We could think of it as a hybrid structure, containing both at least one object and at least one concept. We have already allowed that an object can come before the mind without being subsumed under a concept, and that this can happen in attention. It seems natural to allow that there are, or could be, such hybrid structures. Suppose someone attends to a flower without bringing it under a concept. If the object is before her mind, it seems she could apply the concept PRETTY to it, thereby coming to be in a hybrid state involving the flower and the concept PRETTY. Although this state of mind can be evaluated for truth, we prefer not to count such hybrid structures as thoughts.

More commonly, a thought is counted de re if it involves at least one de re concept. Opinions differ as to how to characterize this special category of concepts. Here are some

---

[14] One might think Tyler Burge held that there were de re thoughts of this kind: "An attitude is de re if it has a content that is not completely conceptualized" (Burge 2007: 68). However, we think "completely" is playing an important role in this sentence: Burge thinks of demonstrative and indexical concepts as incomplete conceptualizations.

examples: demonstrative and indexical concepts, rigid concepts (i.e. ones with the same referent at every world), concepts whose application requires acquaintance with the referent, concepts whose application requires some causal contact or other with the referent, object-involving concepts. The classification may be absolute or, more likely, will be context-relative, classifying a use of a concept on an occasion as de re.

Originalists can accept that some distinction of this kind is well-grounded. A familiar example contrasts the thought that the murderer—whoever it may be—has large feet, with the thought that that man (pointing to a man in sight) has large feet, the latter being de re and the former not. The thoughts certainly feel different in kind: the first can be properly used while "not knowing who the murderer is", while the second cannot properly be used without "knowing who that man is". However, we do not propose to elaborate a precise way of marking the distinction. We simply allow that there are thoughts that are de re thanks to involving concepts that are de re, or that are used in the de re style within the thought in question.

De re ascriptions of thoughts typically imply that the thinker used a de re concept.[15] Setting aside hybrid cases, Sally thinks of Hesperus that it is visible iff for some de re concept C, whose referent is Hesperus, Sally thinks a thought whose first element is C and whose second element is R-related to the concept IS VISIBLE. As before, the R-relation will sometimes but not always be identity.

Attitude attributions may sometimes be implicitly de re, even though the surface form is de dicto. Consider our attribution of attitudes to non-humans, for example:

1. Fido believes we've buried his favorite bone near the sycamore tree.

Some will deny that non-humans have any concepts, in which case they must say, implausibly, that all such attitude ascriptions are false. Even those most anxious to rebut this suggestion may find it hard to swallow the opinion that Fido uses the concept SYCAMORE. One way forward is to hold that the attribution is really intended to be de re with respect to some or all of the concepts in the thought displayed. A modest proposal is that the attribution should be understood along the lines:

2. Concerning the sycamore tree, Fido believes that we have buried his favorite bone near it.

A more drastic application of this idea is consistent with agnosticism about which concepts non-humans use:

3. Concerning us$_1$, burying$_2$, his favorite bone$_3$, and the sycamore tree$_4$, Fido believes that we$_1$ have done it$_2$ to it$_3$ near it$_4$.

The subscripts indicate the heads of the anaphoric pronouns. The rigmarole also reveals why this would be a silly mode of attribution to adopt explicitly. One option is to say that

---

[15] Hybrid de re states may not involve any de re concept, but they could make true a de re ascription (e.g. he believes, of that flower, that it is pretty). We set this possibility aside in the discussion.

the original attribution, (1), is strictly false, and to the extent that we judge it to be true we are imagining it replaced by some more de re attribution, something more like (2) or (3). Another option is to say that the original attribution is strictly true, and is made true by the facts mentioned in the fully de re attribution (3). This second alternative gives a great deal of freedom to the R-relation. Either option could be applied to give an account of why it seemed right to say, of the mistaken climber, that he believed he would make it to the top of K2.

Thoughts de se are thoughts about oneself *as* oneself. To recall a famous example from John Perry:

> An amnesiac, Rudolf Lingens, is lost in the Stanford library. He reads a number of things in the library, including a biography of himself, and a detailed account of the library in which he is lost. He believes any Fregean thought you think might help him. He still won't know who he is, and where he is, no matter how much knowledge he piles up, until that moment when he is ready to say, *This* place is aisle five, floor six, of Main Library, Stanford. *I* am Rudolf Lingens. (Perry 1977: 492)

On the basis of his reading, Lingens knew things about himself, but did not know these things about himself *as* himself.

Both Millian and Fregean theories have difficulties with such examples. Millians start from the position that coreferential simple singular terms, in this case "I" and "Lingens", are semantically the same, and they have difficulty conjuring up further resources on the basis of which to explain Lingens' ignorance. Fregeans have difficulty explaining what the sense of "I" is. Originalists, by contrast, need only insist that Lingens' concept I is distinct from, because different in origin from, the concept LINGENS. This explains why the thought that Lingens is in the library is different from the thought he would express as: I am in the library.

What remains unexplained is the special relation that I-thoughts have to action (and the same for NOW thoughts). We defer this discussion to Chapter 7.

7
The Puzzles Solved

7.1 The Puzzle of Hesperus and Phosphorus

If the usual story is correct, the concepts Hesperus and Phosphorus were introduced on different occasions, and so are distinct.[1] Since the concepts are atomic and have the same referent, they have the same content. The difference in the concepts is enough to explain the data that motivate Fregeans. We'll apply the view using the standard kinds of comparisons between thoughts.

1. (a) Hesperus is visible.
   (b) Phosphorus is visible.
2. (a) Hesperus is Hesperus.
   (b) Hesperus is Phosphorus.

The thoughts in both pairs are, intuitively, different.[2] The intuition can be backed by the way in which their embedding can produce different truth values. Someone could think that Hesperus is visible without thinking that Phosphorus is visible, or it could be obvious that Hesperus is Hesperus without it being obvious that Hesperus is Phosphorus. Taking such data at face value requires finding two of something. The fact that we have two concepts, a fact fixed independently of the comparative phenomena in (1) and (2), provides sufficient explanation. Two concepts generate two thoughts, and different thoughts may have different properties. Nothing more is required to explain the differences in (1) and (2).

There is no need to appeal to any difference in truth conditions between the members of the pairs: both paired thoughts are true at just the same worlds, and, for each pair, the set of associated worlds is determined in a similar way from similar assignments of content to the constituent atomic concepts. But, as the previous paragraph illustrated, thoughts similar in these ways can differ in others.

One contrast between originalism and its main rivals lies in how each view treats the significance of the difference between evening sightings and morning sightings. For originalism, the difference ensures that the concept Hesperus was introduced on a different

---

[1] For discussion of the epistemic possibility that we are mistaken about how many concepts are present in a given case, see section 7.3 below.
[2] The pair in (1) are super-isomorphs. The pair in (2) are isomorphs, but not super-isomorphs.

occasion from, and so is distinct from, the concept PHOSPHORUS. For Fregeans, the difference generates different descriptions which competent users supposedly associate apriori with the concepts. Originalists, by contrast, believe that a competent user may fail to associate the relevant description with the concept. Indeed, in the standard example, competent users had better not associate the concept HESPERUS with being the evening star, since Hesperus is a planet (and so not a star, as this notion is normally used).

Intuitively, it was an astronomical discovery that Hesperus is Phosphorus. Yet on the present account the "discovery" has the same truth conditions as that Hesperus is Hesperus, which was not a discovery. In some sense, no new "fact" was added to knowledge when the fact that Hesperus is Phosphorus was added. This raises interesting issues about knowledge of identities.[3]

Let's say that people make a *cognitive* discovery that p, just if they come to know that p, having not previously known that p. It is a cognitive discovery that Hesperus is Phosphorus. The pre-Babylonians may have entertained the thought that Hesperus was Phosphorus, but they did not believe it, or, if they believed it, they did not have sufficient evidence for it to count as knowledge. When it became known that Hesperus is Phosphorus, a new thought came to be knowledge.

One might think in a different way of what it is to make a discovery. The starting point for the acquisition of knowledge is a state of information that excludes no possibilities at all: it's a state that rules out no possible worlds from being actual. When new information is acquired, the set of worlds consistent with our information shrinks. Let's say that a *possibility-eliminating* discovery is the addition of a piece of knowledge that shrinks the set of worlds that are consistent with what we know. It is not a possibility-eliminating discovery that Hesperus is Phosphorus, for that is true at just the worlds at which Hesperus is Hesperus, that is, at all worlds. Yet, as we said earlier, this is a cognitive discovery. We should not denigrate cognitive discoveries that are not possibility-eliminating discoveries, for all mathematical discoveries are in this category.

It is no objection to originalism that coming to know that Hesperus is Phosphorus is not a possibility-eliminating discovery. This is simply how things are, on any reasonable view, for all "pure identity thoughts"—thoughts in which distinct atomic nominative concepts are combined by the concept IDENTITY. Suppose a community possesses just one of the two nominative concepts in such a thought. Intuitively, that is no barrier to their being omniscient about the referent of the concept. But if they can know everything about this object, those with the additional concept can know no more. So we should expect that there will be an understanding of "discovery" on which adding a pure identity thought to the stock of knowledge is not a discovery: it's not a possibility-eliminating discovery, even if it is a cognitive discovery.

---

[3] These issues are addressed by Ruth Millikan (1997, 2000).

One can never make a possibility-eliminating discovery of a necessary truth. Suppose it's necessary that water is H_2O. Adding this to a stock of knowledge cannot shrink the set of worlds consistent with what is known. Hence research into the composition of water does not issue in a possibility-eliminating discovery. This shows that possibility-eliminating discoveries are not the only discoveries of value; we can certainly value mathematical discoveries though these are cognitive discoveries that are not possibility-eliminating.

If a community has two atomic nominative concepts with the same referent, ignorance of identity can generate ignorance whose rectification requires a possibility-eliminating discovery. For example, someone ignorant of the identity might believe that Hesperus was the only visible star right now, and infer that Phosphorus was not visible. This would be straightforwardly false. So acquiring knowledge of a pure identity thought, even though it is not in itself a possibility-eliminating discovery, is likely to lead to possibility-eliminating discoveries. This is what makes the discovery that water is H_2O empirically significant in a way that mathematical discoveries are not.

Some identity thoughts count as possibility-eliminating discoveries. These are contingent identities, like the thought that Sally Smith is the murderer of Jones.[4] These are impure identity thoughts, ones involving a nonatomic concept. That's part of the explanation of how its discovery can be a possibility-eliminating discovery as well as a cognitive discovery. We can use the test from a couple of paragraphs back: you couldn't know everything about the referent of the concept SALLY SMITH without knowing that she was the murderer of Jones. That's because the nonatomic nominative concept THE MURDERER OF JONES carries information, in a way that an atomic nominative concept does not.

Is the situation symmetrical? Could one know everything about the murderer of Jones without knowing she was Sally Smith? A community that did not possess the concept SALLY SMITH does not thereby count as ignorant of something substantive about the referent of this concept: there need be no possibility-eliminating discovery to be made. A community that did possess the concept, but which was ignorant of the identity, is liable to substantive error, believing for example that Sally Smith was somewhere the murderer was not. Even if learning that the murderer is Sally Smith is not a possibility-eliminating discovery, but only a cognitive one, it is likely to bring possibility-eliminating discoveries in its train.

On the basis of the examples, a simple principle emerges: pure identity thoughts never amount to possibility-eliminating discoveries, though they may be cognitive discoveries. Impure contingent identity thoughts can constitute discoveries of both kinds, when what is discovered is essentially expressed by the application of a nonatomic concept.

---

[4] Russellians would disagree that this thought is an identity thought (as opposed to an existential generalization). The present point could be fashioned to fit this framework. It is assumed that the concept SALLY SMITH is atomic.

Empirical non-possibility-eliminating discoveries may generate possibility-eliminating discoveries.

7.2 The Puzzle of the Twins

Tim and Tom have different concepts, respectively WATER and TWATER. The concepts have different origins, WATER having been introduced in Tim's community, and TWATER having been introduced in Tom's entirely distinct community. The different acts of introduction guarantee difference of concept.

The different concepts refer to different things, respectively water and twater. That is to say, these are concepts with different contents. On this puzzle, originalism and Millian views coincide. The only opponents on our radar would be a particular kind of descriptive Fregean or two-dimensionalist, theorists who think that the concepts WATER and TWATER have the same content, along the lines: the liquid that falls from the skies as rain, collects as puddles on pavements, makes up most of the lakes and oceans.... These theorists have to deny that it's metaphysically necessary that water is H_2O. They have to think that water is twater. Not many theorists fall into this category.

Not all descriptivists are forced into this uncomfortable position. They may, like Jackson (1998b), include an indexical element in the proposed description: the stuff that falls as rain and so on, *around here*. Since "here" will pick out different places on earth and twin-earth, this view is consistent with the claim (indeed, on minimal assumptions, entails the claim) that water is distinct from twater. But the view is prey to standard problems. For example, it seems that someone could grasp the concept WATER while not believing that it falls as rain. If that were to happen, it would be hard to know what to make of the alleged apriori connection between the concept WATER and falling as rain around here. (For more, see the discussion of the pink granular stuff that seems like water in Chapter 2.4.)

7.3 The Puzzle of the Cat and le Chat

Suppose the concepts CAT and CHAT originated independently, and so are distinct.[5] This might well not be historically correct, but we think there are plenty of historically correct examples of different concepts with the same content, like the concepts HESPERUS and PHOSPHORUS. One approach is to find pairs of communities that have always been isolated,

---

[5] Those who react against the proposal that the concept CHAT is distinct from the concept CAT might reflect on the fact that singular non-generic uses of CHAT differ in extension from corresponding uses of CAT, since they apply only to males. "Cela n'est pas un chat, c'est une chatte", can express a literally true thought. This is not a knock-down argument for the distinctness of the concepts. Taking into account gender, case and number (and, for verbs, tense and aspect) would call for a notion of a core concept, variable in such respects. The verbal concept BOTTLE and the nominative concept BOTTLE might be seen as sharing a common core. The substantive question would be whether the core concept CHAT is or is not identical to the core concept CAT.

and which have introduced concepts for common objects, like fire, wood, food, on separate occasions. However, since the CAT/CHAT case has been widely discussed, we will continue to use it as our example.

The concepts have the same content, since they refer to the same property, the property of being a cat. This is what makes Paul's situation puzzling. Under his nanny's influence, he is disposed to assent to "Chats have tails", so we may suppose him to believe that cats have tails. When his parents introduce him to the word "cat", he treats the sentence "Cats have tails" as expressing a new belief. Yet the belief would seem to be the old one, that cats have tails. The options are to say that it really is a new belief, and so Paul did not, under his nanny's influence, form the belief that cats have tails; or that it is not a new belief, though Paul fails to recognize it as familiar.

Given what was said in Chapter 6, section 6.4 about the ascription of beliefs, we have to accept that for Paul, under his nanny's influence, the ascription "Paul believes that cats have tails" is correct. Thus understood, Paul already believes that cats have tails when he meets his parents. Taken this way, we have a ready explanation of why he takes himself to have learnt something new in his parents' company: he forms a new concept, and becomes belief-related to a new thought. When we said he already believed that cats have tails, we were relying on the flexibility in the correctness conditions for ascribing beliefs: we need not express the very thought that is in the belief box of the subject whose beliefs we report; and we did not do so when we said that Paul, under his nanny's influence, believed that cats have tails. In the report, we expressed a super-isomorph of what he came to believe under parental influence, and that was good enough for the truth of the report.

After meeting his parents, Paul makes a cognitive discovery, though not a possibility-eliminating one (see section 7.1 for the distinction). He can rightly think to himself: Now I know something I didn't know before. What I knew before was that chats have tails, whereas I now know, additionally, that cats have tails. It's like someone who says to themselves: What I knew before was that Phosphorus is visible, whereas now I know, additionally, that Hesperus is visible. A new thought comes to be known.

In summary, Paul does form a new belief, since a new thought enters his belief box when he acquires the concept CAT and comes to believe that cats have tails. He therefore makes a cognitive discovery. However, our ordinary practice of ascribing beliefs does not normally require correct ascriptions to mark this difference.

Now suppose that the concept CAT is the same concept as the concept CHAT. Then there is nothing new for Paul to learn. Not only is the thought that cats have tails a super-isomorph of the thought that chats have tails, these are the very same thought. To the extent that Paul has a sense of discovery, it is not explicable in terms of his thoughts; it is not even a cognitive discovery.

For this version of the puzzle, the explanation must be linguistic. In using the word "cat", Paul, before his "discovery," wrongly takes himself to exercise a different concept from the concept he exercises in using the word "chat". The possibility of this kind of mistake should not come as a surprise: we argued at length in Chapter 5 against a thesis to the effect that we can always know how many concepts we are exercising.

Other cases show that an assertion that is about neither language nor concepts (in this case, the assertion that cats have tails) can generate only wholly linguistic knowledge. Stalnaker has a nice example:

> Consider [the] case of the Russian pasta chef with an imperfect grasp of English who is taking a class on cooking pasta. He knows perfectly well how long to cook each kind of pasta, but not what they are called in English. When he is told "cook vermicelli for four minutes, and linguini for six", he already knew the subject matter content of the claim, but learns some facts about English terminology, which are part of the reflexive content of the statement: that "vermicelli" and "linguini", respectively, refer to vermicelli and linguini. (Stalnaker 2008: 41)

Similarly, on this version of the puzzle, when Paul hears the assertion "cats have tails" he gains only the metalinguistic knowledge that "cats" refers to just what "chats" refers to.

The puzzle of Pierre, who believes that Londres is pretty but that London is ugly raises a new issue. As Kripke presents the case, there is a puzzle only on the assumption of Pierre's rationality, which should supposedly preserve him from having inconsistent beliefs. We deny that rationality can be guaranteed to have this preservative effect, and we argue for this in detail in section 7.4 below.

Chapter 4 explained how originalism deals with straightforward Mates cases. The different truth values of

> Nobody doubts that whoever believes that all Greeks are Greeks believes that all Greeks are Greeks
> Nobody doubts that whoever believes that all Greeks are Greeks believes that all Greeks are Hellenes

result from the fact that the concept GREEK is distinct from the concept HELLENE. This means that there are two thoughts, the thought that Greeks are Greeks, and the thought that Greeks are Hellenes, and these thoughts may well have different enough properties to make the displayed thoughts differ in truth value.

As stressed in Chapter 4, it is not apriori that the concepts are different. We applied our rather scanty and uncertain historical views. Hence we must confront the possibility that we are mistaken. Suppose that, contrary to what we in fact believe, there is just one concept, though two words, "Greeks" and "Hellenes", are used to express it. Does not a puzzle remain?

Suppose Pablo wrongly assumes there are two concepts. He may well sincerely assent to the first, but not the second of these sentences:

1. All Greeks are Greeks.
2. All Greeks are Hellenes.

Even if it is known that there is only one concept, it may seem that the following reports are correct:

3. Pablo believes that all Greeks are Greeks.
4. Pablo does not believe that all Greeks are Hellenes.

Assuming there is only one concept, (3) and (4) both affirm and deny that Pablo has a certain belief, the belief whose conceptual structure is that all Xs are Xs, and so they are contradictory. Moreover, since it's part of the assumption that we know there is only one concept, under normal circumstances we should be able to know that we contradict ourselves.

No one will wish to challenge (3), but (4) is dubious for more than one reason. First, there seems nothing intuitively implausible about simply denying it: Pablo does believe that all Greeks are Hellenes, even if he does not recognize this verbal way of expressing something he believes. Secondly, even if sincere assent to an understood sentence, s, which says that p, guarantees that the subject believes that p, sincere dissent works differently. Sincerity is a matter of believing what one says, so the immediate evidence it generates is for belief, not for lack of belief. All that sincere dissent ensures is that the subject believes she does not believe that p. Though such beliefs concerning what one does not believe are normally correct, they are not always. People can sincerely believe they lack a belief they in fact have,[6] and conceptual confusion can be a source of this kind of mistake. Pablo is conceptually confused, and this confusion may lead him to dissent from a sentence which expresses something he believes.

This example does not generate a Mates case. But perhaps one is lurking nearby, for even though anyone who knows the conceptual identity should deny (4), perhaps Pablo should accept it. The response just offered involved the suggestion that Pablo might sincerely believe he lacked a belief he has. Thus:

5. Pablo believes that he does not believe that all Greeks are Hellenes.

It seems consistent to move from (5) to the following:

6. Pablo does not believe that he believes that all Greeks are Hellenes.

It's hardly controversial that Pablo believes (3), that is:

7. Pablo believes that he believes that all Greeks are Greeks.

If (6) and (7) are both intuitively plausible, they constitute a new Mates case. They seem both to be verified by Pablo's belief states, yet they contradict each other. In this case, the pattern of explanation used for straightforward Mates cases would appear to be unavailable: there are no conceptual differences.

In fact, (6) should be denied, even though both (5) and (7) are true. The mistake is similar to the one that made (4) initially seem appealing. In normal cases, one can infer

---

[6] Some racists believe they do not have racist beliefs. See also the discussion of the puzzle of Paderewski in section 7.4 below.

from "She believes that not-*p*" to "She does not believe that *p*". But the cases under discussion are special: Pablo is conceptually confused, and confusion of this kind blocks the inference in which negation is exported from the content believed to the believing. The strengthened Paderewski puzzle (section 7.4 below) is a specially clear case in which the inference fails.

Pablo does indeed believe that he does not believe that all Greeks are Hellenes. In this, he is mistaken, as we have seen. That is, (5) is true, but reports a false belief. It's a belief in the absence of a belief that is in fact present. He may also believe (6); but in this, too, he is mistaken. As before, it's a belief in the absence of a belief that is in fact present.

Hence the supposition, which we take to be counterfactual, that the concept GREEKS is the concept HELLENES does not generate any new Mates cases.

7.4 The Puzzle of Paderewski

Peter hears Paderewski play the piano at a concert, and forms the belief that Paderewski has musical talent. Later he hears Paderewski address the crowd at a political rally. Peter believes that being a politician is inconsistent with having musical talent. Since the Paderewski at the rally is plainly a politician, Peter infers he is a different Paderewski from the pianist, and that he lacks musical talent.

Kripke (1979) invites us to think of the puzzle as our inability to answer a certain question. Everyone agrees, on the basis of the first encounter, that Peter believes that Paderewski has musical talent. One supposedly unanswerable question is whether one should also conclude, on the basis of the second encounter, that Peter believes that Paderewski lacks musical talent. If he does, then he has contradictory beliefs, which appears inconsistent with his being a rational person. But if he does not, his behavior seems hard to explain, for example his apparently sincere assertion: "Paderewski lacks musical talent". That constitutes what we call the "standard" Paderewski puzzle.

There is also a "strengthened" puzzle. There is some inclination to say that, at the rally, Peter does not believe that Paderewski has musical talent. But this produces a contradiction in *our* beliefs. We seem to be committed both to Peter having the belief and not having it. Let's now look in detail at these puzzles.

The standard puzzle can be developed as a set of claims that are jointly inconsistent:

1. Peter believes that Paderewski has musical talent (formed at the concert).
2. Peter believes that Paderewski lacks musical talent (formed at the rally).
3. The belief attributed in (1), that Paderewski has musical talent, contradicts the belief attributed in (2), that Paderewski lacks musical talent.[7]
4. Peter cannot tell that he has contradictory beliefs, "no amount of pure logic or semantic introspection suffices for him to discover his error" (Kripke 1979: 134).

---

[7] We take it that "Paderewski lacks musical talent" is simply a more idiomatic version of "It is not the case that Paderewski has musical talent".

5. "Anyone... is in a position to notice and correct contradictory beliefs if he has them" (Kripke 1979: 122).
6. Peter's ability to "notice and correct" contradictions is unimpaired: if he has such beliefs, he is in a position to come to know this merely by reflection.

(1) through (6) are inconsistent. The puzzle consists in the fact that, according to Kripke, we are in no position to form a stable view about which of these claims to give up.

Kripke spends some time arguing for (1) and (2), drawing on the empirical fact that Peter is disposed sincerely to assent to the sentence "Paderewski has musical talent" in the one case, and "Paderewski lacks musical talent" in the other. One way to support these claims (pre-empting some objections that have been made) envisages two journalists, one who talks to Peter at the concert and another who talks to him at the rally. As experienced reporters, their independent views about Peter's beliefs need to be taken seriously. We find (1) in the notebook of the one journalist, and (2) in the notebook of the other.

On what basis might one challenge the correctness of these reports? Very few people would have any qualms about accepting each were it not for the other. But it's hard to see how the occasions can interfere. Could what happens later make it untrue that, at the first encounter, Peter believed that Paderewski has musical talent? Later events could not affect earlier ones in that way. The more promising line is that although (1) is true at the time of the first encounter, and until the second, the second encounter itself somehow terminates that belief. This termination must be either by a rational process or by a non-rational one. It cannot be by a rational process, for it is built into the example that Peter takes there to be two Paderewskis, so, from his point of view, rally-based information cannot have any evidential bearing on concert-formed beliefs. If in some case the early belief was terminated by an irrational process, then there is a variant in which this process fails to operate, so the variant would still give rise to the puzzle. We think there is certainly a case in which Peter retains the early belief at and after the second encounter. This view could be supported by his behavior even after the rally. "Remember that wonderful concert, when we heard Op. 110?" we ask him at, or after the rally. "Yes indeed," replies Peter, "Paderewski certainly has musical talent."

There is no serious room for doubt that (1) holds throughout the time of the story. But perhaps the second encounter is not enough to ensure the truth of (2). Anyone who accepts what has been said so far will agree that if there had been no first encounter, the second encounter would have ensured the truth of (2). That's because the encounters, taken separately, are essentially the same: either on its own would have been enough to make Peter master of the name "Paderewski", thereby equipping him with the public concept PADEREWSKI, and thereby enabling him to have beliefs involving that concept. How could the presence of the belief attributed in (1) prevent the formation, at the second encounter, of the belief attributed in (2)? From Peter's point of view, they stand in no interesting logical relation. We have a similar choice as before. It can't be a rational process, since Peter thinks there are two Paderewskis, and hence that facts about the one are logically independent of facts about the other. If it's some non-rational process, let's shift to a situation in which that process fails. So there are cases in which it's right to say that both (1) and (2) are true of Peter at the same time.

Are these beliefs contradictory? In other words, is (3) true? A common way to seek to dissolve the puzzle is by denying (3), saying that the concept PADEREWSKI in (1) is different from the concept PADEREWSKI in (2), so the beliefs do not contradict.[8] For example, this line continues, the Paderewski-belief Peter forms at the concert is most accurately expressed using a definite description in the subject position: *the pianist who played Op. 110 has musical talent*. The Paderewski-belief Peter forms at the rally is most accurately expressed using a different definite description in subject position: *the person running for Prime Minister lacks musical talent*. Even though these beliefs cannot both be true, they are not contradictory, so there's nothing puzzling about Peter having both.[9]

Peter might indeed form both these beliefs, but this is consistent with his also forming beliefs each of which involves one and the same concept PADEREWSKI. The basis for this view is the linguistic character of certain concepts. It's part of the story that on the first occasion Peter was introduced to the name "Paderewski". Maybe he sees the name on the program, and its bearer on the stage. By ordinary standards, he has done enough to master the use of the name. For originalists, this is to say that he can exercise the concept associated with the name. This concept, and its content, is fixed in a social way by the linguistic community to which Peter belongs. He now counts as a member of the "Paderewski"-using community. Hence he is in a position to form beliefs which involve the public concept PADEREWSKI. It would be pretty extraordinary if he didn't form any such beliefs. A sincere utterance of "Paderewski has musical talent" is enough to remove any doubt that might remain about whether he believes that Paderewski has musical talent. On the second occasion, he re-encounters the very same concept. So, even though he may also exercise other concepts whose referent is Paderewski, he also counts as exercising the public one, the very same concept that he had encountered previously. To generate the puzzle, you don't need to have any further view about the semantic character of this shared concept: it could be Millian or Fregean or descriptive. The crucial thing is to ensure (3), and we think this cannot be denied. As Kripke stresses, (3) is not rendered false by the supposition, no doubt correct, that Peter also thinks of Paderewski under other concepts as well.[10]

---

[8] Inconsistent thoughts are contradictory iff one is the negation of the other.
[9] Fodor (2008: 73) is among many who take a similar line. We resist the inference from "Peter must have more than one concept for Paderewski" to "Peter does not have a single concept for Paderewski, used on both occasions."
[10] Peter's engagement with a single public concept PADEREWSKI contrasts with the subject of the Perry/Evans example discussed in Chapter 3, in which someone first sees a ship through one window, and then sees what is in fact the same ship through another, without recognizing it. This subject has introduced distinct specific demonstrative concepts, and so the thought accepted is distinct from the thought rejected.

We also agree with Kripke, and everyone else, that (4) is true: Peter is in no position to detect, by reflection on his beliefs, that they are contradictory. Accepting all of (1)–(4) of the inconsistent set puts strong pressure on us to reject one of (5) and (6):

5. "Anyone...is in a position to notice and correct contradictory beliefs if he has them" (Kripke 1979: 122).
6. Peter's ability to "notice and correct" contradictions is unimpaired: if he has such beliefs, he is in a position to come to know this merely by reflection.

The crucial point is that (5) is false, and so is the second part of (6). Both depend on a thesis, rejected in Chapter 5, concerning introspective knowledge of comparative content.

A pair of sentences is inconsistent if they cannot both be true, but this may not be manifest, as with the pair "Hesperus is visible" and "Phosphorus is not visible" (with the same temporal index). Being contradictory is supposed to be a specially manifest way of being inconsistent. Sentences are contradictory only if one is of the form "A" and the other of the form "not-A". Perhaps the form of a sentence is always manifest to anyone who understands it. Yet form alone does not provide a sufficient condition for being contradictory. A further requirement is that the two occurrences of "A" be interpreted in the same way. Hence semantic knowledge is required, not just syntactic knowledge. Moreover, it is *comparative* semantic knowledge: that two sentences, one figuring under negation, have the same content. Hence one should not be surprised to find cases in which rational subjects do not realize that two sentences are contradictory. If there were two dogs called "Fido", then both the sentences "Fido barks" and "Fido does not bark" could be true. The syntactic facts alone do not rule this out.[11] Engaging in suitable communicative linguistic activities would be enough to ensure that someone understands both sentences. If such a person does not know that there is just one Fido, she could rationally take these sentences to be consistent. Hence (5) is false for sentences: a rational person cannot always detect that sentences he understands are contradictory, even if they are.

The same holds for thoughts. Inconsistent thoughts are contradictory iff one consists of the other embedded in a concept for negation.[12] Rational subjects are not always in a position to know whether they are exercising a fresh concept, or the same concept again. Peter thinks, at the rally, that he has learned a new concept PADEREWSKI, different from the PADEREWSKI concept he had earlier acquired at the concert. He is wrong. But if this is a reasonable mistake, it is one that makes it reasonable for him to believe that his thoughts are not contradictory. He reasonably believes that it is not the case that the one thought consists in the other embedded in a concept for negation.

---

[11] Kaplan insists that contradictions are not to be defined merely syntactically, and his reasons lead him to deny axiomatic status to "$\phi(that) \rightarrow \phi(that)$" (Kaplan 1977/1989: 587).

[12] In another version of originalism, the restriction to inconsistent thoughts could be omitted. But in our version, having the form A and not-A does not guarantee being inconsistent. For example the 15th-century thought that spinach is meat is true, and so is the 21st-century thought that spinach is not meat.

Claim (6) comes in two parts. The first is acceptable: Peter is normal as far as his ability to detect contradictions in his beliefs is concerned. It does not follow that he, or anyone, has either of the following two properties: (i) if ever Peter has beliefs which contradict, he is capable of coming to know this by reflection alone; (ii) if ever Peter believes he has beliefs that contradict, then he has contradictory beliefs. In short, being normal as a contradiction-detector is a very different thing from being both infallible and omniscient on this matter. The second part of (6) should be rejected. Rather, Peter does indeed have contradictory beliefs, even though he is in no position to come to know this merely by reflection. We can explain how it is that someone with normal powers can nonetheless be in no position to detect the contradictory character of a pair of his beliefs.

Peter has the false belief that there are two Paderewskis, that is, two people called "Paderewski", so he believes that the name "Paderewski" is ambiguous. If he is rational, he will see that it follows that the sentence he was disposed to utter on the first encounter, "Paderewski has musical talent", does not contradict the sentence he was disposed to utter on the second encounter, "Paderewski lacks musical talent". Hence, given the false belief in two Paderewskis, it's rationally required of Peter to think that the two sentences do not contradict.

There is a similar story to be told about Peter's thoughts. Let's suppose he heard on good authority that no politicians have musical talent, so it's rational for him to believe this, and rational to infer that he has encountered two Paderewskis. If he reflected on his mental states using the originalist apparatus, it would be rational for him to believe that he has two concepts PADEREWSKI. In his eyes, the concepts are two because they have different contents, one involving one person, the other another. Inconsistent thoughts are contradictory iff one consists of the other embedded in the concept of negation. If one thought contains a nominal concept, a contradiction must contain the same nominal concept at the corresponding position in the structure. In the light of Peter's rationally held but false beliefs about his concepts, it's rational for him to believe that the thought formed at the rally is not the negation of the thought formed at the concert. Hence it's rationally required of Peter to believe that the thoughts do not contradict.

To escape Kripke's standard puzzle, it's enough to show that Peter is not irrational, despite having contradictory beliefs. In our discussion, we have said something stronger: Peter is rational to believe that he does not have contradictory beliefs. Indeed, we can regard Peter as rational through and through: rational to believe that Paderewski has musical talent (for the performance of the Op. 110 was really superb), rational to believe that Paderewski lacks musical talent (for the person who told him that no politicians have musical talent was an expert in these matters, and Peter knows that Paderewski is a politician), and rational to believe his beliefs do not contradict (for things he rationally believes entails that there are two Paderewskis, which in turn entails that the beliefs are consistent). Reaching these verdicts does not entail that no one is ever irrational in cases like these. Suppose, for example, that, at the rally, someone else, whom Peter has excellent reason to trust, tells Peter that this politician is an exception to the rule, and is a superb musician. This should give Peter pause. He ought to weigh this testimony against the previous testimony to the effect that no politicians have musical talent. It could well be that the recent testimony should trump the earlier. In that case, Peter is irrational if he does not reconsider his beliefs: his reason for thinking there were two Paderewskis has been undermined.

When all goes well, thinkers are sensitive to sameness and difference of concepts used. This is required in the most humble forms of reasoning, for example modus ponens. One who infers that q, from the premises p and if p then q, does so properly only if she treats the two occurrences of p as occurrences of the same thought; likewise for the two occurrences of q. If we say that the thinker needs to know that the two occurrences are of the same thought, we require the thinker to have meta-conceptual thoughts, ones relating to thoughts. This is excessively demanding: one can find the modus ponens inference compelling without having meta-conceptual thought. In this case, one treats the occurrences of p as occurrences of the same without necessarily forming a corresponding judgment. The mechanism that leads to treating things as the same or different is a pretty reliable one, and is essential to reasoning. One lesson of the puzzle of Paderewski is that the mechanism is not infallible.

One straightforward explanation of the behavior of split-brain subjects in certain experimental situations is that, like Peter, these subjects have contradictory beliefs. This is not the only possible view of their situation, however: some philosophers have held that the right conclusion to draw is that split-brain subjects are really two people. For example, if a split-brain subject fixates on a screen on which the word "pen" is flashed to the left and the word "knife" to the right and the subject is asked to say what he saw, he will say "the word 'knife'"; but if he is asked to reach with his left hand behind the screen and pick out the object corresponding to the word he saw, he will pick out a pen. The verbal behavior is evidence that he believes that he saw "knife" and the nonverbal behavior is evidence that he believes that he saw "pen". This has seemed to some philosophers to generate trouble, since the fact that the split-brain subject says "knife" when asked what he saw suggests that he believes that he saw "knife", yet the fact that he doesn't reach with his left hand for a knife in the group of objects suggests that he fails to believe that he saw "knife". Since one and the same person cannot both believe that p, and not believe that p at the same time, some philosophers have been tempted to conclude that the split-brain subject is really two people (if only for a short period of time).

There is a mistake in this reasoning. The fact that the split-brain subject doesn't reach for a knife, when told to pick out with his left hand the object corresponding to the word he saw, doesn't show that he doesn't believe that he saw "knife". It shows only that he believes that he didn't see "knife". But one and the same individual can certainly believe that p, and believe that not-p at the same time. Peter is one such individual.

We turn now to the strengthened puzzle: despite having formed at the concert, and never rejected, the belief that Paderewski has musical talent, it seems that, at the rally, Peter does not believe that Paderewski has musical talent. All theorists have to deal with this contradiction, and the only attractive approach is to deny that, at the rally, Peter doesn't believe that Paderewski has musical talent. But in that case, how should we understand Peter's sincere denials, when asked such questions as "Does Paderewski have musical talent?" or "Do you believe that Paderewski has musical talent?"?

The answer is that Peter falsely believes that he does not believe that Paderewski has musical talent. The second-order belief is false: he formed the belief that Paderewski has musical talent at the concert, and has not abandoned it. So his belief that he lacks this belief is false. But it is enough to explain his sincere denials. Peter is asked if Paderewski has musical talent. In responding negatively, he is being sincere; sincerity means he believes what he says; what he says is that he does not believe that Paderewski has musical talent; so we can infer that he believes that he does not believe that Paderewski has musical talent. To express it metaphorically, let's imagine that Peter queries his database of relevant Paderewski beliefs with: does Paderewski have musical talent? The database returns a negative answer. This in turn justifies Peter in also returning a negative answer: No, I don't believe that Paderewski has musical talent. But his database is inaccurate: in fact he does believe that Paderewski has musical talent, though he does not believe he believes this.[13]

Our treatment of this case presupposes that people can have false beliefs about what they believe.[14] We think that there are plenty of uncontroversial cases which show that this is sometimes the right description. For example, Freudians say that many men believe they would be better off with their father dead, so that they could have unrestricted access to their mother; but that few men believe they have this belief. However the theory of the Oedipus complex may be disputed, we are not aware of anyone having objected merely on the grounds that it attributes to subjects false beliefs about their beliefs. There are endless further examples: most of us believe that we don't have racist beliefs. But various kinds of subtle testing may reveal (to our shame) that in fact we do have racist beliefs, which we have managed to hide from ourselves. Most of us believe we don't believe that some human lives are intrinsically less valuable than others. But we support policies of killing innocent civilians in Afghanistan (in pursuit of "bad guys") that we would never support if the same number of casualties were caused to our fellow citizens.

This resolution of the strengthened puzzle depends upon denying that we can generally rely on dissent as evidence for absence of belief. However, in typical cases, in which the

---

[13] Kripke (1979: 113) considers a principle (he calls it the strengthened disquotation principle) which, setting aside details, treats dissent as evidence for absence of belief. One could regard the strengthened Paderewski case as simply a disproof of this principle (Salmon 1986: 132). We do better to treat dissent from a sentence which says that p, as evidence that the subject believes that not-p. In general, presence of belief is easier to establish than its absence.

[14] If the earlier split-brain subject is asked "Do you believe that you saw 'pen'?" he will say "No". This is evidence that he believes that he doesn't believe that he saw "pen". Given that he does believe that he saw "pen" (see above), his second-order belief is false.

subject is fully sincere and under no error, conceptual or otherwise, dissent provides good evidence for absence of belief. This is the basis on which we can properly treat dissent by the ancient astronomers as good evidence for their not believing that Hesperus is Phosphorus, thus preserving some of the Fregean data that originalism explains.[15]

The Paderewski examples are consonant with originalism, but finding a suitable description of the cases makes little use of details of the theory. Rather, what's needed are correct views about rationality, about the capacity to know when our beliefs are contradictory, and about the capacity to know what we don't believe. It's consonant with our generally externalist views that our knowledge of these things may well be imperfect.

7.5 The Puzzle of the Two Tubes

Jonathan, with tubes attached to each eye, is seeing a single red patch with each eye, but is led on good authority to believe that he cannot reliably tell on the basis of vision where objects are located or which eye he is seeing with. He asks himself whether *that* (referring to the red, circular region that he is actually seeing with his left eye) is identical with *that* (referring to the red, circular region that he is actually seeing with his right eye). The answer is yes, but the question is substantive for Jonathan: he may not know the answer, or know how to improve on his ignorance.

From what was said in Chapter 3 about distinguishing specific demonstrative concepts, it follows that Jonathan uses two specific concepts THAT. The second occurrence of the specific concept THAT in his wondering whether *that is that* is not intended to be deferential with respect to the first, nor is Jonathan disposed to bring forward information associated with the first and amalgamate it with information associated with the second. If he had these dispositions, he would be thinking a trivially true identity; clearly that is not what he is doing. Rather, he introduces a fresh concept to fill the second nominative position. Although the concepts are different, it follows from the case that they have the same content: both refer to the same red patch.

This shows that we have a Hesperus/Phosphorus case: Jonathan makes a cognitive discovery, though not a possibility-eliminating one. The original intention was that the case would indeed be a Hesperus/Phosphorus one, with the variation that the restrictions on Jonathan's cognitive powers would make a Fregean descriptivist answer unavailable. There's supposed to be no descriptive material that could make for an appropriate difference between the two concepts THAT. But, as we've seen, descriptive material is not required. It's enough that the concepts are distinct.

The other demonstrative puzzle concerned Mary, the color scientist imprisoned from birth in a black and white room, and released only after she had learned everything there was to know about the physical facts pertaining to colors. The aspect of Mary's situation

---

[15] In ordinary conversation, it is hard to detect much sensitivity to the distinction between believing that not-*p* and not believing that *p* (as Hans Kamp has emphasized). That's because, normally, one can infer the second from the first. Theoretical purposes, however, require the distinction to be stressed.

described in Chapter 1 was as follows. When she emerges from her room, she might see something red while at the same time checking on the state of her brain using an autocerebroscope. If physicalism is true, the experience is (we'll assume) the brain state. In connection with the experience of red she might introduce one specific demonstrative concept THIS. In connection with the brain state seen on the cerebroscope she might introduce another specific demonstrative concept THAT. We asked how she could sensibly wonder whether this is that, and how it could count as a discovery that this is that. The answer should now be clear: since these are distinct specific demonstrative concepts, then, even if the demonstrated experience is identical to the demonstrated brain state, we have nothing more problematic than the puzzle of Hesperus and Phosphorus or of the two tubes: Mary makes a cognitive but not a possibility-eliminating discovery.

7.6 The Puzzle of Empty Thoughts

There are two main ways in which a concept can fail to have a content. One is error, exemplified by the usual story about the concept VULCAN. Leverrier postulated a planet lying between Mercury and the sun, in order to explain a feature of Mercury's orbit, and he introduced the name "Vulcan", and the concept VULCAN, for this supposed planet. It turned out that there was no such thing (and the problematic feature of Mercury's orbit was subsequently explained in terms of Relativity Theory). The concept was at one time widely used (the Boston *Daily Globe* for 29 July 1878 promised its readers a sighting of Vulcan) and is still used, as in this paragraph. Only philosophical prejudice could lead to the opinion that empty concepts have no intelligible use.

Another source of emptiness is pretense, of which the most conspicuous form is fiction. The concept SHERLOCK HOLMES was introduced by Conan Doyle for his fictional detective. When we engage in the pretense, we pretend that the concept has a referent, but we know that in fact it does not.

Even specific demonstrative concepts may be empty for either of these reasons. One might use a specific THAT-concept in the mistaken belief that there was a bat swooping across one's yard when there was nothing at all. The thought that that is a bat is perfectly coherent, though on originalist semantics (negative free logical) it comes out false. Or one might start a game with a child. Showing an empty hand, one closes it into a fist: "That's a red one in there. [Now holding out the other fist.] What color do you think that one is?"

Empty concepts are manifestly valuable in describing mental states. Leverrier really did believe that Vulcan was involved in the explanation of Mercury's orbit. Some children really do believe that Santa Claus brings them presents. Empty concepts may also have significant uses in other contexts. There are no witches; there is no such thing as phlogiston.[16] One needs to appreciate these truths to understand aspects of culture and aspects of combustion. Why might anyone think that there can't be intelligible empty concepts?

---

[16] These are empty concepts only if there is no property of being a witch or of being phlogiston. There is room for a different view on that issue.

We think the explanation lies in philosophical prejudice. For example, there is a tendency to make inferences of the following kind:

X represents so-and-so.
Hence so-and-so is such that X represents it.

An example of this reasoning is found (implicitly) in Gareth Evans' discussion of Frege (Evans 1982: 1.6). He says that in introducing sense as a way of thinking of an object, Frege was committed to the position that there is no sense without a referent.[17] The commitment holds only if "thinking of" supports for senses the kind of inference just displayed for representations in general. Evans has to be understood to be arguing as follows: Fregean senses are ways of thinking of objects; if a sense is a way of thinking of an object, there must be an object such that this way of thinking is a way of thinking of it; hence every sense requires an object.

This reasoning should be rejected: one can think of Vulcan without there being a thing, Vulcan, of which one thinks, just as one can search for the fountain of youth without there being a thing, the fountain of youth, for which one searches.

The prejudice against empty concepts is also found among theorists attracted to Millianism. These theorists insist, rightly, that the point of having representations is typically to enable us to interact effectively with the things they represent. At the same time, they rightly recoil from Fregean descriptivist accounts of representation. But it's just a mistake to move from these positions to the conclusion that there cannot be intelligible empty representations. One does not have to be a descriptivist to allow that there can be representations of unicorns yet no unicorns, or a representation of Vulcan and yet no Vulcan; and one can allow that representations typically do have objects, and even that this is typically their main point, without allowing that they always have objects.[18] A map can be of a purely imaginary land, so there is no land of which it is a map. A painting can represent a purely imaginary landscape, and so no landscape is one it represents. We are familiar with pictorial and cartographic representations failing to represent; we should extend the same indulgence to conceptual representations.

It is reasonable, however, to require an account of how empty concepts contribute to truth conditions. We have already given an answer for straightforward extensional cases (in Chapter 3). To repeat the truth condition for atomic thoughts:

a unary atomic thought is associated with the set W of worlds meeting this condition: $w \in W$ iff both concepts have a content with respect to w, and the content of the

---

[17] "It is really not clear how there can be a mode of presentation associated with some term when there is no object to be presented. On my interpretation of the metaphor the difficulty remains acute: it certainly does not appear that there can be a way of thinking about something unless there is something to be thought about in that way" (Evans 1982: 22).

[18] One version of Millian views relies on "structured propositions", set theoretic entities whose elements are worldly objects—individuals and properties—corresponding to sentences or thoughts. One response from such theorists to the problem of empty concepts is to allow for "gappy propositions", where the gap corresponds to the empty concept. We show in Chapter 8 that this idea is unworkable.

nominative concept at w possesses the property that is the content of the predicative concept at w.

This ensures that the following thoughts are false—a result we regard as happy:

Vulcan is Vulcan[19]
Pegasus flies
Holmes is a detective.

Negation operates in the usual way, so, for example, the thought that Vulcan doesn't exist is true; we have no trouble at all with the so-called "puzzle of negative existential truths".

The negative free logical approach adopted in Chapter 3 has the consequence that the only way for a thought containing an empty concept to feature in a truth is for that concept to be within the scope of some operator. We have just seen that negation can create a true thought from a false one containing an empty concept. More interesting operators which have the same effect are attitude verbs and fiction operators. The thought that Leverrier believed that Vulcan has a diameter in excess of 1,000 km can be true, because the conceptual structure corresponding to "Leverrier believed that" can generate a true whole thought, even if the part on which it operates is false. Essentially the same goes for the thought that, in the stories, Holmes is a detective. The thought-component corresponding to "In the stories" has no interest in whether the thought it embeds is true or false, but only whether it is faithful to the stories; and a thought can be faithful to the stories without being true. Recognition of empty concepts is thus consistent with false atomic thoughts containing them, and true nonatomic thoughts in which they are embedded under an operator.

What the originalist approach as so far characterized does not make room for is true *atomic* thoughts containing empty concepts. Intuitively, there are such thoughts, and accordingly we will modify originalism to make room for them.

There's room for disagreement about which are the most telling examples of thoughts in this category, but we think everyone should agree that at least one of the following could be true:

1. James is thinking of Pegasus.
2. Ponce de León looked for the fountain of youth.
3. Sally wants a unicorn.
4. Holmes is famous.
5. The concept VULCAN represents Vulcan.

Believers in empty concepts need to explain how truth is possible in such cases. The problem is not unique to originalism: it has given rise to much philosophical striving, under the heading of problems concerning "intensional transitives".

---

[19] Given that there is no such thing as Vulcan, there is nothing it is identical with. Similarly, the fact that everything is self-identical should not suggest that Vulcan is.

While the problem is not unique to originalism, originalists have a distinctive resource for giving an answer. According to originalism, empty concepts are unproblematic, and they are interestingly different from one another despite not differing in content. This suggests a strategy for dealing with intensional transitives: their truth-makers will be states of their subjects involving a special relation to the *concept* used in the problematic position in the thought (that occupied by the concept Pegasus in (1) above).

When James thinks of Pegasus, he entertains a representation of Pegasus in his thought, viz, the concept Pegasus. When he thinks of Austin, he entertains a representation of Austin in his thought, very likely the concept Austin. There is a difference, of course, for the concept Austin is non-empty, so in entertaining the concept in thought, there's a city on which his thought is focused. This doesn't follow just from the fact that he thought of Austin, as is easy to see by the comparison with his thought of Pegasus. The additional requirement is that the relevant concept be non-empty.

When Ponce de León looked for the fountain of youth, he engaged in searching activities guided by a representation of the fountain of youth, perhaps the concept THE FOUNTAIN OF YOUTH. When Sally wants a unicorn, she has a desire (a species of thought) in which what she desires is represented as a unicorn. In the usual case, she will exercise the concept UNICORN in thinking what she wants. Understanding the claim that Holmes is famous in a sociological way, as a truth following from the immense popularity of the Holmes stories, it amounts to saying that many people exercise a representation of Holmes (typically, the concept Holmes) in thinking favorable thoughts featuring that representation.

The general strategy is to understand the truth-makers for thoughts seeming to involve relations to nonexistent entities (Pegasus, the fountain of youth, Holmes), in terms of relations to appropriate concepts. Since we allow for empty concepts, we can allow that these relations may not generate relations to anything, existent or nonexistent. There remain two hurdles. One is that we need to make sure that we are happy with our own theoretical uses of such claims as that the concept Vulcan represents Vulcan. The other is that the approach requires a case-by-case analysis of the problematic predicative concepts. Ponce de León did not look for a representation of the fountain of youth, and no representation would have satisfied him as the terminus of his quest. Sally wanted a unicorn, not a representation of a unicorn. So the problematic cases can't merely be treated as ones in which we refer to a concept rather than to an object.

"Represents" is itself an intensional transitive verb, and the concept it expresses is to be classified analogously. We need to be happy that this classification does not lead to an unacceptable regress, for we appeal to it routinely in explaining the other cases. We should have no qualm about the emptiness of certain concepts which represent; the qualm relates to understanding how, when an empty concept is in question, we can *truthfully* fill in the dots in "the concept represents...". The objection is that if the dots can be filled in so as to make a truth, then the concept represents something. But it was meant to be an empty concept, one that represents nothing.

The scope differences already mentioned contribute to easing perplexity, but we can add something more substantive: the free logical framework allows us to say not only *that* an empty concept represents something, but *what* it represents. The canonical explanation of the representational properties of the concept VULCAN is given by the free logical truth:

for all x, the concept VULCAN represents x iff x = Vulcan.

In fact, "x is Vulcan" is false of everything and so, if the biconditional is to be true, "the concept VULCAN represents x" needs also to be false of everything. This is the desired result. We do not undermine it if we add that the concept VULCAN represents Vulcan. Since there is no such thing as Vulcan, this is consistent with there being nothing the concept VULCAN represents: it is an empty concept. What holds for the concept VULCAN holds for empty atomic concepts generally.[20]

The other hurdle is that every intensional verb or concept will require a made-to-measure analysis. Wanting a unicorn is having a desire essentially involving a unicorn representation; looking for a unicorn is engaging in search activities guided by intentions essentially involving unicorn representations. It doesn't look as if there will be a single transformation, applicable to every case, from the original intensional verb or concept to one which trades not in objects, but rather in representations of objects. Desire is for an object, not for a representation; likewise for searches. But the way in which the concept DESIRE is modified to bring out its more direct connection to representations seems not to be the same as the way in which the concepts LOOKING FOR or BEING FAMOUS are modified to bring out their more direct connection to representations. Hence although we may have a fully general semantic clause for simple thoughts formed from two-place extensional atomic concepts, there will be no analog for simple thoughts formed from two-place intensional atomic concepts, no true generalization beginning

for all intensional atomic concepts C, and nominative concepts a and b, the thought consisting of $a \frown C \frown b$ is true iff . . . .

We recognize that this makes the semantics in some sense unsystematic. However, all the semantic accounts of intensional transitives of which we are aware have this feature (e.g. Montague 1973; Thomason 1980; Forbes 2006). More importantly, we do not regard our essential task in this area as providing systematic semantics. Rather, our main task was to show that simple thoughts built around intensional transitive concepts can be true, even when the concept in the second place is empty. We have shown in various cases how facts involving empty concepts can make such thoughts true, and we are not aware of cases for which this cannot be done. Our main task has been carried out.

The main conclusions are these: empty concepts can be intelligible; even though they all have the same content, originalism ensures they are different concepts; empty concepts can be used to construct true complex thoughts in which the empty concepts are

---

[20] We rely on the notion of a *canonical* explanation of representational properties. The free logical truth for the concept VULCAN is just as true if we replace the word "Vulcan" at the end by "Pegasus". Just as true; but not a canonical explanation of the representational features of the concept VULCAN.

embedded under an operator; and, for the case of intensional transitives, there are true atomic thoughts containing empty concepts.

7.7 The Puzzle of Thinking About Oneself

How can there be different ways of thinking about oneself? Can some of these ways generate "immunity to error through misidentification" (IEM)? When Mach saw himself in the omnibus mirror he thought about himself in one way; when he realized the object of his thought was none other than himself, he thought about himself in another way. This exemplifies the basic contrast we have to clarify. When Mach thought about the shabby pedagogue, he thought it was not himself, and so made a mistaken identification. When he thinks he has toothache, such a mistake seems impossible: there seems no room for him to be wrong about who has toothache. This exemplifies IEM, which places a constraint on the adequacy of what we say about different ways of thinking about oneself. In many cases (especially Paderewski), we have stressed possibilities for unnoticed error about one's thoughts. Are we committed to the view that there is, after all, a possibility of error through misidentification even in those cases usually said to be immune?

We'll begin by applying originalism to some features of self-identification, and then review the connection with IEM.

According to originalism, Mach has more than one concept of himself, including one he expresses with the word "I" (or "Ich"), and a concept THE SHABBY PEDAGOGUE (looking towards the mirror). The difference between these concepts is guaranteed by the fact that one is atomic and the other not. The concept THE SHABBY PEDAGOGUE has the concept SHABBY as a constituent, whereas the concept I does not. How do these concepts compare for content? The content of his concept I is just Mach himself. We have given no account of the content of nonatomic nominative concepts, and originalism as such has no commitment to any particular theory: it could move in a Russellian direction, according to which they "have no meaning in isolation", or in the direction of complex referring expressions. We'll move in the latter direction, at least for the present kind of nonatomic concept, and identify its content with its referent. As in many previous examples, we have two concepts with the same content. Mach's failure to recognize the shabby pedagogue as himself is essentially like the failure of early astronomers to recognize Hesperus as Phosphorus.

The generic I-template, the one shared by all English speakers (and also, let's suppose, by Mach), is governed by the following rule: one should use it to think of oneself.[21] Acquiring a specific I-concept involves mastering this rule. Each person's use of their specific concept I is special: only that person can use it to think of him or herself. You can refer to yourself, and no one else, with your I-concept, and no one else can use it to refer to

---

[21] The generic I-template is not a concept, in the originalist sense: see Chapter 3, section 3.6. Each person's specific I-concept, however, really is a concept.

anything. Moreover, an I-thought can be of distinctive value: you use it in knowing who you are (as in the case of Lewis's gods), and this is linked to its role in action.

Action and the first person: If Sally thinks something she could express by the words "I need to leave" she is thereby in a motivating state. If she thinks something she could express by the words "Sally needs to leave" she might not thereby be in a motivating state (if she does not know that she is Sally). We can express the contrast in this way: when she's in the motivating state, she thinks of herself as herself; but she might think of a person who is in fact herself without thinking of that person as herself, in which case her state may not be motivating. This was Mach's fate: he thought of himself as the shabby pedagogue, but not as himself. It's a constraint on any theory of thought that it can provide, or at least not block, an adequate account of what it is for a person to think of herself as herself.

A common view (found in some interpretations of Perry 1979) is that the content Sally expresses when she forms a belief she could express in the words "I need to leave" is a special content, a first-person indexical content. On this view, to think of yourself as yourself is to think a special content, one distinctively *as yourself*. It's a feature of this special content that it motivates. This picture is not available to originalists. Where reference is the same, there is no room for difference of content. An originalist explanation must draw on difference of concept. The special nature of a specific first-person concept ensures that when its subject uses it, the subject thereby thinks of himself as himself.

Every subject who properly grasps an I-concept, as user or as understander, treats it as governed by the rule recently noted: a subject is to use it to think of herself, and she can use it to think of no one else. One who explicitly exploits this rule as a user must therefore think on the following lines (we shift to their perspective): I must use my I-concept to think of myself. As we may say (shifting back to our own perspective): she knows she must use her I-concept to think of herself. We claim that being in this state guarantees, and explains, thinking of yourself as yourself. The reason is simple: thinking the rule requires the subject to think of herself as herself. Sally would not be thinking the right rule if she thought: I must use the I-concept to think of Sally. Her I-concept is not governed by that rule. But if Sally thinks a thought in which she applies the rule for the I-concept correctly, she does think of herself as herself, and so is in a potentially motivating state.

Immunity to error through misidentification (IEM): The thesis is that there are ways of making judgments about oneself that are immune to error through misidentification (IEM). The claim is standardly attributed to Wittgenstein, in a passage quoted more fully in Chapter 1:

> there is no question of recognizing a person when I say I have toothache. To ask "are you sure it's *you* who have pains?" would be nonsensical.

Wittgenstein's main concern is to show that there is a kind of self-knowledge, that expressed by the subject-centered use of the first person, whose grounds do not involve any judgment of identity. I may become aware that my arm is broken by seeing a mangled arm among a pile of limbs and forming the judgment: that arm is my arm. The identity judgment would be part of the grounds of my judgment that my arm is broken, and my use of "my" would be "as object". This is not how things are in normal first-person judgments about one's own mental states. My judgment that my tooth hurts does not depend in any way on an identity judgment, neither one of the form "that tooth is my tooth", nor one of the form "that sufferer is me".

Originalism would ideally help justify, and at a minimum be consistent with, any true thesis in this area.[22] We'll single out four candidates for discussion:

1. Some self-knowledge is subject-free.
2. Some self-knowledge is identification-free.
3. Self-reference is guaranteed to succeed.
4. IEM, a thesis which we'll try to formulate more precisely shortly.

7.7.1 *Some self-knowledge is subject-free*

Think of some simple measuring instrument, like a fuel gauge or a thermometer. Such devices don't immediately deliver proposition-shaped information. The thermometer reads 85°. One could think of the reading as like a predicate: "is 85°". But what is the subject? What is said to be at 85°? Although the thermometer can give different readings, the device itself is in a sense invariant concerning its subject: it simply tells the temperature of its sensitive tip. This in turn indicates the temperature of wherever the tip happens to be: in your coffee, or just out in the room. We say that the information the thermometer provides is *centered* on its tip, meaning by this that the thermometer reading is accurate just if the temperature it indicates is the temperature at the tip. The information is "subject-free": it's just predicative, and the subject, though essential to the accuracy condition of the information, is not represented in the information.

We think it's theoretically possible that some self-knowledge is of this kind (we do not commit to whether this is actually so). It would be presented to the subject purely predicatively: *hungry, thirsty*. It would be centered information in the sense that it is accurate iff *the subject* satisfies the predicate. If there is self-knowledge of this kind, it would be free from error through misidentification in the sense that the only way for the information to be inaccurate is for it to be inaccurate information *about the subject*. There is no question of the information *mis*identifying the subject, for the information does not so much as represent the subject.

Nothing in originalism precludes subject-free self-knowledge. But it's not distinctive of self-knowledge: temperature information provided by a thermometer is also subject-free, but is not self-knowledge.

---

[22] Wittgenstein himself wanted to conclude that first person judgments are not really "about" anything. We do not follow him down this road.

7.7.2 Some self-knowledge is identification-free

Say that the knowledge that a is F is identification-free iff it is not grounded on any distinct identity judgment of the form $a = b$. In this case, the putative knowledge cannot be defeated by the information that $a \neq b$. This seems the main point Wittgenstein wished to stress.

We agree that some self-knowledge is identification-free. This imposes no constraints on the first-person concept or its content. One way to see this is to appreciate that there must be identification-free knowledge not involving the first person. Suppose I know that a is F, where a is not myself. If this is not grounded on any identity judgment of the form $a = b$, then it is identification-free. If it is grounded on some judgment $a = b$, we can ask whether this judgment in turn is identification-free. It is iff there is no distinct judgment, say $b = c$, on which it is grounded. If it is identification-free, we have our conclusion. If it is not, we can push the argument a stage further, and so on, but this process must end somewhere. The general point is straightforward and intuitive: there must be acts of identification that don't depend on other acts of identification, else we would have an endless regress.

The argument also makes plain that identification-free knowledge is not distinctive of self-knowledge.

7.7.3 Self-reference is guaranteed to succeed

This thesis is true. It is entailed by the fact that to use the I-concept is to use the concept of oneself. The subject who thinks the right rule for the first person has already thought of herself, as herself, so in applying the rule there is no risk of failure.

It may be objected that there cannot be success without the possibility of failure, and hence the conclusion must be rejected (compare Anscombe 1975). We agree with the principle, but in the present case the possibility of failure is the possibility that one might fail to think the rule for using the I-concept. Once one has thought it, one has self-referred.

Another objection is that it seems clearly possible for self-reference to fail. Looking at an old school photograph, someone might misidentify a person as himself: he tries to refer to himself, but in fact refers to another student. Or he might have delusional beliefs about his identity, thinking, for example, that he is Napoleon: in referring to Napoleon, he thinks he is referring to himself when he is not. These examples miss the nature of the claim: the guarantee of self-reference comes from using the I-concept to refer to oneself. The concept NAPOLEON is not the I-concept even for Napoleon himself, let alone for the subject of the delusion. This subject refers to himself perfectly well using the I-concept: that's what makes his belief that he is Napoleon false: he wrongly thinks of *himself* as Napoleon, which means that he thinks of himself. Similarly, when someone uses a demonstrative to single out a student in the photograph, he is not using his I-concept. However, when he thinks that that student is him, he does, in what follows the "is", think of himself using his I-concept; that's why what he thinks is mistaken.

The phenomenon of guaranteed reference does seem to be confined to the first person, and is thus fit to enter into a partial characterization of the nature of self-knowledge. However, it is neither necessary nor sufficient for IEM. Seeing a person you take to be yourself in a mirror, you think that you are wearing a yellow hat. This kind of example is standardly taken not to manifest IEM. The reason is that the person you see in the mirror might not be yourself. You could sensibly wonder: someone is wearing a yellow hat, but is it me? Even so, self-reference is guaranteed: when you think that you are wearing a yellow hat, you can but think of yourself. So guaranteed self-reference is not sufficient for IEM.

It is not necessary for IEM, since IEM can arise even when no person is referred to, and so, afortiori, in the absence of self-reference. There's an example in the next subsection.

7.7.4 IEM

The intuitive idea is that, when IEM obtains for a belief of the form a is F (as formed under specific circumstances), one can't be right about something being F yet wrong about the thing in question being a. There's no separating out the information one is receiving into distinct components, one component delivering the predicative information, and another providing an identificatory link to a subject; the information is, as one might say, consolidated. We agree that in this sense some judgments are IEM. Information about one's sensory states is typically information that is in this way consolidated. If you judge on the normal introspective basis that you have a headache, your state can't justify the judgment that someone has a headache without also justifying the judgment that you have a headache.

IEM can obtain even when the belief one forms is mistaken. The point is that the mistake is not misidentification. Here's an example. In a hazing situation, you are told that a red hot poker is going to be applied to your back. Given that many unpleasant things have been happening, you fully believe this. You hear the poker being prepared, while you are held in such a position that you cannot see what is going on behind you. Then you feel a sensation in your back and for a moment take it to be pain. After a short while you realize that ice cubes have been applied, not something hot. For a moment, though, you wrongly thought your skin was burning hot. The sensations on which this erroneous judgment are based can't ground the view that someone's skin is burning hot, except to the extent that they ground the view that one's own skin is burning hot. Putting it the other way, even when a self-judgment is false, it's not that the predicative informational basis is fine, and only the identificatory link erroneous. The information is consolidated. So one could not reasonably believe, on the basis of one's experience, that someone's skin was burning hot while wondering whether it was one's own.

We accept that some self-knowledge, and even some (false) self-belief, is IEM. However this is not confined to cases of self-knowledge. Consider a perceptually-based demonstrative judgment that that is a cat. In this case, too, the information is consolidated. That is to say, it can't be that there is a correct predicative element, *there is a cat in the vicinity*, and then a potentially incorrect identificatory link, connecting being a cat with a specific object. Hence one can't be justified, on the basis of this experience, in thinking that something is a cat, but it's not *that*. The justification of the singular thought and of the existential generalization stand or fall together. This is an interesting phenomenon. We do not, however, see it as placing a constraint on a theory of concepts. In particular, it places no constraint on a theory of the I-concept.

Let us summarize the relation between IEM and the originalist theory of the first-person concept. There is only one thesis in this area that is special to our concept of the self, and that's the guarantee of self-reference possessed by one who uses the I-concept correctly. This is consistent with originalism. Indeed, the originalist distinction between concept and content makes it particularly straightforward to present the relevant phenomenon. The other related issues (subject-free or identification-free knowledge, and IEM) are not distinctive of the first person, and place no constraints on a correct theory of concepts.

8

Further Applications: Originalism and Experience

Originalism has consequences for a number of issues and arguments pertaining to experience. In this chapter, we show how originalist views naturally lead to some new and interesting theses with respect to the content of hallucinatory experience and the justificatory role played by experience. We also draw out the implications of originalism for two famous arguments against physicalism with respect to experience: the knowledge argument and the appeal to the conceivability of zombies.

8.1 The Content of Hallucinatory Experience

Consider a case of veridical perception. Suppose that you are seeing a ripe tomato. The view of naïve realism is that you see the tomato directly. You are in direct contact with the perceived object. There is no tomato-like sense impression that stands as an intermediary between the tomato and you. Nor are you related to the tomato as you are to a pig when you see its footprint in the mud. You do not experience the tomato by experiencing something *else* over and above the tomato and its facing surface. You see the facing surface of the tomato *directly*.

Some disjunctivists have suggested that to do proper justice to the above thought, we need to suppose that the objects we perceive are *components* of the contents of our perceptual experiences in veridical cases. This supposition is supported further by the simple observation that if you see an object, it must look some way to you; and if an object looks some way to you, then intuitively it is experienced *as* being some way. On pain of losing direct contact with the object, that again suggests that the object itself figures in the content of the experience, assuming that experience is representational at all.

In cases of illusion, the perceived object appears other than it is. In such cases, intuitively, the perceptual experience is inaccurate,[1] precisely because the object is not as

---

[1] Not everyone accepts this claim. One notable exception is Travis (2004). See also Brewer (2008).

it appears to be. The simplest explanation of this, it is natural to hold, is that where there is a perceived object, a perceptual experience has a content into which the perceived object enters along with its apparent properties.[2]

Once it is acknowledged that in veridical and illusory cases the seen object is a component of the content of the experience and thus that the content itself is singular, a puzzle arises.[3] In standard hallucinatory cases there is no object with which the subject is in perceptual contact and correlatively no singular content.[4] So, if you hallucinate a tomato, what is the representational content of your experience?[5]

One possible answer is that the content is existential in the hallucinatory case. When you hallucinate a ripe tomato, your visual experience represents that there is something red, round and bulgy before you, and since there is no such thing, your experience is inaccurate. The combination of views that results is unlovely and implausible; for it is forced to postulate a displeasing and radical asymmetry in cases that pre-theoretically seem alike.

Another possible answer is that your experience has no content at all in the hallucinatory case.[6] You are simply sensing a red, round, bulgy sense-datum, or you are sensing redly, roundly, and bulgily. Again, the resulting combination of views for the veridical and hallucinatory cases is unlovely and implausible. And there are other well-known difficulties which we shall not rehearse here.

These reflections suggest that in the hallucinatory case we should say that there is content of the very same sort as in the veridical and illusory cases—content that is just like singular content, but with a gap or hole in it where the object is supposed to go: it is "gappy content".[7]

---

[2] On this view, the content is a structured entity. Not all disjunctivists grant that in cases of illusion, perceptual experiences have contents of the same sort as veridical perceptual experiences (e.g. Martin 2006). Obviously, those disjunctivists who take this view cannot use the present consideration to motivate their position.

[3] McGinn (1982) and Davies (1992) deny that the content is singular for any perceptual experiences. For criticisms of this position, see Tye (2009, ch. 4).

[4] Assuming that the term "singular content" is used in the usual way. For an opposing usage, see Sainsbury (2005b).

[5] In what follows, we ignore the case of de re hallucinations. These may be regarded as illusions of a special sort. As to how we are using the expression "representational content", in sections 8.2 and 8.3 below we take it that a visual experience v, in having the representational content that p, is related to an entity picked out by "that p" that is v's representational content. We further take it that v has accuracy conditions and that v's having the accuracy conditions it does, follows from its having the representational content it does. We also hold that hallucinatory visual experiences are not accurate—though below we briefly mention (and reject) two views on which this is denied—and we intend the question, "What is the content of a hallucinatory experience?" to be asking for an elucidation of the nature of that content.

[6] On this view, it is not the case that Keith's experience is not accurate. The question of accuracy, at the level of his experience, simply does not arise.

[7] See Bach (internet essay); Burge (1991); Loar (2003); Tye (2009).

8.2 The Trouble with Gappy Content

Consider the singular content that object, O, is red. On the Russellian view, this content is complex, having object, O, and redness as its components.[8] A visual experience (or other mental state) having that content is accurate if and only if O is red. Content of this kind can be thought of as an ordered pair having O as its first member and redness as its second. Alternatively, it could be thought of as a structured, possible state of affairs built out of O and redness.

The guiding idea behind gappy content is that a hallucinatory visual experience has a content just like a singular content except that there is a gap or hole where the object should go. But does this really make sense?[9] On the ordered-pair conception of singular content, there must be two items to form the pair. Since a gap or a hole is not an item, or so it seems, there is no first member of the ordered pair and so no ordered pair at all. On the possible state of affairs conception, the relevant complex is structured out of O and redness in the singular case. But in the gappy case, there is no object O. So, how is there a *complex* entity structured out of its components?

A possible reply is to say that the missing item in both cases is the empty set. Where one hallucinates, the content is a complex entity built out of the empty set and various properties. But intuitively this is a bizarre proposal indeed. If the empty set is the gap filler, then the hallucinatory experience is about the empty set. So, in a hallucination, one experiences the empty set just as, in the veridical and illusory cases, one sees an object. Furthermore, if the hallucinatory experience is about the empty set then it is experienced as being some way or other, for example, red. So then the empty set looks red, just as the seen object, O, looks red when one sees O and experiences it as red! This is more than a little hard to swallow. Furthermore, the proposal effectively reconfigures hallucinations as illusions of a special sort. Instead of there being no object perceived, there is now an object of a special sort that is perceived, or if not perceived, at least experienced, and this object is not as it is experienced to be.

The empty set proposal is a desperate attempt to save the gappy content view. It confuses the truth that in hallucination one does experience something—for example, a ripe tomato—with the falsehood that there exists some thing one experiences, the empty set being proposed as the relevant thing, since no ordinary object is available to do the job.

Another possible reply is that the missing item is an absence. This needs a little explanation. Roberto Casati and Achille Varzi (1994) make an interesting case for the view that holes exist. If, for example, I say truly that there is a hole in the cheese, on their view, what makes my remark true is the existence of a hole surrounded by the relevant piece of cheese. What Casati and Varzi show (at a minimum) is that it is not at all easy to

---

[8] Obviously, there are other views of singular content. For ease of exposition, we shall stick with the Russellian conception for the time being.
[9] This question is a pressing one for gappy proposition theorists (e.g. Braun 2005) generally.

paraphrase away apparent commitment to holes in our ordinary talk. Analogously, it might be suggested, a case can be made for the view that there exist absences. Even if such a case were successful, however, there is a pressing question for anyone who appeals to an absence in the context of a hallucinatory experience, namely which absence is relevant?

For you, since you are hallucinating, there is no ripe tomato that you are seeing. So, on the absence view, the relevant absence is that of any ripe tomato. *That* is what you experience as red. The content is an ordered pair of an absence of any ripe tomato and redness, or a possible state of affairs structured out of these items,[10] where the relevant absence presumably is a concrete entity existing wherever ripe tomatoes do not and thus varying in its location with variations in the locations of ripe tomatoes. But then how can you experience that entity? How can *that* entity look any way to you?

A third possible proposal is that the gap filler in the ordered pair is a spatio-temporal region. On this proposal, in hallucinating a red object, one is experiencing a particular spatial region as red. This seems plainly misguided, however. Spatial regions do not look red, so one cannot experience them as red. Perhaps it will be suggested that, in hallucination, one experiences a specific spatial region as filled by *an* object having so-and-so properties, for example, redness. The trouble now is that if one says this for the hallucinatory case, one should say it for the veridical case too, at least if one wants to avoid the earlier mentioned implausible and unlovely asymmetry. The price paid is that the seen object in the veridical case is no longer in the content. In its place is the spatial region occupied by the object. But that is not what one sees.

Another difficulty for the spatial region proposal is that it is very unclear which region is to serve to fill the gap in the content. Suppose, for example, you are in a dark room and you hallucinate a sudden bright pinpoint of light. It could be that your experience does not locate the light at any particular distance away from you. So, which spatial region in the room is the one that you are experiencing as being occupied by the light? There is no obvious answer.

It seems to us that the net effect of these reflections is to cast serious doubt on the wisdom of the idea that the gap in a gappy content should be filled. Whatever role gappy content plays in hallucinations, it can't be a species of ordered-pair content. What are the remaining alternatives?

Perhaps we should try to think of gappy content as something that aspires to be an ordered pair of a certain sort, but fails to achieve that status. With this in mind, let us consider next what we shall call "the mailbox proposal". A mailbox has a slot that is designed to take letters. The slot may be empty or it may have a letter placed in it. Perhaps we should think of the content of a visual experience as being like a mailbox. In the veridical and illusory cases, there is a structure (the mailbox) containing an object (the letter placed in the slot). In the hallucinatory case, there is the same structure but no object (letter in the slot).

---

[10] Obviously we are over-simplifying here, since the content of visual experience is extremely rich. But this makes no difference for present purposes and so we ignore it.

The immediate trouble with this proposal is that, as it stands, it offers no illumination as to truth or accuracy conditions and so one may reasonably ask what it has to do with content at all. However, this worry can be overcome by complicating the mailbox model a little. Suppose that the mailbox is designed to take letters for a certain range of zip codes and only for those zip codes. Then no mistake has been made by the person posting a letter just in case the letter in the mailbox has one of the right set of zip codes. Analogously, it may be suggested, a visual experience is accurate (true) if and only if the seen object (the "letter" in the "mailbox") has the property it appears to have (a "zip code" within the allowed range). Now where there is no "letter" in the "mailbox" or a disallowed "zip code", the condition on the right-hand side of the bi-conditional is not met and the experience is inaccurate or false.

Leaving aside the point that the model proposed here is grossly oversimplified given the richness of perceptual content, a general worry remains.

Just what IS gappy content here? It isn't the mailbox. As already noted, that isn't content at all. Nor is it an ordered pair consisting of the mailbox and a range of zip codes. For that is present in veridical cases (cases in which there is a letter in the mailbox with a permissible zip code for delivery from that mailbox). Clearly, something further needs to be added. But what? Perhaps we should say that gappy content is an ordered pair of the empty slot in the mailbox and a range of zip codes. The trouble now is that we are back to a variant of one or other of the earlier ordered-pair proposals: in place of the empty set or an absence or a spatio-temporal region, we now have an empty slot. And the person who is hallucinating experiences (and thus is conscious of) that slot! No genuine progress has been made.

It might be suggested that what the mailbox model is really gesturing towards is a view of gappy content as schematic content of a certain sort. Consider an open sentence of the form "Fx", where "x" is a variable and "F" a predicate for a specific property (or cluster of properties). The initial thought is that in the hallucinatory case, the visual experience is like the open sentence, "Fx", whereas in the veridical and illusory cases, it is like the closed sentence "Fa", where "a" refers to the object seen. Since in the hallucinatory case, there is no value for the variable—no seen object—the visual experience is either false, or neither true nor false, depending on the semantics devised for open sentences. If, for example, it is held that "Fx" is true iff the value of "x" is F, then where there is no value, the right-hand side of the bi-conditional is false, so the left-hand side is false too, in which case, on a two-valued semantics, "Fx" is false.

These remarks do not yet provide us with a clear account of what the gappy content is supposed to be in the hallucinatory case. And here there remains a puzzle. To appreciate this, note that in the open sentence "Fx", there are two component parts: the predicate "F" and the variable "x". The counterpart to "F" in the gappy content of a visual experience is the property of being F, as it is in the singular content case. What is the counterpart to the variable "x"? It looks as if we have to say, as before, that it is something like a slot in a mailbox. Gappy content, then, presumably is an ordered pair consisting of the empty slot and the relevant property or complex of properties. But now we are back with a version of the ordered-pair view and all of the obscurity that goes with it.[11]

Furthermore, if we do make this proposal about gappy content then, to preserve uniformity, we ought to say that singular content is an ordered pair consisting of the filled slot and the relevant property. Unfortunately, this is too general. Not just any old filling of the slot will do in the singular case. We need one particular filling—that provided by the seen object—so that the singular content is now something like the following structure (where P is the relevant property and CONJ the truth function for conjunction):

< CONJ << the relation of filling, < a, the slot >>, < the property P, a >>>

Modifying the account of gappy content correspondingly, we have:

< CONJ << the relation of filling, < –, the slot>>, < the property P, – >>>

where – is the absence of any seen object or some other dubious item. Obviously, we are getting nowhere.

Perhaps we should think of the content of a hallucinatory experience as being like a tree structure. The model in this case is the tree structure linguists take sentences to have. On this proposal, in veridical and illusory cases, when one experiences an object O, as red, the structure has two branches, each of which has an entity at the end:

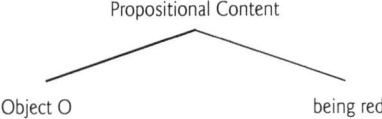

Figure 2a

The left-hand branch is reserved for objects and the right-hand one for 1-place properties. In the hallucinatory case, there are the same two branches but the left-hand one is empty:

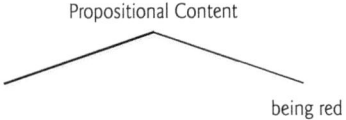

Figure 2b

---

[11] Barwise and Perry (1981) call the propositional analogs of variables "indeterminates". As applied to the case of the content of hallucinatory experience, this does not help with the earlier worries.

In linguistics, the tree structure for a sentence is not a part of the sentence. Rather when linguists talk of a sentence as having a certain tree structure, they are saying that the parts of the sentence are related in a certain tree-like way. On this view, in the veridical and illusory cases, the content is to be understood as follows:

< Quasi-branching relation Q, < O, the property of being red>>

Here Q is the worldly counterpart of the linguistic branching relation connecting the constituents of the sentence "O is red". Accuracy conditions are now straightforward. The experience is accurate just in case O bears quasi-branching relation, Q, to redness. Given that the same two-term relation, Q, is part of the content in the hallucinatory case, it seems that the gappy content must be this:

< Quasi-branching relation Q, < -, the property of being red>>

But this isn't coherent unless "–" picks out an entity, in which case we have made no progress. By definition, every branch in a tree (as understood in graph theory) needs two nodes: there cannot be a branch with just one node.

There is also a lack of clarity in the appeal to quasi-branching relation Q. Perhaps Q is supposed to be what some have called "the exemplification tie" linking objects and properties. If so, then, in the veridical and illusory cases, the visual experience must be counted as accurate just in case O exemplifies redness, in which case the ordered pair of O and redness would serve just as well as the content and we really are back to square one.

There is a more complicated alternative in the general area of the last proposal worth considering. Suppose, following Jeff King (2007), we take the propositional content that O is red to be a worldly *fact* (or obtaining, actual state of affairs), specifically, the fact of O's standing in relation R to the property of being red, where this is to be unpacked as follows:

> The propositional content that O is red = the fact of there being lexical items *a* and *b* of some language L such that O is the semantic value of *a*, where *a* occurs at the left terminal node of the sentential relation S that in L encodes the instantiation function, and *b* occurs at S's right terminal node and has as its semantic value the property of being red.[12]

Then it might be proposed that we can extend King's view to handle the case of hallucinatory content in the following way. Where the person hallucinating seems to see O and it seems to her that O is red, the content of her experience is the fact of there being lexical items *a* and *b* in a language L such that *a* has no semantic value and *a* occurs at the left-hand terminal node of the sentential relation S that in L encodes the instantiation function and *b* occurs at S's right terminal node and has the property of being red as its semantic value.

---

[12] This oversimplifies King's proposal minimally. For King's motivations for such a view, see his (2007). King takes his account to explain the unity of a proposition as well as the constitutive link (as he sees it) between propositions and language.

This does seem to us coherent. But it is complicated and it requires that facts about language be part of the content of visual experience. This seems to us counterintuitive, especially if it is accepted that experiences themselves are more like maps or pictures than linguistic representations (see below). Perhaps the proposal could be made more viable by allowing the relevant scheme of representation to be internal and nonlinguistic in character; but obviously this would necessitate further revisions since there would be no relevant sentential relation S. And there would still be the counterintuitive requirement that facts about the system of representation be part of the content.

The upshot is that the prospects for understanding the putative gappy content of visual experience are very gloomy. It behooves us to look for a better alternative.

8.3 An Alternative View of the Content of Visual Experience

Visual experiences are not like conscious thoughts. As we observed earlier, one can think that there is a ball on a box without one's thought representing anything further about the ball and the box; but one cannot have a visual experience of a ball on a box without one's experience representing such things as the color of the ball, the color of the box, the relative size of the two, the shape of the box, the viewer-relative locations of the ball and the box, and so on. Visual experiences, in representing one thing, represent many. In this way, visual experiences are like maps or pictures whereas thoughts are like sentences. Visual experiences are representationally rich. It is tempting to infer from this that the content of visual experience must be correspondingly rich. But this is a mistake. It falsely assumes that a property of the vehicle of representation (the experience) must be a property of its content. Structure in a representation need not be mirrored in structure in its content.

This point applies not just to experiences but to thoughts as well, even though they lack the representational richness of experiences. Consider the thought that Vulcan is a planet. The thought is structurally complex, being composed of the concept VULCAN and the concept PLANET, combined in a certain way (rather as the sentence "Vulcan is a planet" is composed of the words "Vulcan" and "planet" in a certain order). However, according to originalism, the content of the thought is not structurally complex. The content is just a set of possible worlds—the set of worlds in which the referent of the concept VULCAN has the property referred to by the concept PLANET (the property attributed by the thought). Since the concept VULCAN has no referent either in the actual world or in any other possible world, the relevant set of possible worlds is empty.

Correspondingly, experiences are complex. They have representational parts. Some parts represent objects seen (if there are any); others represent properties of which the subjects of the experience are conscious. The latter representational parts are arguably more like features (as is the case with real pictures), and so in one sense they are not really parts at all but rather features of parts. But however this is developed further, a complexity in representational structure for experiences need not be reflected in a corresponding complexity in representational content.

Once this point is appreciated, given the difficulties already encountered in trying to understand gappy content, a natural suggestion is that the content of a visual experience is simply a set of possible worlds, namely the set of worlds at which the experience is accurate. On this view, the content of a visual experience is unstructured in the sense that it has no component *parts*.

This suggestion preserves uniformity in content for all experiences. Experiences, whether they are veridical, illusory, or hallucinatory, have associated with them an appropriate set of possible worlds. An experience is accurate if and only if the actual world belongs to the appropriate set of possible worlds. Which is the appropriate set? Answer: the set of worlds at which the objects picked out by representational parts of the experience have the properties the experience aims to attribute to those objects (however this is further cashed out). The objects thus picked out are the objects (if any) that are seen. Where there are no seen objects, as in a hallucination, there are no possible worlds at which the objects picked out by the representational parts of the experience have the experienced properties. So, the set of worlds associated with a hallucinatory experience is the empty set.[13]

What, then, of the reasons given at the beginning of the chapter for the view that seen objects are components of the contents of visual experiences? Consider first this reasoning from earlier on:

1. If person P sees an object, it looks some way to P.
2. If an object looks some way to P, then it is experienced *as* being some way.
3. If an object is experienced as being some way, then it is a component part of the content of the experience (assuming that the experience has a content).

So,

4. If P sees an object, the seen object itself is a component part of the content of the experience, assuming that experience is representational at all.

The premise we reject is (3). If a given object, O, is experienced as being some way then the experience represents O as being some way (e.g. red). But this is now cashed out further in terms of the experience having as its representational content the set of possible worlds at which O is that way (red). And O is not part of the content of the experience.

Of course, the set of possible worlds at which an experience that is about O is accurate has members, namely possible worlds, each of which has O as a component part (whether

---

[13] On this view, (rather obviously) experiences are not to be individuated simply by their phenomenal character. The experience of seeing something, O, and experiencing it as red, has a different content (set of possible worlds associated with it) than does the experience of hallucinating something red, even though the experiences have (or may have) the same phenomenal character. The former experience has the set of possible worlds at which O is red as its content (and there are many such worlds); the latter experience has the empty set as its content.

one supposes that worlds are maximal states of affairs or (implausibly) concrete configurations of objects). But O is not a component part of that set, any more than my heart is a component part of the set whose members are me and my mother.[14] So, O is not a part of the content of the experience.[15]

Even though O is not a part of the experience, the experience remains crucially dependent on O. This is because the content of the experience is specified by reference to O as the set of worlds at which O is red. Thus, given that in actuality there is such an object as O, had things been different and O not existed, neither would the experience occasioned in actuality by P's seeing O (assuming the content of the experience is essential to it).

The same points can be made in the case of thought on originalism's austere view of thought content. The thought that Cicero is an orator is a thought about Cicero. It is about Cicero in virtue of its having an atomic nominative concept that refers to Cicero. The thought attributes the property of being an orator to the person so referred to. The content of the thought is the set of possible worlds at which Cicero is an orator and the thought is true since the actual world is a member of that set. That content does not contain Cicero as a component part even though the thought is about Cicero, and even though that thought would not have existed had Cicero not existed.

The second piece of reasoning offered earlier for the view that the seen object is in the content of the experience went as follows:

5. In cases of illusion, the seen object appears other than it is.
6. If the seen object appears other than it is, then the visual experience is inaccurate.

The best explanation of such inaccuracy is

7. Where there is a seen object, a visual experience has a content into which the seen object enters along with its apparent properties, so that the experience is accurate if and only if the object has those apparent properties.

We deny that (7) really is the best explanation of the relevant inaccuracy. If the content of a given visual experience is a set of possible worlds at which the seen object, O, has the properties, P_1-P_n, attributed to it by the experience then we have an equally good explanation of the inaccuracy for the case in which O appears other than it is. In that case, the actual world is not a member of the set of worlds at which O has the properties, P_1-P_n and O is not a component part of the content.[16,17]

---

[14] Set membership should not be confused with the part–whole relation. The former is irreflexive, asymmetric and intransitive; the latter reflexive, asymmetric and transitive.

[15] Earlier, we assumed that the members of an ordered pair are parts of the ordered pair. This assumption might be challenged on the grounds that ordered pairs can be defined set-theoretically (e.g. on Wiener's definition, <a,b> := (((a), the empty set), ((b))), in which case they have sets as their parts. The trouble here is that there are too many equally good definitions and thus too many equally good candidates. We should accept all or none of them. We can't accept all of them because they are in conflict. So, we should accept none.

[16] As above, the experience will remain dependent on O even though O is not part of the content.

[17] It may be wondered whether the views we have sketched above with respect to the content of visual experience have consequences for the thesis of representationalism (Tye 1995, 2000), with respect to the phenomenal character of visual experience. For a discussion of this issue, see Tye forthcoming.

8.4 The Epistemic Role of Experiences

Traditional empiricist views of experiences take experiences to be mere sensations—states without any representational content. If, for example, something looks red and round to you then, according to the empiricist view, you are subject to a red, round sense impression. The Given consists in such sense impressions. Your senses deliver up to you impressions in a mechanical way and, on the basis of these sense impressions, you then go on to form beliefs about your environment. In *Mind and World*, John McDowell objects to the Given on the grounds that it cannot account for how "experience [can] count as a reason for holding a belief" (14). He says: "We cannot really understand the relations in virtue of which a judgment is warranted except as relations within the space of concepts: relations such as implication or probabilification, ... " (1994: 7).

McDowell's target is wider than traditional empiricism. He also argues that the view that perceptual experiences have nonconceptual contents is susceptible to the same criticism. In making this charge he is not alone. Bill Brewer (2005), following McDowell, puts the complaint as follows:

1. Sense experiences supply reasons for empirical beliefs.
2. Sense experiences supply reasons for empirical beliefs only if they have conceptual content.

So,

3. Sense experiences have conceptual content.

McDowell himself says much the same thing:

[W]e can coherently credit experiences with rational relations to judgement and belief, but only if we take it that spontaneity is already implicated in receptivity; that is, only if we take it that experiences have conceptual content. (1994: 162)

Both McDowell and Brewer are Fregeans about belief content. They suppose that belief contents involve Fregean senses and thus individuate in a very fine-grained way. In claiming that experiences must have conceptual contents in order to enter "the space of reasons", what they are supposing is that experiences must also have Fregean contents. In their view, there aren't two sorts of content, nonconceptual and conceptual, mysteriously related, but one shared by both experience and belief (or judgment). McDowell comments:

A judgment of experience does not introduce a new kind of content, but simply endorses the conceptual content, or some of it, that is already possessed by the experience on which it is grounded. (McDowell 1994: 48–9)

The first thing to note about this criticism of the nonconceptual content thesis for experiences, is that it assumes that those who endorse that thesis hold that experiences have a different sort of content from belief. Matters are not so simple, however.

Consider the case of visual experience. On the usual minimal understanding of the nonconceptual content thesis, a visual experience E has a nonconceptual content if and only if (i) E has correctness conditions; and (ii) the subject of E need not possess the concepts used in a canonical specification of E's correctness conditions. This thesis does not preclude the nonconceptual content of a visual experience from being the content of a thought of another subject. For what makes the content nonconceptual for subject, S, is simply the fact that S need not herself have the relevant concepts and thus need not herself be in a position to form the relevant thought. Moreover, the nonconceptual content of an experience E, of a subject S, can even be the content of a thought of S, given the above thesis. All that is required in such a case is that S *need not* possess the pertinent concepts in order to undergo the experience: were S to lose the concepts and with them the capacity to have such a thought, that would not preclude her from having the experience, if the content of the experience is nonconceptual.

Given the minimal (but also widely held) understanding of the thesis of nonconceptual content, there need be no distinction between the nature of conceptual content and that of nonconceptual content. All the minimal thesis requires is that visual experiences be contentful nonconceptual states, where a contentful nonconceptual state is a contentful state, the tokening of which does not involve the exercise of concepts. So, understood, the criticisms by McDowell and Brewer simply miss the point.

There is a second more robust understanding of the thesis that experiences have nonconceptual contents. On this understanding, experiences have contents that are non-Fregean and coarse-grained in their individuation conditions. As such, their contents are supposedly fundamentally different from the contents of beliefs. It seems clear that it is really this version of the nonconceptual content thesis, traceable to Evans (1982), that McDowell and Brewer are opposing in the remarks quoted above. They hold that experiences provide reasons for beliefs and, whatever else reasons are, they are surely things that can be believed, whether or not they are actually believed by the subjects of the experiences. So, the McDowell/Brewer criticism in a nutshell is that if the contents of experiences are themselves robustly nonconceptual then they cannot provide reasons for beliefs—they cannot enter the space of reasons.

What is to be made of this criticism? From the perspective of the views developed in this book, it is largely misguided. It assumes that beliefs have Fregean contents and then chastises the nonconceptual content thesis for making the contents of experience non-Fregean, thereby undermining their justificatory role. On the originalist account, however, belief content is not Fregean. It does not individuate in a fine-grained way. The content of a belief is simply the set of possible worlds at which the belief is accurate or true. Given our remarks in the earlier sections of this chapter, the same holds for the content of an experience. So, there is no fundamental difference between belief content and experience content. This being the case, when a belief is formed in the normal way on the basis of an experience, there is no difficulty in grasping how the content of the experience can imply or probabilify the content of the belief.[18] In the case of implication, *every* world at which the experience is accurate is a world at which the belief is true. In the case of probabilification, *most* possible worlds that are relevantly similar to the actual world and at which the experience is accurate are worlds at which the belief is true.[19] So, there is no difficulty in grasping how the experience can provide a reason for having the belief.

Of course, to say that a person's experience *provides* a reason for holding a given belief is not to say that the person *has* a reason to hold that belief. *Having* a reason, q, to believe that p requires that one believe q; q's *providing* a reason to believe that p does not.[20] Suppose, for example, that Edgar has a heart condition. That Edgar has a heart condition provides a reason to believe that Edgar will die early; but it may not be a reason Edgar actually has to believe that he will die early. Perhaps Edgar has never seen a doctor and is unaware of his heart problem.

This point is relevant to the following worry. Suppose that you are standing before Dr Jekyll, dressed in his customary physician's garb. Your visual experience warrants you in believing that Dr Jekyll is present. But does it warrant you in believing that Mr Hyde is present, if you have no idea that Dr Jekyll is Mr Hyde?

The right thing to say here, it seems to us, is that on at least one understanding of "warrant," your experience does indeed warrant or justify the belief that Mr Hyde is present; for the content of your experience probabilifies the content of the belief. Given that in actual fact Dr Jekyll is Mr Hyde, at most of the possible worlds that are relevantly similar to the actual world and at which your experience is accurate, Mr Hyde is present. Accordingly, your experience provides a reason for believing that Mr Hyde is present. Even so, if the only pertinent evidence you have is that supplied by your visual experience, you do not *have* a reason to believe that Mr Hyde is present. Having a reason, as noted above, involves belief, belief involves concepts, and thus a situation in which certain concepts are not triggered will be one in which, even if *there is* a reason involving those concepts, you will not *have* it. It follows that in any stronger sense of "warrant" that requires that you *have* a reason for the belief, you are *not* warranted in believing that Mr Hyde is present.

There remains a potential worry. Suppose you are facing a tomato in good light; intuitively your experience at least *puts you in a position* to have a reason to believe of

---

[18] In our view, talk of contents implying or probabilifying contents is best understood in terms of content bearers standing in such relations. In this case, the relevant content bearers are experiences and beliefs. This view is reflected in the accounts of implication and probabilification in the text.

[19] Probabilification is relative to a contextually determined condition of relevance. Suppose a subject sees a real barn in fake barn country, and so has an accurate experience, and on this basis believes (truly, as it happens) that there is a barn before him. Suppose all the other 9 barns within 100 ft are fakes, and that it was equally likely that he would at that moment have seen any of the 10 barns. Then 9/10 "relevantly similar" worlds are ones in which his belief that there is a barn before him is false, so the experience does not probabilify the belief. Now suppose that apart from the 9 fakes within 100 ft, all the other 990 barns within 1,000 ft are real, and he was as likely to have seen any one of these. If we consider this larger circle, 991/1,000 "relevantly similar" worlds are ones in which his belief that there is a barn before him is true. The issues are evidently tricky, but not specially so for our theory.

[20] Cp. Byrne (2005). See also ibid. for further discussion of the reason-playing role of experiences.

the tomato that it is red, whether or not you actually have such a reason, or indeed whether or not you endorse your experience and believe that the tomato is red. How does your experience do that on the nonconceptualist view?

The answer, it seems to us, is that your experience supplies a reason to believe that the tomato is red. So, if you also have the concepts needed to have some particular reason for believing that the tomato is red, your experience puts you in a position to have that reason. If it is now replied that for the experience to put you in a position to have a reason, you should be able to recognize the reason *as* a reason to believe that the tomato is red, we disagree. In general, subjects are very bad at recognizing their reasons. But whatever one thinks of the merits of introducing a reason-recognizing condition, it should be clear that this presents no special problem for nonconceptualism. Recognizing a reason as a reason is itself a belief-like state and there is nothing in the thesis of nonconceptualism about visual experiences that precludes the subject from being in a belief-like state of this sort.

If our objector continues by claiming that no general account is available to the nonconceptualist of how the transition is made from experiences to beliefs or belief-like states, we respond that the transition is straightforward at least in the simplest case. The content of the experience is conceptualized by the subject and then endorsed. The process of conceptualization respects content preservation. What could be simpler than that?

Obviously this is not the place to flesh out these suggestions into a full epistemological theory. Even so, we maintain that once originalism, as we have developed it, is embraced, there is no obvious difficulty in seeing how experiences could have a suitable place within the space of reasons. And this is the case notwithstanding the fact that experiences, in our view, have nonconceptual contents.[21]

8.5 The Knowledge Argument

This famous argument was laid out informally in Chapter 1 (pp. 15–16). Mary is a color scientist who has been trapped in a black and white room for her entire life. By studying the books in her room and consulting her many computers (with grayscale monitors), she comes to know all the physical facts pertaining to color vision. Yet there is something she doesn't know: what it is like to experience red. This Mary finds out when she leaves her room and is shown something red for the first time. Since she knows all the physical facts, what she discovers must be a non-physical fact. Therefore, physicalism is false.

One way of regimenting the argument that fits nicely with Jackson's original essay (1982) and also with some more recent statements (e.g. Nida-Rümelin 2002) is as follows:

---

[21] We hold that experiences have nonconceptual contents both in the minimal sense distinguished earlier and in the stronger sense of having coarse-grained, non-Fregean contents. Beliefs, on our view, do not have nonconceptual contents in the minimal sense, but they do have nonconceptual contents in the stronger sense.

1. In her room Mary knows all the physical facts pertaining to color vision.
2. After Mary leaves her room and sees something red, she comes to know something new (something she cannot know in her room).

Therefore,

3. After Mary leaves her room, she comes to know a non-physical fact.

Therefore,

4. Physicalism is false.[22]

8.6 Knowing What It Is Like

What is it exactly that Mary comes to know? The obvious answer is that when she is shown a red object, she comes to know what it is like to see red; when she is shown a green object, she comes to know what it is like to see green; and so on. But what is it to know what it is like to see a given color?

The semantic treatment usually accorded in linguistics to sentences containing embedded questions (that is, embedded clauses that are interrogatives) has it that they are true if and only if the relevant subjects know some proposition that is a legitimate or acceptable answer to the embedded question. Thus,

Rupert knows where the pub is

is counted as true if and only if Rupert knows some proposition that is a legitimate or acceptable answer to the question, "Where is the pub?"

In general, what counts as an acceptable answer to an embedded question is context-relative. Consider Rupert. Suppose that all Rupert knows is that *here* is where the pub is. Rupert has been blindfolded and taken to the relevant pub. Since he has no idea as to where the pub is located, it seems strange to count what he knows as an acceptable answer to the question "Where is the pub?" But we can imagine a context in which it is an acceptable answer. Imagine that Rupert is not blindfolded and that he has been searching for hours for a particular pub. Finally, he sees a side street that seems familiar to him and, convinced that the pub is nearby, he goes into a building with the intention of asking where the pub is. Suddenly out of the blue it dawns on him that he is actually inside the relevant pub. "The pub is here!" he announces wearily to a friend. Rupert now knows where the pub is.

If the standard semantics is correct, knowing what it is like to see red is knowing an acceptable answer to the question, "What is it like to see red?" But what is an acceptable

---

[22] The above statement of the knowledge argument is not the only one. Sometimes, the argument takes a different form that ties it to apriori reasoning (see, e.g., Chalmers 1996, 2004a; Jackson 2004). For more detail, see Tye (2009).

answer? Philosophers generally agree that Mary in her black and white room does not know what it is like to see red. But, of course, Mary does know various facts about the experience of red and its phenomenal character; for she can "triangulate each color experience exactly in a network of resemblances and differences" (Lewis 1990: 502). She knows, for example, that seeing red is like seeing orange but not like seeing green, that seeing red is like seeing purple but not like seeing lime, and so on. So, citing these similarities and differences cannot count as providing an *acceptable* answer to the question, "What is it like to see red?", else Mary would know what it is like to experience red. What, then, would?

It seems to us that intuitively the right thing to say is that an acceptable answer for this case is that seeing red is (phenomenally) like *this*, where *this* is an experience having the phenomenal character of the experience of red.

It might be objected that one can know what it is like to see a given color at times when one is not experiencing the color either via the use of one's eyes or via a phenomenal memory image. Right now, for example, both of us know what it is like to experience red, but neither of us is imaging or seeing anything red either. So, it might be held, right now we do not know that seeing red is like *this*, where this is an actual experience of red.

A natural reply is that a person's knowledge of the relevant demonstrative fact does not require that she now undergo an occurrent, conscious thought deploying the concept THAT. It suffices that she be in a dispositional epistemic state that *can* manifest itself in consciousness in the appropriate demonstrative thought, whether or not it actually does so (where the demonstrative concept at play in the thought refers to the phenomenal character of the experience of red). The knowledge state thus is one she can be in even when she is fast asleep.

When Mary comes to know that this is what it is like to experience red (and thereby what it is like to experience red), the demonstrative concept she uses in her knowledge is one that she did not possess or exercise in her room. It is a new concept, the identity of which is tied to its origin. That origin derives from Mary's attending for the first time to her own experience of red when she leaves the room. Of course, Mary in the black and white room does possess *a* demonstrative concept that she can apply, via a cerebroscope or some such other device, to the physical state with which the physicalist identifies the phenomenal character of the experience of red, as it occurs to someone outside the room whose physical make-up Mary is remotely viewing. But this is a different demonstrative concept having a different origin.

The upshot is that while Mary, located in her black and white room and viewing a cerebroscope trained on the brain of someone experiencing red, does know *an* answer to the question, "What is it like to experience red?", this answer would not be counted as acceptable in normal contexts. By the usual standards, the demonstrative concept operative in her knowledge has the wrong kind of origin and thereby is a contextually inappropriate demonstrative concept.

By contrast, you do know what it is like to experience red (unless you are an achromotope), since you know an answer to the above question that *is* acceptable in normal contexts. What you know is that experiencing red is like this, where the demonstrative concept your knowledge draws upon originates in an act of attending to the relevant phenomenal character in your own experience. The answer you know here is a *different* answer from the one Mary knows in her room viewing a cerebroscope. It uses a different (and contextually appropriate) demonstrative concept. So, there is no difficulty in holding that your answer is acceptable and Mary's is not.

8.7 Mary's Discovery

On this view, Mary makes a discovery when she leaves the room. But if physicalism is true, her discovery is a cognitive discovery yet not a possibility-eliminating discovery.[23] In this respect, it is like the discovery that Hesperus is Phosphorus or that Cicero is Tully. Everyone agrees that the last two discoveries are significant, even though they do not eliminate possibilities; so too is Mary's. If Mary's room is to ground an anti-physicalist conclusion, however, what is required is that Mary's knowledge in the black and white room leave some possibilities open: she needs to make a possibility-eliminating discovery when she steps outside.

Some physicalists say that the reason that Mary makes a cognitive discovery is that she acquires a new concept RED when she sees red for the first time. This is a position we emphatically reject. In her room, Mary has the concept RED. She acquired it by reading her books on color and color vision and scanning her computer screens. This concept is not one Mary herself introduced. She acquired it by being a member of our linguistic and concept-using community, a community in which there is a word expressing the concept. The concept RED Mary has in her room is one that originated long ago and whose identity is not tied to any facts about Mary's own color experience. Furthermore it is the very same concept RED she has outside the room. After all, the word "red" is surely not ambiguous. It expresses a concept that Mary has, on the originalist view, simply in virtue of being part of the community of users of the term "red". This position is bolstered by the further observation that the thought Mary has in her room, and that she expresses in a pessimistic mood one day by saying, "I'll never know what it is like to experience red", intuitively is logically inconsistent with the thought she expresses after leaving, when she sees something red and remarks, "I now know what it is like to experience red". This would not be the case if two different concepts for red were operative in her thought (one tied to experiencing red and one not). Intuitively the situation here is not like that which obtains with the thought that Cicero is an orator and the thought that Tully is not, where there are two concepts for a single individual and no logical contradiction (even though both thoughts cannot be true).[24]

The case of Marianna (Nida-Rümelin 1996, 2010) may seem to present a difficulty for the position we are taking on Mary. Marianna, like Mary, is also kept in a black and white room. One day she leaves the room and enters a Technicolor vestibule in which there are

---

[23] The distinction between these species of discovery is explained in Chapter 7, section 7.1.
[24] See Ball (2009); Tye (2009).

various patches on the walls of different colors. Staring at the red patch, it may be said, Marianna then knows for the first time what it is like to experience red. But since she does not know that the patch is red, she does not know that this (referring to the phenomenal character of her experience) is what it is like to experience red.

Marianna, as she stares at the red patch, does not know what it is like to experience red. Rather she knows what it is like to experience *that color*. For she knows that this (referring to the phenomenal character of her experience) is what it is like to experience that color. The general point here is that "knowing wh—" contexts are non-extensional. Co-referential terms may not safely be substituted salva veritate. Thus, for example, Samantha can know who John is without knowing who is the richest man in Austin, even if John is the richest man in Austin. When it comes to knowing-wh—, as for knowledge more generally, thoughts matter, not just their contents.

One final point remains. We hold that the new knowledge Mary acquires when she starts to see the hues is not only knowledge-that. She also acquires some new object knowledge. In particular, she comes to know the phenomenal character of the experience of red, and this is not a form of propositional knowledge at all. It requires personal acquaintance with the given phenomenal character. But it does not require any propositional knowledge.[25] We cannot argue for this claim here (see Tye 2009). It is the combination of these two kinds of new knowledge and their relationship that makes the case of Mary's epistemic change special.

In summary, we maintain that Mary makes a cognitive discovery but not a possibility-eliminating one. In coming to know what it is like to experience red, she comes to know that experiencing red is (phenomenally) like this, where the demonstrative concept at play in her knowledge was introduced into her mental economy via an act of attending to the relevant phenomenal character in her own visual experience. By attending to the phenomenal character in this way, she became acquainted with it and via her acquaintance, she knows it. So, knowing what it is like does involve object knowledge, or at least requires it. But object knowledge does not suffice for knowing what it is like. Physicalism is not refuted by the knowledge argument.

8.8 Conceivability: Preliminary Remarks

Before we can take up the case of zombies, some general stage setting is necessary. Recall the case of Peter and Paderewski. Peter, in the grip of an empirical falsehood (namely, that there are two Paderewskis), cannot detect the contradictory character of his beliefs. No amount of apriori reflection will tell Peter that the concept he expresses by "Paderewski," when he assents to "Paderewski has musical talent", is the same as the concept he expresses by "Paderewski" when he assents to "Paderewski lacks musical talent". On the

---

[25] We thus distinguish between knowing what it is like to experience red and knowing the phenomenal character of the experience of red. Marianna in the Technicolor vestibule knows the phenomenal character of the experience of red as she stares at a red patch but she does not know what it is like to experience red.

originalist view, Peter is in this situation because concept identity is tied to identity of origin and facts about origin are not available apriori to Peter.

The moral of the Paderewski story for present purposes can be brought out as follows. Philosophers usually suppose that if something is logically impossible then it can be revealed as such at least by an ideal apriori reasoner. However, the case of Paderewski shows us that something that no amount of apriori reflection reveals to be impossible may be impossible, even logically impossible and logically impossible in a very straightforward, potentially obvious way. Peter can calmly go through the things he believes and he won't discover any contradiction. It is certainly conceivable to Peter that both his belief that Paderewski has musical talent and his belief that Paderewski lacks musical talent can both be true. He believes that in fact both *are* true. But it's logically impossible for both to be true. Conceivability, even by an ideal apriori reasoner, does not entail logical possibility. At best, it provides a defeasible guide.

Perhaps it will be replied, following Kripke (1972), that a distinction needs to be drawn between veridical and illusory conceivability. Illusory conceivability occurs just in case we are under the illusion that we are conceiving of a situation, S, when in reality we are conceiving of a distinct situation, S'. We confuse S and S' because they are "epistemic duplicates": the world is presented in the same way to us no matter which situation we are in. On the Kripkean view, conceivability does guarantee logical possibility (indeed metaphysical possibility), but only when the conceivability is veridical or non-illusory.

A natural question to ask here is this: what is the relationship between S' and S? The answer is illustrated by a standard example. When we think of water, for example, we think of it as the colorless, odorless liquid that comes out of taps and fills lakes (or the watery stuff, for short). And so when we illusorily conceive of water without H_2O, we are really conceiving there being a unique watery stuff without H_2O. In such cases, we are in the grip of an illusion. What happens is that the world we are conceiving is presented to us in our thought (in part) via a contingent reference-fixer (e.g. "the watery stuff"), whose satisfaction in the conceived world misleads us into supposing that the thing satisfying the reference-fixer in the actual world (water) is thereby present in the conceived world.

One possible proposal, then, is that in the Paderewski case, when Peter conceives of a world in which Paderewski has musical talent and Paderewski lacks musical talent, the conceivability is illusory.

We offer two reasons for rejecting the claim that non-illusory conceivability entails possibility. First, consider the claim that there is a being whose essence includes existence. This claim has been advanced by those theists who take necessary existence to be part of supreme perfection. It is certainly conceivable that there is such a being. And this is the case even though there is no term in the sentence "There is a being whose essence includes existence", whose reference is fixed by a contingent reference-fixer (Yablo 1999). So, the conceivability is non-illusory. If non-illusory conceivability is a guarantee of metaphysical possibility then it follows that it is metaphysically possible that there is a being whose essence includes existence. Since it is necessarily true that there is such a being if it is true at all, given (S5), it follows that there actually is a being whose essence includes existence. This surely is not an acceptable proof. Non-illusory conceivability is not a guarantee of metaphysical possibility.[26]

Secondly (and more generally), the appeal to contingent reference-fixing for concepts or terms presupposes that it is apriori that the thing denoted by the expression or concept whose reference is fixed by a contingent reference-fixer is the thing having the properties attributed in it. In the case of water, for example, the idea is that water is presented to us in thought as the watery stuff and this could not be the case if it were not apriori that water is the watery stuff. Unfortunately it isn't apriori that water is the watery stuff; for we could discover that in the actual world, water isn't the watery stuff. There are perfectly coherent though far-fetched scenarios about the actual world in which it turns out that water isn't the watery stuff (see Chapter 2.4).

Returning now to Paderewski, there are no contingent apriori reference-fixers for the concept PADEREWSKI. It is not apriori that Paderewski is:

the famous musician called "Paderewski"
the politician named "Paderewski"
the man widely held to be a musician who is called "Paderewski"

and so on. For we can describe coherent scenarios in the actual world in which it turns out that Paderewski isn't any of these. When Peter thinks that Paderewski has musical talent, Paderewski is presented in his thought in exactly the same way as when he thinks that Paderewski lacks musical talent. Paderewski is presented as Paderewski.[27] So, there is no illusory conceivability in the Paderewski case. Peter non-illusorily conceives something impossible.

8.9 The Zombie Argument

The above claims about conceivability and possibility have consequences for the well known zombie argument against physicalism.[28] This argument can be laid out in several closely related ways, but the differences make no difference as far as our general response goes. We shall take the argument to go as follows:

1. A zombie replica of the actual world is conceivable.
2. If a situation S is conceivable in a non-illusory way then it is metaphysically possible.
3. A situation S is illusorily conceivable just in case it is not conceivable but an epistemic duplicate situation S' is conceivable.

---

[26] It is also non-illusorily conceivable that there is *no* being whose essence includes existence. So, if non-illusory conceivability entails metaphysical possibility, it follows that it is metaphysically possible that there is no such a being. Since (as noted in the text) the claim that there is a being whose essence includes existence is necessarily true, if it is true at all, it follows that the claim is false. We take it that this is not a satisfactory *disproof* of the existence of a being whose essence includes existence.
[27] Likewise in the case of water. When we think that water is wet, water is presented in our thought as water.
[28] Zombies are beings who are physically just like us down to the smallest detail but who lack phenomenal conciousness. There is nothing it is like to be a zombie.

4. There is no distinction between pain and an epistemic duplicate of pain (put another way: there is no distinction between pain and the way pain is presented in thought); likewise for other experiences.

So,

5. A zombie replica of the actual world is not illusorily conceivable (from (3) and (4)).

So,

6. A zombie replica of the actual world is conceivable in a non-illusory way (from (1) and (5)).

So,

7. A zombie replica of the actual world is metaphysically possible (from (2) and (6)).

But

8. If a zombie replica of the actual world is metaphysically possible then physicalism is false.

So,

9. Physicalism is false.

Our objection to this argument rests not with (4), which we are happy to accept. Our objection is that (2) is false. That, we maintain, is the upshot of the Paderewski example.[29]

One possible reply to our evaluation of the zombie argument is to grant that non-illusory conceivability is no guarantee of metaphysical possibility, but to insist that it is a defeasible guide. This is relevant, of course, only if in the zombie replica case there is no defeater. However, according to the physicalist, there *is* a defeater, namely the empirical hypothesis that every experience or phenomenal state is one and the same as some (broadly) physical state. This hypothesis, which is supported by causal considerations (specifically, evidence for the view that the physical world is causally closed), is necessarily true, if it is true at all and so it rules out the metaphysical possibility of a zombie replica of the actual world.

A second possible reply is to say that what really matters in arguing for possibility is imaginability. Chalmers (2002), for example, appeals to what he calls "primary positive conceivability" in arguing against physicalism, and as far as we can see, this amounts pretty much to imaginability. But even if the zombie argument is understood in this way, it is still unsuccessful.

This may be brought out by distinguishing two different senses of the term "imagine." There is a broad sense of "imagine" under which no imagery need be present. This can be illustrated by some examples from Alan R. White (1964): you can imagine that someone is trying to kill you; you can imagine a difficulty or an objection; you can imagine being

---

[29] It is also shown by the theistic example of Yablo's mentioned earlier.

Figure 3

persecuted. In this sense, one imagines something if and only if one supposes that something is the case and, as one thinks through one's supposition and its consequences, no contradiction reveals itself directly or indirectly in one's thought. Imagining in this broad sense is like conceiving, as discussed previously, and it adds nothing of significance to the appeal to conceivability in arguing against physicalist theories of consciousness.

There is a second kind of imagining: perceptual imagining. In this case imagery plays a crucial role. If one of us imagines a black dog, for example, the imagining involves an image. This is a case of perceptual imagination. However, imagining in this narrower partly imagistic sense is not a guarantee of possibility any more than conceivability is; for one can image the impossible just as one can perceptually experience it.

Here's a perceptual example. Consider Figure 3 above. Viewing such a figure in the right contrived perceptual circumstances, you can perceptually experience an impossible 3-D structure in space before you. It will seem to you that there is such a structure before you. Since there is plenty of evidence that the representations involved in visual imagery are similar to visual representations generated via the use of the eyes, one should expect that imagistic experiences can represent impossibilities too.

Here's a somewhat different example. We hold that in the perceptual sense, one can imagine a situation in which there are unicorns, even though such a situation is metaphysically impossible. We hasten to add that, in saying this, we are not supposing that a situation in which there are horses with horns on their heads is metaphysically impossible. Imaging a unicorn is not the same as imaging a horse with a horn on its head, any more than imaging a man carrying a pot of gold is the same mental act as imaging a man carrying a pot of fool's gold. Our assumption is that unicorns form a mythical species supposed to be uni-horned and horselike in appearance, just as tigers form an actual species with a characteristic striped appearance. We take it, then, that the concept UNICORN is empty and that, given its introduction in the context of a piece of myth telling, according to originalism and the essentiality of origin, the concept is necessarily empty. So unicorns are metaphysically impossible.

The upshot is that insofar as perceptual imaginability provides any evidence for what is possible, the evidence is defeasible. So again there is no mileage here for the anti-physicalist with respect to consciousness. The physicalist can insist that a zombie replica of the actual world, though imaginable, is metaphysically impossible and thus the argument against physicalism fails as before.

9

Objections and Replies

1. Objection (due to Paul Horwich): Your view entails that if two words express the same concept, replacing one by the other anywhere within a thought-expressing sentence will not affect the thought expressed. But this will give rise to versions of Mates cases. For example, assuming the concept GREEK = the concept HELLENE, if Pablo doubts whether all Greeks are Hellenes, he also doubts whether all Greeks are Greeks; but he does not!

Reply: Under the supposition, Pablo doesn't doubt whether all Greeks are Hellenes, and doesn't believe he doubts it. Before rushing to object that this is "counterintuitive", recall that the case depends upon a supposition which we regard as very improbable, and which we suspect has not been so much as considered until now: that the concept GREEK = the concept HELLENE.

Even under this supposition, originalism allows us to say that Pablo genuinely believes the falsehood that the concept GREEK ≠ the concept HELLENE, and so believes the falsehood that the thought that Greeks are Greeks is distinct from the thought that Greeks are Hellenes, and so believes the falsehood that the latter but not the former thought is open to doubt.

2. Objection (due to Mark Richard): Your solution to Mates cases is inadequate. For the following principle holds generally:

    (a) If S believes that *p*, then the thought that *p* is such that S believes it.

If the thought that *p* is the thought that *q*, then if the one is such that S believes it, so is the other. Applying to the "hard" Mates case (in which the concept HELLENE is in fact the concept GREEK, though Pablo does not know this), it seems one can move from

    (b) Pablo believes that he does not believe that all Greeks are Hellenes

to

    (c) the thought that all Greeks are Hellenes is such that Pablo believes he does not believe it.

But, on the present supposition, the thought that all Greeks are Hellenes is the thought that all Greeks are Greeks. Since Pablo believes (and believes he believes) that all Greeks are Greeks, it follows that

   (d) the thought that all Greeks are Greeks is such that Pablo does not believe he does not believe it.

Hence

   (e) the thought that all Greeks are Hellenes is such that Pablo does not believe he does not believe it.

Since (c) and (e) contradict, there remains a Mates paradox.

Reply: The objection conflicts with originalism in various ways. First, (d) is presumably derived as follows:

   (i) Pablo believes that he believes that Greeks are Greeks.
   (ii) Pablo does not believe that he does not believe that Greeks are Greeks.
   (iii) (d) [from (ii), applying (a)].

We reject the move from (i) to (ii). It's not in general the case that *anything* about what someone does *not* believe follows from what they *do* believe. This point, crucial to achieving a stable and satisfactory view about Paderewski cases, can be obscured by the fact that the relevant wide scope negation ("not believe") is hard to hear in English and other natural languages. "John doesn't believe that Fido barks" is normally not distinguished from "John believes that Fido does not bark".[1]

We are skeptical of principle (a), as should be apparent from the treatment of attitude ascriptions in Chapter 6. The thought in the mind of a subject that renders an attitude ascription true may not be the same as the thought displayed in the ascription. Principle (a), as naturally understood, and as it must be understood if the objection is to get off the ground, is inconsistent with this latitude.

3. Objection (due to Paul Boghossian): Two scientific groups, at different times, "come up with the same idea", introducing a new concept, say the concept NEUTRINO (for team A) and the concept NEUTRINO (for team B). By originalism, these are distinct concepts. Initially, the result might seem welcome, since

   Are neutrinos (as thought of by team A) neutrinos (as thought of by team B)?

is a substantive question (and so like "Is Hesperus Phosphorus?," rather than like "Is Hesperus Hesperus?"). But on your version of originalism, a concept may change its referent, giving rise to substantive questions like

   Is meat (as thought of in the fifteenth century) meat (as thought of today)?

---

[1] Hans Kamp stressed this point.

Hence there is no good reason to think that the teams came up with different concepts. We should therefore revert to the intuitive view that they reached the same concept independently, and this is inconsistent with originalism.

Reply: There is nothing in this case that makes it implausible to say that the teams introduced different concepts. As with Leibniz, Newton, and the concept INTEGRATION (Chapter 3), it may well be that the concepts are very similar, in that they have the same content and were introduced in response to the same problem. It also may well be that one concept comes to dominate (one team gets the Nobel prize, the work of the other is ignored); or that the two concepts fuse.

4. *Objection (due to Steven Schiffer):* Intuitively there are non-denumerably many true propositions. For example, for every number there is a true proposition to the effect that it is a number. But it seems there cannot be non-denumerably many thoughts, given the finite character of thinkers. So thoughts can't be the bearers of truth. We need propositions after all. These can be true even if they cannot be thought.

Reply: Propositions, as Schiffer thinks of them, are simply sequences of objects and properties. We are happy to agree with him about how many such sequences there are, but this has no relevance to originalism.

What matters for originalism is that the theory should not place incorrect restrictions on what is thinkable or on what is true. For each thinkable number, it is thinkable that it is a number. If there is a restriction on thinking this thought of a thinkable number, it is imposed by human psychology, not by the system of thoughts made available in an originalist theory.

Not all real numbers are thinkable, even "in principle". This is common ground, not specific to originalism. Unthinkable things are not describable, cannot figure in a humanly accessible proposition, and cannot be expressed by a sentence in any language with a finite base. Unthinkable propositions do not correspond to thoughts (or to sentences).

If there is an objection in this area, it is presumably that some unthinkable propositions are true, but are not thoughts. We regard truth as a relation between a representation and a fact (individuated in a coarse-grained way). There are unthinkable facts, but no truths that are *in principle* unthinkable, that is, truths whose unthinkability does not derive from contingent limitations of thinkers. We think anyone who agrees that truth is a property of representations must accept this. An unthinkable truth would involve a representation that in principle cannot be thought (yet that would be true). Originalism does indeed preclude such representations.

Schiffer introduces propositions as objects of propositional attitudes. If this is intended as a constitutive feature of propositions, he too should reject the view that there are unthinkable propositions.

5. *Objection (due to Hans Kamp):* Does not using a concept require knowing the analog of the grammatical category to which it belongs? For example, someone who took the concept

VULCAN to function as a verb (and who tried to think things like: Mercury is getting badly Vulcaned tonight) surely cannot use it correctly?

Reply: We agree that this person will not be able to think a true thought that contains the concept VULCAN, and so in that sense uses the concept VULCAN incorrectly (see also Objection 13). It is consistent with originalism to require that knowledge of the analog of grammatical category is needed for concept use, but we need further persuasion before imposing that requirement.

6. *Objection (due to Ruth Millikan):* When a child learns the public concept CAT, it presumably brings forward the information it already has about cats, however conceptualized. So it should follow, on your view, that the child is still using its prelinguistic concept for cats.

Reply: Accumulating information from the subject's past uses is not sufficient for sameness of concept. The central notion is deference to other uses. The child's dominant deference will be to uses by others in her surrounding community, from whom she will, for example, accept correction concerning which things are cats.

7. *Objection:* "[T]here has to be something that explains why John [aka Peter] isn't prepared to infer from his thoughts that Paderewski was a politician and that Paderewski was a pianist that someone was both a politician and a pianist. I can't think of anything...that will do so that isn't itself equivalent to the idea that Paderewski has two names in Mentalese" (Fodor 2008: 77).

Reply: Our alternative, adapted to Fodor's framework, is that Peter takes two occurrences of the same "mental name" to be occurrences of distinct "mental names". This response depends upon rejecting of *IKCC* (see Chapter 5), and is consistent with Peter using the same public concept on two occasions.

8. *Objection:* You have no adequate account of Peter's mental state when he believes that there are two Paderewskis. If the belief exercises the single concept PADEREWSKI, then it's not merely false, but obviously so. But it doesn't seem it can involve two concepts for Paderewski, and it was crucial to your account that there is just one concept.

Reply: There are two ways to give a more detailed characterization of Peter's mental state when he believes that there are two Paderewskis. One is metalinguistic: he believes that there are two people called "Paderewski". Alternatively, it may be that he thinks there is a person x who is Paderewski, and a person y who is Paderewski, and $x \neq y$.[2] These are both ways to characterize Peter's mental state without attributing to him a belief which, from his

---

[2] Brian Cutter stressed this option.

point of view, is obviously false, and without appealing to his having distinct concepts for Paderewski.

One would expect Peter to have many concepts for Paderewski (THAT PIANIST, THE MAN ON THE PLATFORM, etc.). This is consistent with his also using just one concept for Paderewski in forming the belief that Paderewski has musical talent and in forming the belief that Paderewski lacks musical talent.

9. *Objection:* You say that the content of a thought is a set of worlds. But why choose sets rather than their characteristic function? In general, is there not a Benacerraf-style problem with your choice of contents for thoughts: there are various options, with no good reason to choose among them?

Reply: This does raise a problem, but it is not special to originalism: anyone who uses possible worlds or sets thereof is exposed to the same issue. Originalists should adopt whatever turns out to be the best general resolution of it.

10. *Objection:* Swampman comes into existence with our concepts. But on your view this is impossible. This must count against originalism.

Reply: This issue affects most externalist views which assign relevance to history. Since, on one view,[3] belonging to a species is a matter of an individual's origin, and swampman has no origin of the right sort, he is not a member of any species; in particular, he is not human. Ruth Millikan has said that swampman does not have eyes, since an eye is an organ whose presence is to be explained in terms of descent from creatures whose fitness was increased in certain specific ways by the operation of that organ. Swampman's eye-like structures are present merely by chance, and so do not count as eyes. The implications are far-reaching: swampman doesn't see anything, assuming seeing constitutively involves using eyes, doesn't walk, assuming that walking involves use of legs, and legs, like eyes, are individuated historically; and so on.

The surprising character of this view can be diminished by reflecting that something just like an eye, but which is not an eye, can be as useful as an eye; and likewise for all the other features. Something just like a human, though not human, may be as loveable as a human, and as worthy of a place in our moral scheme. One might go further: in ordinary contexts, it would be silly to object to using the word "eyes" of swampman's light-sensitive frontal protuberances. They are not strictly eyes; but for most purposes we should engage in some loose talk.

These points apply equally to the question of whether swampman starts out with, or acquires, concepts. He certainly does not start out with them, assuming that originalism is true. While there is some temptation to say that he acquires them, in strict accuracy this

---

[3] Swampman would count as human on the view that one is a member of species S if one can produce fertile offspring in conjunction with a member of species S.

temptation must be resisted. Swampman does not have the appropriate kind of mental life to acquire concepts from interactions with others, or to create them for himself. He does not have the right kinds of deferential intentions unless he has intentions, but he has intentions only if he already has concepts. He does not have the right kind of perceptual attention to use as a basis for introducing concepts since, strictly speaking, he has no sense organs, and so does not perceive, and so lacks perceptual attention.

Just as non-eyes that are indistinguishable from eyes may be as good as eyes, so states that are just like conceptual states, but not strictly conceptual, may be just as useful. In most contexts, it would be silly to insist that swampman lacks concepts; we should engage in some loose talk. But in strict accuracy, we should say that swampman has as many concepts as eyes.

11. Objection: Events that occur at different times are distinct. So if Gell-Mann had introduced a concept for quarks at some other time, it would have been a different event of concept introduction, and so a different concept would have been introduced. But it is wildly implausible to say that if the introduction had happened a little earlier or later, the concept QUARK would never have been introduced.

Reply: The objection as stated is not cogent: from the principle that events that occur at different times are distinct, it does not follow that an event could not have occurred at any time distinct from the time at which it actually occurred.

It is hardly controversial to say that Gell-Man could have spent a couple of years studying law before becoming a physicist, so that his development of quark theory could have occurred two years later than it actually did. It is not obvious that it follows that the actual introduction of the concept QUARK could have occurred two years later—that depends on the scope of the modal operator in the uncontroversial claim.[4] So it seems there is likely to be controversy about whether concept-introductions could have occurred at times other than their actual times.

Suppose events are very modally fragile with respect to their time of occurrence, so that an event that in fact occurred at time t could not have occurred at any time t′, unless t′ is very close to t. Then if there are putative cases in which a concept could have been introduced at a significantly different time, they will need to be reinterpreted as cases in which a very similar concept could have been introduced at another time.

12. Objection: If, as you admit to be possible, the concept CAT is distinct from the concept CHAT, a Frenchman, Jacques, who believes something he would express with the words, "Les chats ont des queues", does not think the same as we think when we think that cats have tails. This is already wildly implausible, and leads to the further absurdity that it is strictly false that Jacques believes that cats have tails.

---

[4] As Brian Cutter stressed.

Reply: "Thinking the same" is a tricky notion, from every point of view (do Hume and Heimson think the same in thinking, as each does, that he is Hume?). One way to understand it is this: two subjects think the same iff there is a thought ascription true of both. On the originalist account of attitude ascription in Chapter 6, both we and Jacques think that cats have tails. In this sense, we think the same.

13. *Objection:* How do you distinguish between merely using a concept (possibly incorrectly) and using it correctly?

Reply: One may use a concept incorrectly in that one may apply it to something to which it does not apply; more generally, the concept may play a distinctive role in a number of false thoughts. Originalism has no place for any other view of "incorrect use". In the days when analyticity was more fashionable than it is now, it might have been supposed that a thinker who took the concept FORTNIGHT to refer to a period of ten days could not be using the concept "correctly", even in a thought that is in fact true (for example, the subject might truly think that his guests would stay for a fortnight). Originalism rejects this kind of distinction between correct and incorrect use. Similarly, as emphasized in Chapter 4, originalism has no use for any notion of grasping or understanding a concept that goes beyond simply using it.

14. *Objection:* Conceptual fusion is hard to understand. Suppose Gell-Mann's concept QUARK fused with Zweig's concept ACES to form the concept QUARK we now have. On your view, this means that Gell-Mann unwittingly switched from using his original concept QUARK to using the new concept QUARK. But there is no manifestation of this in his thought or behavior.

Reply: The objection depends on a behavioristic notion of manifestation, which we reject. In a sense, there is no manifestation that Tom is using the concept TWATER, rather than Tim's concept WATER. In a slow switching example, there is no manifestation of the change in the switched subject's conceptual repertoire. The example is more pertinent to externalism than originalism.

Conceptual fusion is probably not at all common. More commonly, one concept swamps another, which is perhaps what happened in the case in question.

15. *Objection:* Even if your originalism solved Frege-type puzzle for thoughts, it can't solve analogous puzzles for language. You need to explain why what is said by "Hesperus is visible" differs from what is said by "Phosphorus is visible". On your semantics there is no distinction of content. Since two words may express the same concept, your distinction of concepts will not be adequate to this task. So you have no resources to explain Frege-puzzles for language.

Reply: "What is said" is a slippery phrase, whatever one's theory (see the reply to Objection 12). A natural interpretation takes the phrase to refer to the thought expressed, rather than the content of the thought expressed. (This needs qualification in cases of indexicality.) Thus understood, what is said by "Hesperus is visible" differs from what is said by "Phosphorus is visible".

16. *Objection (due to Derek Anderson):* Suppose that one population P1 of users of the concept MEAT continues to use it with its original broad extension (so that their thought that spinach is meat is true), whereas in another population P2 the extension shrinks (as it has in fact in ours). It seems you are committed to the implausible view that if a member of P1 thinks that spinach is meat, and so does a member of P2, they think the same thought and yet the first thinks a true thought whereas the second thinks a false one.

Reply: That truth is a property of thoughts means that truth is a property of thought-tokens, rather as, in language, truth is a property of sentence-tokens not sentence-types. Tokens of the same thought-type may differ in truth value.

17. *Objection:* The several sons of Ali are gathered together to receive their names. The eldest will have the root name with the addition "Primus", and so on down to the tenth son ("Decimus"). Ali says "Your root name is Maji". The eldest son is thereby baptized Maji Primus, the second eldest Maji Secundus, and so on. Corresponding to the names, ten new concepts are introduced. But there is a single act of introduction, which is impossible according to originalism.

Reply: Ali has ten intentions: to name his eldest Maji Primus, his second Maji Secundus, and so on. His uttering the words "Your root name is Maji" is a complex event, with ten co-located component events. One analogy is with a billiard ball striking two adjacent balls. On one way of counting, there's just one event; on another way of counting there are two events, the striking of the one ball and the striking of the other. In Ali's case, the different intentions have different causes and effects, so are distinct. Hence the concepts corresponding to each of Ali's sons have different origins.

18. *Objection:* You say that concepts are individuated by their origins. But if that's right, then for the most part we can't individuate our concepts, since, as you admit, we typically don't know how or when they originated.

Reply: The objection runs together a metaphysical notion of individuation and an epistemic notion. Metaphysically, individuation is determined by principle (O) in Chapter 3 above:

(O) Necessarily: concept C1 = concept C2 iff the originating use of C1 = the originating use of C2.

This metaphysical principle is silent on the question of how we in practice individuate concepts in the epistemic sense.

As emphasized in Chapter 3, section 3.2, this epistemic question is quite different from the metaphysical one. On one interpretation, epistemic individuation involves knowing some metaconceptual fact, for example that the concept HESPERUS is distinct from the concept PHOSPHORUS. If it is granted that these concepts have different origins, one requires only Leibniz's Law to infer that they are distinct. That's one possible route to knowledge of individuative facts concerning concepts. Another route exploits distinctness of thoughts. For example, given that the thought that Hesperus is visible is distinct from the thought that Phosphorus is visible, distinctness of the concepts can be inferred. As we have emphasized, knowledge of this kind is not incorrigible.

Originalism thus makes room for various ways of attaining individuative knowledge of concepts. A concept can be used by a subject who has no relevant metaconceptual knowledge (as with small children). Which concept a subject is using is fixed, not by what metaconceptual knowledge the subject possesses, but by causal facts about the ancestry of the use.

19. Objection (due to Alex Byrne): Suppose someone introduces a concept for a certain kind of plant and then, in a single utterance, introduces two hitherto entirely unfamiliar distinct words usable to express the concept: "gorse" and "furze". Standard Mates and Frege cases will arise: reasonable people might wonder whether furze is gorse, but not whether furze is furze. By hypothesis, there is only one concept, so originalists cannot appeal to differences among concepts to explain the phenomenon.

Originalists presumably must classify this case as conceptual ignorance in the following sense: people use two words without realizing that the words express a single concept. But if originalists have to adopt this strategy for this case, why not adopt it for all, and so revert to a Millian view of concepts? The Millian will individuate concepts by their referents, and say that Frege cases are ones in which two words are wrongly taken to express distinct concepts. Applying the idea, the concept expressed by "Hesperus" is the concept expressed by "Phosphorus", but those who sincerely assert things like "Hesperus is seen in the evening, but not in the morning", do not realize this.

Reply: We can't accept the example in precisely its present form. Words are introduced for objects, not for the concepts they express. If someone introduces the words "gorse" and "furze" for what is in fact the same plant, two concepts for that plant are thereby introduced. Even if the introductions take place within what can be counted as a single event, say an utterance of "let's use 'furze' and 'gorse' indifferently for that plant", there are two concepts, and two originating events. The larger event is made up of a sub-event in which a concept expressed by "furze" is originated, and a distinct sub-event in which a concept expressed by "gorse" is originated. Compare my sweeping the beans into the pot. There is one event of sweeping the beans, but also many events of sweeping specific beans—sweeping bean A, sweeping bean B, and so on. As Frege famously said, counting is relative to a predicate, and the predicate "sweeping bean A" is distinct from the predicate "sweeping the beans". So we deny that Byrne's case is really one in which there is just one concept.

We do allow that there can be distinct words that express the same concept. (Such a case is discussed in Chapter 7, section 7.3.) However, we are not aware of any definite examples. If there are any, they are rare, and we deny that "intuitions" concerning them can be very robust. But let's waive these considerations, and pretend that the example works as stated. Would this make originalism no better than Millianism? There are two reasons for a decisive negative answer. (1) Millians still confront the problem of empty concepts, which are unproblematic for orginalists. (2) Millians of the kind envisaged in the objection confront the problem of cases in which not only are the concepts the same (by their lights), so too are the words. For example, in Evans' case of the long ship, the subject both accepts something expressed by "that ship was built in Japan" and rejects something expressed by the same words. A satisfying account requires two of something to explain the subject's different attitudes. In contrast to Millianism, originalism entails there are two concepts, and thus supplies a straightforward account of such cases. Millianism has nothing immediately on offer.

From the originalist perspective one would expect two kinds of error, one more common than the other. The common kind of error is failure to realize that two concepts have the same content. These are the Frege cases. But, as we argued in Chapter 5, people may also make mistakes about how many concepts are before their minds. This is a less common kind of error, and is exemplified by Paderewski cases as well as by the case Byrne aimed to introduce. Our distinction between mistakes about contents and mistakes about concepts corresponds nicely to the intuition that Frege cases primarily involve some kind of world-related ignorance, whereas Paderewski cases primarily involve ignorance about representations. Peter thought there were two Paderewskis, that is, two people called (represented by) "Paderewski".

20. *Objection (due to Paul Boghossian):*[5] Suppose that Peter is switched from earth to twin-earth but is not aware of the change. Suppose also that "cohabitationism" is the correct account of his subsequent conceptual state: he retains his old concept WATER, acquires the new concept TWATER, and he uses the word "water" for both concepts. Oversimplifying in a respect that will not affect the present discussion, typical past tense thoughts trigger uses of the concept WATER, as required for his remembering pre-switch episodes involving water, whereas uses involving all other tenses trigger applications of the concept TWATER, under the influence of his current conceptual community. Hence the Pavarotti argument

---

[5] We would like to thank Paul Boghossian, Agustin Rayo and Mark Richard for their valuable comments at the author-meets-critics session on the book at the Pacific Meeting of the American Philosophical Association, March 2013. We regret that space limitations prevent us responding to the other insightful criticisms we received on that occasion.

discussed on p. 99 ("Whoever floats on water gets wet, Pavarotti once floated on water, so Pavarotti got wet") is invalid, though Peter cannot detect this.

This example was initially offered as a reason to accept a thesis of transparency: rational thinkers have introspective access to sameness and difference among their thoughts (Boghossian 1992). Accepting transparency was offered as a reason to reject externalism. But if originalists commit to externalism, an argument for transparency can become an argument against originalism. The challenge is to explain how Peter can be rational, while being unable to detect the invalidity of Pavarotti-like arguments.

Originalists have the option of adopting either first-order or higher-order solutions. A first-order solution will say that Peter is rational provided he rationally holds some first-order belief that would make his reasoning valid. In the present case, this will involve his rationally believing that twater (figuring in the first premise) is water (figuring in the second). A second-order solution will say that Peter is rational, even if his first-order reasoning isn't valid, provided he rationally believes that it is. This would be so if, for example, he rationally believes the meta-conceptual proposition that the concept expressed by "water", as it occurs in the first premise, is the same as the concept expressed by "water" as it occurs in the second.

Against a first-order account, it is impossible to see how Peter could think the thought that twater is water. Given the kind of cohabitationist externalism being taken for granted, he cannot tell, given his ignorance of the switch, whether a use of "water" expresses the concept TWATER or the concept WATER. (Indeed, if we take the simplified cohabitationist's view about tenses seriously, a tenseless relevant identity thought must involve the concept TWATER both sides of the identity concept.) At a minimum, he would be unable to recognize the thought that twater is water. This makes it hard to see how his rationality could depend upon his thinking it rationally. It is also unclear how this idea might be extended to Paderewski cases.

There are various options for higher-order accounts, but they all lead to difficulties. For example, the critical false but rational-making belief cannot be that, in the Pavarotti argument, the occurrence of the concept WATER in the first premise is an occurrence of the same concept as the occurrence of the concept WATER in the second, since the concept WATER does not occur in the first premise. Moreover, attributing meta-conceptual thoughts faces two general difficulties: one is that they are highly sophisticated (and perhaps even embedded in originalist, or at least deeply theoretical, opinions), and so cannot be ascribed to every subject capable of Peter-like thinking; the other is that attaining these meta-conceptual thoughts involves inference, which raises anew the question of rationality and the possibility of rational logical error.

Since originalists cannot successfully appeal either to first-order or to higher-order accounts of Peter's rationality, they have no such account, and their theory needs modification.

The underlying worry is this. Good reasoning involves sensitivity to patterns of recurring elements and so involves the ability to recognize sameness and difference among occurrences of concepts. Simply adding more beliefs does not guarantee this ability unless the pattern of concept recurrence in the beliefs themselves is manifest to the thinker. Transparency reflects this need for the manifest character of patterns.

Reply: We agree that, in earlier chapters, we tended to give unduly meta-conceptual accounts of the rationality of some of the problematic subjects (e.g. Peter in twin earth cases, Peter in Paderewski cases). We also agree that, even if meta-conceptual beliefs may sometimes appropriately feature in explanations, the basic phenomenon may arise in subjects not capable of meta-conceptual thought. There are two crucial points: one is that a subject may be rational in *not* believing something; the other is that a subject may rationally *treat* concept-uses as uses of the same concept, or uses of a different concept, without having meta-conceptual beliefs. Not believing something does not require the exercise of concepts; and *treating* uses as uses of the same concept does not require *believing* that the uses are uses of the same concept (such a belief would require possession of the concept CONCEPT).

These considerations can be applied to the question of whether *we* are rational in believing that the Pavarotti argument is valid. By "we" we mean ordinary people, who may have no philosophical training and may never have heard of twin earth or switching. Just as it is rational for you not to believe that the book you are now holding in your hands will explode in ten seconds time, it is rational for us not to believe we have been subject to switching. Suppose the very idea of switching has never entered our heads (we have not had the benefit of a philosophical education). Without addition to our stock of concepts, we cannot form beliefs about switching, and so our rationality cannot depend upon having rational beliefs about it. We are rational in not having any beliefs on the subject of switching; and we are also rational in not having any other beliefs that would throw doubt on the validity of the argument. The argument strikes us as valid and we rationally lack defeaters for that opinion. Hence we are rational in believing it to be valid.

We claim that switched Peter is in exactly the same position as we are regarding what it is rational for him not to believe. Just like us, he is rational in not believing he has been switched, for the idea of switching has never entered his head; just like us, it is rational for him not to have any other belief that would defeat his opinion that the argument is valid. For example, just like us, he is rational in not believing that his word "water" expresses one concept on some occasions, another concept on others. He is as rational as we are, and for the same reasons; we are rational; so he is rational. Our opinion about validity is correct and Peter's is not (assuming cohabitationism[6]). There is a distinction between us and Peter concerning truth; but not one concerning rationality.

There remains a further issue which Boghossian alludes to in the final paragraph of his objection (as we have presented it above). We need to see both ourselves and Peter as treating the occurrence of the crucial concept in the first premise as an occurrence of the

---

[6] We ourselves do not think that cohabitationism is the right description of switching cases, and we regard Boghossian's observation that, on this view, Peter could not bring the two concepts together to form an identity claim (that twater is water) as a novel argument against it. But we set this issue aside in this note.

same concept as the crucial one in the second premise. That is bound up with our intuitive judgment of validity. But what does this "treating as the same" consist in? Boghossian is right that it cannot consist in some further belief which attempts to express sameness or difference of concepts. A belief is a structure of concepts and we still need to know what it is for the subject of the belief to treat the concept-occurrences in that structure as occurrences of the same concept or different ones.[7] We think that "treating as the same" is revealed in such cognitive behavior as forming the false belief about the validity of the Pavarotti argument. If this were all that could be said, its explanatory value would be small. But a wide variety of behavior can manifest "treating as the same". For example, we and Peter would not only rationally count as valid the following version of the Pavarotti argument, but would also be rational if we judged the rewording to make no substantive difference:

Whoever floats on water gets wet
Pavarotti once floated on it
so Pavarotti got wet

The reworded argument is valid (though, as thought by Peter, unsound, assuming Pavarotti never encountered twater). It is as rational for Peter as for anyone else to believe that it is valid. Like us, he treats it as equivalent to the original argument, and has no beliefs that would make it rational for him to make any distinction between the validity or soundness of the one and the validity or soundness of the other. It is as rational for Peter as for us to believe that both arguments are valid.

We agree with Boghossian that "treating as the same" cannot be cashed out just in terms of further beliefs that attempt to specify sameness and difference among concepts. It does not follow that treating the same is inerrant, in the sense that it's impossible to treat as the same what is not the same, or that facts of sameness and difference of concepts are transparent. Nothing can make error logically impossible: it's logically possible that what we treat as the same should not be the same, and that what we treat as different should not be different. That an ability is not aptly described as an ability to form beliefs does not require that it is either omniscient or infallible within its range.

The account extends naturally to Paderewski cases, except that the Peter in this case treats concept-uses as uses of different concepts when in fact they are uses of the same one. Given that it's rational for Peter to believe that he has encountered distinct Paderewskis, it's rational for him to treat his different concept-uses as uses of different concepts. This treatment does not require any meta-conceptual beliefs.

---

[7] In discussion, Boghossian referred to John Campbell as making essentially this point from a Fregean perspective.

References

Anscombe, G.E.M. (1975) "The first person." In: Samuel Guttenplan (ed.) *Mind and Language*. Oxford, Clarendon Press: 45–65.
Austin, David (1990) *What is the Meaning of "This"? A Puzzle about Demonstrative Belief*. New York, Cornell University Press.
Azzouni, J. (2010) *Talking About Nothing: Numbers, Hallucinations, and Fictions*. Oxford, Oxford University Press.
Bach, K. (1997) "Searle against the world: how can experiences find their objects?" http://userwww.sfsu.edu/~kbach/Searle.html
Ball, D. (2009) "There Are No Phenomenal Concepts." *Mind* 118: 935–62.
Barwise, J. and Perry, J. (1981) *Situations and Attitudes*. Berlin and New York, Walter de Gruyter.
Bealer, George (1998) "Propositions." *Mind* 107: 1–32.
Boghossian, Paul (1989) "Content and Self-knowledge." *Philosophical Topics* 17: 5–26.
—— (1992) "Externalism and Inference." *Philosophical Issues* 2: 11–28.
—— (1997) "What the Externalist Can Know A Priori," *Proceedings of the Aristotelian Society* 97: 161–75.
Braun, David (2005) "Empty Names, Fictional Names, Mythical Names," *Noûs* 39: 596–631.
Brown, Jessica (1995) "The Incompatibility of Anti-individualism and Privileged Access," *Analysis* 53: 149–56.
Burge, Tyler (1979) "Individualism and the Mental," *Midwest Studies in Philosophy* 4: 73–121.
—— (1980) "Truth and Singular Terms." In: Mark Platts (ed.) *Reference, Truth and Reality*. London. Routledge and Kegan Paul.
—— (1982) "Other Bodies." In: A. Woodfield (ed.) *Thought and Object: Essays on Intentionality*. Oxford, Oxford University Press: 97–120.
—— (1988) "Individualism and Self-knowledge," *Journal of Philosophy* 85: 649–63.
—— (1991) "Vision and Intentional Content." In: E. LePore and R. Van Gulick (eds) *John Searle and his Critics*. Oxford: Blackwell: 195–214.
—— (1996) "Our Entitlement to Self-Knowledge," *Proceedings of the Aristotelian Society* 96: 91–116.
—— (2007) *Foundations of Mind*. Oxford, Clarendon Press.
Brewer, B. (2005) "Perceptual Experience has Conceptual Content." In: E. Sosa and M. Steup (eds) *Contemporary Debates in Epistemology*. Oxford, Blackwell: 217–30.
—— (2008) "How to Account for Illusion." In: A. Haddock and F. Macpherson (eds) *Disjunctivism: Perception, Action, Knowledge*. Oxford, Oxford University Press.
Byrne, A. (2005) "Perception and Conceptual Content." In: E. Sosa and M. Steup (eds) *Contemporary Debates in Epistemology*. Oxford, Blackwell: 231–50.
Carey, S. (2009) *The Origin of Concepts*. New York, Oxford University Press.
Casati, Roberto and Achille Varzi (1994) *Holes and Other Superficialities*. Cambridge, Mass., MIT Press.
Chalmers, D. (1996) *The Conscious Mind*. Oxford, Oxford University Press.

—— (2002) "Does Conceivability Entail Possibility?" In: T. Gendler and J. Hawthorne (eds) *Conceivability and Possibility*. Oxford, Oxford University Press: 145–200.
Chalmers, D. (2004a) "Phenomenal Concepts and the Knowledge Argument." In: Ludlow *et al.* (2004): 269–98.
—— (2004b) "Epistemic Two-dimensional Semantics," *Philosophical Studies* 118: 153–226.
—— (2006) "Two-dimensional Semantics." In: E. Lepore and B. C. Smith (eds) *The Oxford Handbook of Philosophy of Language*. Oxford, Oxford University Press: 574–606.
Crimmins, M. and Perry, J. (1989) "The Prince and the Phone Booth," *Journal of Philosophy* 86: 685–711.
Davidson, D. (1968) "On Saying That," *Synthese* 19: 130–46.
Davies, M. (1987) "Tacit Knowledge and Semantic Theory: Can a 5% Difference Matter?" *Mind* 96: 441–62.
—— (1992) "Perceptual Content and Local Supervenience," *Proceedings of the Aristotelian Society* 92: 21–45.
—— and Humberstone, L. (1980) "Two Notions of Necessity," *Philosophical Studies* 38: 1–30.
—— and Stoljar, Daniel (2004) "Introduction," *Philosophical Studies* 118: 1–10.
Dretske, Fred (1970) "Epistemic operators," *Journal of Philosophy* 67: 1007–23.
Evans, G. (1973) "The causal theory of names," *Proceedings of the Aristotelian Society, Supplementary Volume* 47: 187–208.
—— (1982) *The Varieties of Reference*. Oxford: Oxford University Press.
Falvey, Kevin, and Owens, Joseph (1994) "Externalism, Self-knowledge, and Skepticism," *The Philosophical Review* 103: 107–37.
Fine, K. (2007) *Semantic Relationism*. Malden, Mass., Blackwell Publishing Ltd.
Fodor, J. (1975) *The Language of Thought*. New York, Crowell.
—— (1978) "Propositional Attitudes," *The Monist* 61: 501–23.
—— (1987) *Psychosemantics*. Cambridge, Mass., MIT Press.
—— (1990) "A Theory of Content." In: J. A. Fodor *A Theory of Content and Other Essays*. Cambridge, Mass., MIT Press: 51–136.
—— (1998) *Concepts*. Oxford, Clarendon Press.
—— (2008) *LOT 2: The Language of Thought Revisited*. Oxford, Clarendon Press.
Forbes, G. (2006) *Attitude Problems*. Oxford, Clarendon Press.
Frege, G. (1892) "On Sense and Meaning." In: B. McGuiness (ed.) *Collected Papers on Mathematics, Logic and Philosophy*. Oxford, Basil Blackwell, 1984: 157–77.
—— (1918/1984) "Logical Investigations: Thoughts." In: B. McGuiness (ed.) *Collected Papers on Mathematics, Logic and Philosophy*. Oxford, Basil Blackwell: 351–72.
Geach, P. T. (1976) "Two Kinds of Intentionality?" *Monist*, 59: 306–20.
Gell-Mann, Murray (1994) *The Quark and the Jaguar*. New York, Freeman.
Goldman, Alvin (1976) "Discrimination and Perceptual Knowledge," *Journal of Philosophy* 73: 771–91.
Jackson, Frank (1982) "Epiphenomenal Qualia," *Philosophical Quarterly* 32: 127–36.
—— (1998a) *From Metaphysics to Ethics*. Oxford, Clarendon Press.
—— (1998b) "Reference and Descriptions Revisited," *Philosophical Perspectives* 12: 201–18.
—— (2004) "What Mary Didn't Know." In: P. Ludlow, Y. Nagasawa, and D. Stoljar (eds) *There's Something about Mary: Essays on Frank Jackson's Knowledge Argument Against Physicalism*. Cambridge, Mass., MIT Press: 409–16.

Kamp, H. (1971) "Formal Properties of 'Now'," *Theoria* 37: 227–74.
Kaplan, D. (1977/1989) "Demonstratives." In: Joseph Almog, John Perry, and Howard Wettstein (eds) *Themes From Kaplan*. Oxford, Oxford University Press.
—— (1990) "Words," *Proceedings of the Aristotelian Society* 64: 93–119.
King, J. (2007) *The Nature and Structure of Content*. Oxford: Oxford University Press.
Korcz, Keith Allen (1997) "Recent Work on the Basing Relation," *American Philosophical Quarterly* 34: 171–91.
Kripke, S. (1972/1980) *Naming and Necessity*. Cambridge, Mass., Harvard University Press.
—— (1977) "Speaker's Reference and Semantic Reference." In: P. A. French, T. E. Uehling, and H. K. Wettstein (eds) *Midwest Studies in Philosophy, Volume II: Studies in the Philosophy of Language*. Minneapolis, University of Minnesota Press: 255–76.
—— (1979) "A Puzzle about Belief." In: A. Margalit (ed.) *Meaning and Use*. Dordrecht, Reidel: 239–83.
Landau, B. (1994) "Object Shape, Object Name, and Object Kind: Representation and Development." In: D. L. Medin (ed.) *The Psychology of Learning and Motivation, Vol. 31*. San Diego, Calif., Academic Press.
Langford, C. H. (1949) "The Nature of Formal Analysis," *Mind* 58: 210–14.
Lepore, E. and Hawthorne, J. (2011) "On Words," *Journal of Philosophy* forthcoming.
Lewis, David (1979) "Attitudes De Dicto and De Se," *Philosophical Review* 88: 513–43.
—— (1986) *On the Plurality of Worlds*. Oxford, Basil Blackwell.
—— (1990) "What Experience Teaches." In: W. Lycan (ed.) *Mind and Cognition: A Reader*. Oxford, Basil Blackwell: 447–60.
Loar, B. (1987) "Social Content and Psychological Content." In: R. H. Grimm and D. D. Merrill (eds), *Contents of Thought*. Tucson, University of Arizona Press: 99–110.
—— (2003) "Phenomenal Intentionality as the Basis of Mental Content." In: M. Hahn and B. Ramberg (eds) *Reflections and Replies: Essays on the Philosophy of Tyler Burge*. Cambridge, Mass., MIT Press: 229–58.
Ludlow, Peter (1995a) "Externalism, Self-knowledge, and the Prevalence of Slow Switching," *Analysis* 55: 45–9.
—— (1995b) "Social Externalism, Self-knowledge, and Memory," *Analysis* 55: 157–9.
—— Nagasawa, Y. and Stoljar, D. (eds) (2004) *There's Something about Mary: Essays on Frank Jackson's Knowledge Argument Against Physicalism*. Cambridge, Mass., MIT Press.
Margolis, E. (1998) "How to Acquire a Concept," *Mind and Language* 13: 347–69.
Markman, E. and Hutchinson, J. (1984) "Children's Sensitivity to Constraints on Word Meaning: Taxonomic Versus Thematic Relations," *Cognitive Psychology* 16: 1–27.
Martin, M. G. F. (2006) "On Being Alienated." In: T. S. Gendler and J. Hawthorne (eds) *Perceptual Experience*. Oxford, Oxford University Press: 354–410.
Mates, B. (1952) "Synonymity." In: L. Linsky (ed.) *Semantics and the Philosophy of Language*. Urbana, Ill., University of Illinois Press: 111–38.
McDowell, J. (1977) "On the Sense and Reference of a Proper Name," *Mind* 86: 159–85.
—— (1994) *Mind and World*. Cambridge, Mass., Harvard University Press.
McGinn, Colin (1989) *Mental Content*. Oxford: Basil Blackwell.
McKinsey, Michael (1991) "Anti-individualism and Privileged Access," *Analysis* 51: 9–16.
McLaughlin, B. and Tye, M. (1998a) "Is Content-Externalism Compatible with Privileged Access?" *Philosophical Review* 107: 349–80.

McLaughlin, B. and Tye, M. (1998b) "Externalism, Twin-Earth and Self-knowledge." In: Cynthia Macdonald, Peter Smith, and Crispin Wright (eds) *Knowing Our Own Minds*. Oxford, Oxford University Press: 285–320.

—— (1998c) "The Brown-McKinsey Charge of Inconsistency." In: Peter Ludlow (ed.) *Externalism and Self-Knowledge*. Cambridge, Cambridge University Press: 207–14.

Mill, J. S. (1843) *System of Logic*. London, Parker.

Millikan, Ruth (1984) *Language, Thought, and Other Biological Categories*. Cambridge, Mass., Bradford Books/MIT Press.

—— (1993) *White Queen Psychology and Other Essays For Alice*. Cambridge, Mass., Bradford Books/MIT Press.

—— (1997) "Images of Identity: In Search of Modes of Presentation," *Mind* 106: 499–519.

—— (2000) *On Clear and Confused Ideas*. Cambridge, Cambridge University Press.

—— (2004) *Varieties of Meaning: The Jean-Nicod lectures 2002*. Cambridge, Mass., MIT Press.

—— (2005) *Language: A Biological Model*. Oxford, Oxford University Press.

—— (2011) "Loosing the Word-Concept Tie," *Proceedings of the Aristotelian Society, Supplementary Volume* 111: 125–43.

Moltmann, F. (1997) "Intensional Verbs and Quantifiers," *Natural Language Semantics* 5: 1–52.

Montague, Richard (1973) "The Proper Treatment of Quantification in Ordinary English." In: Jaakko Hintikka, Julius Moravcsik, and Patrick Suppes (eds) *Approaches to Natural Language*. Kluwer, Dordrecht: 221–42.

Moser, Paul (1989) *Knowledge and Evidence*. New York, Cambridge University Press.

Murphy, G. (2002) *The Big Book of Concepts*. Cambridge, Mass., MIT Press.

Nida-Rümelin, M. (1996) "What Mary Couldn't Know." In: T. Metzinger (ed.) *Conscious Experience*. Exeter, Imprint Academic: 219–41.

—— (2002) "Qualia: The Knowledge Argument." In: E. Zalta (ed.) *Stanford Encyclopedia of Philosophy*. http://plato.stanford.edu

—— (2010) "Qualia: The Knowledge Argument," *The Stanford Encyclopedia of Philosophy (Summer 2010 Edition)*, Edward N. Zalta (ed.). http://plato.stanford.edu/archives/sum2010/entries/qualia-knowledge/

Perry, J. (1977) "Frege on Demonstratives," *The Philosophical Review* 86: 474–97.

—— (1979) "The Problem of the Essential Indexical," *Noûs* 13: 3–21.

Prinz, J. J. (2002) *Furnishing the Mind*. Cambridge, Mass., MIT Press.

Prior, A. N. (1968). "'Now'," *Noûs* 2: 101–19.

Putnam, H. (1975) "The Meaning of 'Meaning'." In: K. Gunderson (ed.) *Language, Mind and Knowledge*. Minneapolis, University of Minnesota Press: 131–93.

Pylyshyn, Z. (2007) *Things and Places: How the Mind Connects with the World*. Cambridge, Mass., MIT Press.

Roseveare, N. T. (1982) *Mercury's Perihelion from Le Verrier to Einstein*. Oxford, Oxford University Press.

Russell, B. (1905) "On Denoting," *Mind* 14: 479–93.

—— (1912) *Problems of Philosophy*. Oxford, Oxford University Press (1959).

Ryle, Gilbert (1930) "Are There Propositions?" *Proceedings of the Aristotelian Society* 30: 91–126.

Sainsbury, R. M. (2005a) "Pleonastic Explanations." Critical notice: Stephen Schiffer *The Things We Mean*, *Mind* 114, 2005: 97–111.

—— (2005b) *Reference without Referents*. Oxford: Oxford University Press.

Salmon, N. (1986) *Frege's Puzzle*. Cambridge, Mass., MIT Press.
Schiffer, Stephen (1987) "The 'Fido'–Fido Theory of Belief," *Philosophical Perspectives* 1: 455–80.
—— (1992) "Belief Ascription," *Journal of Philosophy* 89: 499–521.
—— (2003) *The Things We Mean*. Oxford, Clarendon Press.
Segerberg, K. (1973) "Two-dimensional Modal Logic," *Journal of Philosophical Logic* 2: 77–96.
Shoemaker, Sydney (1994) "Introspection," *Cambridge Companion to the Philosophy of Mind*. Cambridge, Cambridge University Press: 395–400.
Stalnaker, R. (2008) *Our Knowledge of the Internal World*. Oxford, Oxford University Press.
Stich, Stephen (1978) "Beliefs and Subdoxastic States," *Philosophy of Science* 45: 499–518.
Thomason, R. (1980) "A Model Theory for Propositional Attitudes," *Linguistics and Philosophy* 4: 47–70.
Travis, Charles (2004) "The Silence of the Senses," *Mind* 113: 57–94.
Tye, M. (1995) *Ten Problems of Consciousness*. Cambridge, Mass.: Bradford Books/MIT Press.
—— (2000) *Consciousness, Color, and Content*. Cambridge, Mass.: Bradford Books/MIT Press.
—— (2005) "Nonconceptual Content, Richness, and Fineness of Grain." In: T. Gendler and J. Hawthorne (eds) *Perceptual Experience*. Oxford, Oxford University Press.
—— (2009) *Consciousness Revisited: Materialism without Phenomenal Concepts*. Cambridge, Mass., MIT Press.
—— (2010) "Attention, Seeing and Change Blindness," *Philosophical Issues* 20: 410–37.
—— (forthcoming) "What is the content of a hallucinatory experience?" In: B. Brogarde (ed.) *Does Perception Have a Content?* Oxford, Oxford University Press.
Tymoczko, T. (1979) "The Four-color Problem and its Philosophical Significance," *Journal of Philosophy* 76: 57–83.
Vlach, F. (1973) "'Now' and 'Then': A Formal Study in the Logic of Tense Anaphora." PhD Thesis, University of California, Los Angeles.
Warfield, Ted A. (1992) "Privileged Self-knowledge and Externalism are Compatible," *Analysis* 52: 232–7.
Wetzel, L. (2009) *Types and Tokens: On Abstract Objects*. Cambridge, Mass., The MIT Press.
White, Alan R. (1964) *Attention*. Oxford, Blackwell.
Wittgenstein, Ludwig (1958) *The Blue and Brown Books*. Abingdon, Basil Blackwell.
Wright, C. (1986) "Theories of Meaning and Speakers' Knowledge." In: S. G. Shanker (ed.) *Philosophy in Britain Today*. London and Sydney, Croom Helm: 267–307.
Yablo, S. (1999) "Concepts and Consciousness: Comments on Chalmers' *The Conscious Mind*," *Philosophy and Phenomenological Research* 59: 455–64.

Index

The index entries appear in letter-by-letter alphabetical order.

ACES 67–8, 179
acquisition, of concepts 55, 66, 177–8;
  see also learning
aluminium, and molybdenum twin puzzle 6–7
AND 82–3
Anderson, D. 180
apriority
  conceivability and logical possibility 168
  contingent reference fixers 169
  externalist thesis 105, 106–9
  necessity distinction 30–2
  two-dimensional semantics 34, 36–8
arthritis/tharthritis twin puzzle 7–8, 47
atomic concepts
  nonatomic concept distinction 20–1
  types of 45
attention, reference indeterminancy
    reduction 69–70
attitude ascriptions 116–23

beliefs
  absence of 137–8
  content of 113, 160–3
  contradictory 13, 98–9, 133–5, 138, 167–8
  experience and 160–3
  explicit/implicit distinction 111–12
  false 55, 135, 137
  kinds of 61
  metaphysics of, see metaphysics (of thought and belief)
Boghossian, P. ix, 91, 102, 107, 174–5, 182–5
Brewer, B. 150, 160, 161
Brown, J. ix
Buchanan, R. ix
Burge, T.
  conceptual ignorance 55
  de re thoughts 121
  externalism 102, 108–9
  partial understanding 9, 82
  twin puzzles 4, 7, 102
Byrne, A. ix, 181

Cappelen, H. ix
cat and le chat puzzle 9–12, 127–31, 178–9
Chalmers, D. 30–8, 164, 170
Cicero and Tully puzzle 12–13, 88–9, 108, 159, 166
cogito thoughts 90, 102

cognition 53–4
cognitive discovery
  cat and le chat puzzle 128
  demonstrative puzzles 138–9, 166–7
  Hesperus and Phosphorus puzzle 125–6
Cohen, J. ix
'color scientist' pure demonstratives puzzle 15–16, 138–9, 163–7
colors twin puzzle 8–9
compositionality 49, 73–4
conceivability 167–70
concept externalism
  Burge's 108–9
  introspective knowledge of comparative concepts (IKCC) and 93–5
  McGinn's 105–8
  originalist (OCE) 109
  privileged access incompatibility argument 102–9
  semantic externalism distinction 47, 90
concept-templates 51, 55–6, 63, 85, 144
concepts
  content of 21–2, 26–7, 30, 45–9, 72–6
  terminology of 1–2
conceptual mastery 55–6, 81–5
conformity 42–3
conjunctive thoughts 48
content
  of beliefs 113, 160–3
  of concepts 21–2, 26–7, 30, 45–9, 72–6
  empty, see empty thoughts puzzle
  gappy 151–7
  nonconceptual content thesis 160–3
  singular 151–2, 155
  of thoughts 47–9, 73–5, 110–11, 157, 159, 177
  of visual experience 150–63
contradictory beliefs 13, 98–9, 133–5, 138, 167–8
creation, of concepts 65–6, 69–70
Cutter, B. 44, 176

Dancy, J. ix
deference
  Burge's externalism 108–9
  cat and le chat puzzle 9–10
  fusion and 68
  objection and reply 176

deference (cont.)
    originating/non-originating usage differences 42
    reference fixation and preservation 70
    twin puzzles 8–9
    in word-learning 60
    see also linguistic community, influence of
demonstratives puzzles, pure, see pure demonstratives puzzles
de re hallucinations 151
de re thoughts 121–3
descendant uses 44
descriptivism, see Fregeanism/descriptivism
de se thoughts 123; see also thinking about oneself puzzle
difference, transparency of 91
discoveries, see cognitive discovery; possibility-eliminating discovery
disjunctivism 150–1
dissent 137–8
Dorr, C. ix
double indexing 33–4

empty thoughts puzzle 16–17
    free logical character of atomic thoughts rule 48, 49
    Fregean views 23–4
    imaginability 171
    knowledge and conceptual mastery 83, 84
    Millian views 22, 30
    objection and reply 176
    reasons for lack of content 46
    reference 62
    solution 139–44
Evans, G. 23, 46, 51–3, 63, 69, 133, 140, 161, 182
existence, being whose essence includes 168–9
expectations, falsified 42
experience
    conceivability background 167–9
    content of 150–9
    epistemic role of 160–3
    the knowledge argument 163–7
    the zombie argument 169–72
extensions 32, 58, 127, 180
externalism
    concept, see concept externalism
    semantic 47, 90

false beliefs 55, 135, 137
falsified expectations 42
fiction 27, 46, 108, 139–44; see also empty thoughts puzzle
Fine, K. 26, 76
first-person concept, see thinking about oneself puzzle
first-person concept-template 51, 63, 144

fission, conceptual 66–8
Fodor, J.
    cognitivist views 53, 82
    comparison with originalist theory 85–7
    individuation 73
    knowledge and conceptual mastery 55
    origin of concepts 42
    Paderewski puzzle 176
    'fountain of youth' example 111, 114–15, 141–2
Fregeanism/descriptivism
    content 4, 17, 23–4, 73–6, 127, 133, 138, 160–1
    Hesperus and Phosphorus puzzle 3, 125
    indexicality 51–2
    Mates cases 57, 76–9, 80, 81
    multi-level 79–81
    overview 22–6
    sense 3, 22–3, 25, 73, 76–81, 140
    two-dimensional semantics 30–9, 76–9
FURZE and GORSE 101, 181–2
fusion, conceptual 66–8, 179

gappy content 151–7
gappy propositions 140
Gell-Mann, M. 41–3, 44, 65, 68
generic names 61–3
Given, the 160
Glick, E. ix
GOLD, concept of 82
GORSE and FURZE 101, 181–2
GREEKS and HELLENES 11
    cognition 54
    content 74
    isomorphism 50
    objections and replies 173–4
    origination 59
    sense 78–9, 80
    solution 129–31
    truth value 77, 80
guises 29

hallucinatory experience 150–9
HELLENE, see GREEKS and HELLENES
HERE 25
Hesperus and Phosphorus puzzle 2–4, 124–7
    Cicero and Tully puzzle similarity 13
    cognition 53–4
    content 45, 47, 49, 74, 75
    Fregean/descriptivist views 23, 24–6, 31, 77–8
    isomorphism 50, 124
    knowledge and conceptual mastery 84
    Millian views 22, 30
    objections and replies 174, 179–80
    sense 77–8, 79–80
    solution 124–7

hidden indexical theory 26–30
HOLMES, SHERLOCK 46, 139, 141, 142
Horgan, T. ix
Horwich, P. ix, 173

I, *see* thinking about oneself puzzle
I/first-person concept-template 51, 63, 144
identification-free knowledge 147
identity thoughts, pure and impure
  contingent 125–6
illusion 150–1, 158, 159, 168
illusory conceivability 168–9, 170
imaginability 170–2
immunity to error through misidentification
  (IEM) 19, 144, 148–9
impure contingent identity thoughts 126
inconsistent thoughts 131–4
indexical concepts
  attitude attribution 119–20
  concept-templates 55–6, 63, 85
  hidden indexical theory 26–30
  knowledge and conceptual mastery 55–6,
    83, 85
  originalist theory overview 51–3
  reference 35–6, 63
  in twin-earth puzzle 127
individuation of concepts
  Fodor's views 85–6
  Millian views 181, 182
  objections and replies 180–2
  by origin 44, 58–61, 180–1
inference
  introspective knowledge of comparative
    concepts (IKCC) thesis and 99–100
  two-dimensional semantics 38
informativeness 3, 53–4, 74–6, 78
INTEGRATION 66, 67–8, 175
intension, primary and secondary 31–2, 34–8
intensional transitives 141–4
intentional actions 43, 64–5
intrinsic duplicates 5–6, 8–9, 47, 90;
  see also twin puzzles
introduction, of concepts/words, *see* origins
introspection 90
  introspective evidence thesis 103–5
  introspective knowledge of comparative
    concepts (IKCC) thesis, *see* introspective
    knowledge of comparative concepts (IKCC)
    thesis
introspective knowledge of comparative concepts
  (IKCC) thesis
  empirical implausibility of 95–8
  formulation of 91–2
  privileged access thesis and rejection of 101–2
  rationality and 98–101
  switching and 92–5
intuition 94, 124, 150–1, 182

isomorphism 50, 54, 120–1, 124
  sub-isomorphism 50, 120
  super-isomorphism 50, 54, 124, 128

judgments
  of experience 160–3
  first-person 146, 148

Kamp, H. ix, 33, 138, 174, 175–6
Kaplan, D. 41, 55–6, 59, 61, 63, 85, 134
King, J. 156
knowledge
  conceptual mastery and 55–6, 81–5
  identification-free 147
  introspective, *see* introspective knowledge
    of comparative concepts (IKCC) thesis
  reference fixation and 70
  self-knowledge 145–7, 148
  tacit 56
  the knowledge argument 15, 163–7
Kripke, S. 3, 11, 12–13, 26, 30, 71, 81, 105, 129,
  131–7, 168

language-less concept users 66
learning
  of concepts 87, 176; *see also* acquisition
  of words 59–60
Lewis, D. 18
Lingens (Rudolf), de se thought example
  18, 123
linguistic community, influence of 9, 10, 43–4,
  108–9, 133; *see also* deference
London and Londres puzzle 11, 129

Mach, E. 18, 144, 145
Madagascar, concept of 46, 69, 71–2
manifestation, behavioristic notion of 179
Marianna case, demonstratives puzzle 166–7
MASS 66, 67
Mates, B./Mates cases 11, 57, 76–9, 80, 129–30,
  173–4, 181; *see also* GREEKS and HELLENES
McDowell, J. 25, 160–1
McGinn, C. 105–8, 151
McGlynn, A. ix
McKinsey's recipe, privileged access and
  105–8, 109
MEAT 46, 69, 71, 72, 180
memory, introspective knowledge of
  comparative concepts (IKCC) thesis
  and 92, 94–5
metaphysics (of thought and belief)
  arguments for orthodox view and
    evaluation 112–16
  attitude ascriptions 116–23
  positive account 110–12
Mill, J.S. ix, 20–22
Miller, B. 68

Millianism
  empty thought puzzles 140
  hidden indexical theory 26–30
  naïve 21–2
  originalism and 57
  Rudolf Lingens example 123
Millikan, R. 58, 72, 73, 87–9, 176, 177
modes of presentation 14, 22–3, 27–30, 140
modus ponens 136
molybdenum, and aluminium twin puzzle 6–7
motleys 7
Müller–Lyer diagram 96–7

names (proper)
  as definite descriptions 3
  generic and specific 61–3
  Millian views 21–2
natural kind terms/concepts 4, 7, 106–8
necessity, apriority distinction 30–2
negation/negative thoughts 48–9, 131, 133–5, 141
nominative concepts
  content for atomic 48
  definition 21
  reference in 40
nonatomic/atomic distinction 20–1
nonconceptual content thesis 160–3
non-eternal abstract continuants 63–6
NOW 25, 52–3

OBJECT 46, 66
object-dependent thoughts 107–8
objections and replies 173–82
occurrent thought 90; *see also* cogito thought
ontological commitment 114–16
ordered pairs 152–5, 159
origin
  of concepts 41–4, 66–8, 127, 178, 180
  individuation by 44, 58–61, 180–1
  of words 41, 58–9, 181–2
originalist theory of concepts
  concept externalism and privileged access 90–109
  defence and elaboration 58–89
  objections and replies 173–82
  overview 40–57
  see also specific concepts/puzzles/topics

Paderewski puzzle 12–13, 131–8
  conceivability 167–9
  introspective knowledge of comparative concepts (IKCC) and rationality 99
  number of concepts error 182
  objections and replies 176–7
  solution 131–8
paradox of analysis 74
partial understanding 9–10, 82
PEGASUS, VULCAN 45, 46, 47, 141–3

perception
  perceptual experience 150–1
  perceptual imagining 171–2
  reference fixation 69–70
  sameness and difference 96–7
Perry, J. 18, 51, 123, 133
phenomenal character 158, 159, 165–6, 167
PHLOGISTON 45, 65, 83, 139
Phosphorus, and Hesperus puzzle, *see* Hesperus and Phosphorus puzzle
physicalism, arguments against 15–16, 163–72
Ponce de León example 111, 114–15, 141–2
possibility 168–72
possibility-eliminating discovery
  demonstratives puzzle 166
  Hesperus and Phosphorus puzzle 125–7
predicative concepts
  content of atomic 48
  definition 21
presentation, modes of 14, 22–3, 27–30, 140
primary intension 31, 32, 34, 35–8
Prinz, J. ix, 73, 82
privileged access thesis
  concept externalism incompatibility arguments 102–9
  introduction to related questions 90–1
  introspective knowledge of comparative concepts (IKCC) thesis and 91–2, 101–2
probabilification 162
properties, terminology of 2
propositional attitudes
  attitude ascription 49, 79, 116–23
  hidden indexical theory 29
  metaphysics of thought views 110, 113
  objections and replies 175
  synonym substitution in 11
propositions
  gappy 140
  hidden indexical theory 27, 29–30
  metaphysics of thought views 110–11, 113
  objections and replies 175
  structured 140
pure demonstratives puzzles 13–16
  'color scientist' puzzle 15–16, 138–9, 163–7
  two tubes puzzle 14–15, 138
  see also THAT; THIS
pure identity thoughts 125–6
Putnam, H. 4, 10, 42, 55, 70, 105, 106

quantifier phrases, ontological commitment 114–16
QUARK 41–3, 44, 65, 68, 179

rationality
  introspective knowledge of comparative concepts (IKCC) thesis and 95, 98–101
  Paderewski puzzle 134–6, 138

realism, naïve 150
recursive clauses 48–9
reference
    of atomic concepts 40–1
    change of referent 174–5
    fixation and preservation of 35–7, 69–72, 87, 169
    Fregean/descriptivist views 22–3, 25, 34–7, 79–81
    generic and specific names 62
    indexical concepts 63
    individuation by referent 181–2
    Millian views 21–2, 27, 29–30
    Millikan's views 88
    modes of presentation 14, 22–3, 27–30, 140
    self-reference 147–8
represent, as intensional transitive verb 142–3
representational content
    experience 151, 158, 160
    thoughts and concepts 1–2, 4, 14, 17
representationalism thesis 159
Richard, M. 173–4, 182
Rosen, G. ix
Rudolph Lingens example 18, 123
Russell, B. ix, 24–5
Russellian 25, 51, 110, 136, 144, 152

Salmon, N. 29
sameness, transparency of 91
Santa Claus, empty thoughts puzzle 16, 17, 139
scenarios, notion of 32–7
Schiffer, S. ix, 26–9, 113, 175
secondary intension 31, 32, 34
self-knowledge 18, 91, 145–9
self-reference 147–8
semantic externalism 47, 90, 91, 101, 102, 179
semantic rules 56
sense
    difference of concept versus difference of 54
    Fregean/descriptivist views 3, 22–3, 25, 73, 76–81, 140
    sense experiences, see experience
Shea, N. ix
ship example 51–2, 53, 133, 182
singular content 151–2, 155
Smith, B. ix
Sosa, D. ix
split-brain subjects 136–7
spoken words, written word differences 61
Stahl, G. 65
strengthened disquotation principle 137
structured propositions 140
sub-isomorphism 50, 120
substitution, principle of unrestricted 74
super-isomorphism 50, 54, 124, 128

swampman 177–8
switching cases, see twin puzzles
synonyms, *salva veritate* substitution 11

THAT 14–15
    creation of 66
    demonstrative puzzle solutions 138–9
    empty concept 139
    indexicality 51–2
    knowledge and conceptual mastery 83–4
    see also pure demonstratives puzzle
thinking about oneself puzzle 18–19
    first-person concept-template 51, 63, 144
    indexicality 51
    metaphysics of de se thoughts 123
    reference 63
    solution 144–9
'thinking the same', notion of 179
THIS 15–16, 52, 139
thoughts
    contents of 47–9, 73–5, 110–11, 157, 159, 177
    metaphysics of, *see* metaphysics (of thought and belief)
    see also specific types of thought
time of occurrence, events and concept introduction 178
truth conditions 1, 16, 56, 72–3, 124–5, 140–1
truth value 29, 32, 54, 72–4, 77, 80
Tully, puzzle of Cicero and 12–13, 88–9, 108, 159, 166
twin puzzles 4–9
    aluminium/molybdenum puzzle 6–7
    arthritis/tharthritis puzzle 7–8, 47
    colors puzzle 8–9
    content 47, 75–6
    introspective knowledge of comparative concepts (IKCC) thesis and 92–5, 99–101
    manifestation and 179
    privileged access and concept externalism 102–8
    solution 127
    water/twater puzzle, *see* water/twater twin-earth puzzle
two-dimensional semantics 30–9, 76–9
two tubes puzzle 14–15, 138

unary atomic thoughts 48, 49, 140
understanding
    of a concept 55–6
    partial 9–10, 82
unicorn, concept of 140, 141–3, 171
unrestricted substitution principle 74
unthinkability 175

visual experience, content of 150–63
VULCAN, PEGASUS 45, 46, 47, 141–3
Vulcan, empty thoughts puzzle 16–17
　free logical character of atomic thoughts rule 49
　Fregean/descriptivist views 23–4
　knowledge and conceptual mastery 83
　Millian views 22, 30
　objection and reply 176
　reference 62
　solution 139–44

water
　knowledge and conceptual mastery 82
　two-dimensional semantics 31, 33–6, 38
　see also water/twater twin-earth puzzle
water/twater twin-earth puzzle 5–6
　content 47, 75–6

　introspective evidence 104–5
　introspective knowledge of comparative concepts (IKCC) thesis and 92–5, 99–101
　manifestation and 179
　privileged access and concept externalism 102–8
　solution 127
WE 120
'what is said' 179–80
WITCH 139
Wittgenstein, L. 19, 71–2, 145–7
words 41, 58–63, 181–2
　word-learning 59–60
written words, spoken word differences 61

Zimmerman, A. ix
zombie argument, the 169–72
Zweig, G. 41, 68

The manufacturer's authorised representative in the EU for product safety is
Oxford University Press España S.A. of el Parque Empresarial San Fernando de
Henares, Avenida de Castilla, 2 – 28830 Madrid (www.oup.es/en or product.
safety@oup.com). OUP España S.A. also acts as importer into Spain of products
made by the manufacturer.

www.ingramcontent.com/pod-product-compliance
Ingram Content Group UK Ltd.
Pitfield, Milton Keynes, MK11 3LW, UK
UKHW021319180426
11947UKWH00015B/1324